Spiritual Guides
of the Third Century:

A Semiotic Study of
the Guide-Disciple Relationship
in Christianity, Neoplatonism,
Hermetism, and Gnosticism

Harvard Dissertations in Religion

Editors

Margaret R. Miles
and
Bernadette J. Brooten

Number 27

Spiritual Guides of the Third Century:
A Semiotic Study of
the Guide-Disciple Relationship
in Christianity, Neoplatonism,
Hermetism, and Gnosticism

Richard Valantasis

Spiritual Guides of the Third Century:

A Semiotic Study of
the Guide-Disciple Relationship
in Christianity, Neoplatonism,
Hermetism, and Gnosticism

Richard Valantasis

Fortress Press   Minneapolis

For Janet, ἡ ὁδηγήτρια

SPIRITUAL GUIDES OF THE THIRD CENTURY:
A SEMIOTIC STUDY OF THE GUIDE-DISCIPLE RELATIONSHIP
IN CHRISTIANITY, NEOPLATONISM, HERMETISM, AND GNOSTICISM

Copyright © 1991

The President and Fellows of Harvard College

Write to: Permissions, Augsburg Fortress, 426 S. Fifth St., Box 1209, Minneapolis, MN 55440.

Internal design: Chiron, Inc.

Library of Congress Cataloging-in-Publication Data

Valantasis, Richard, 1946–
  Spiritual guides of the third century : a semiotic study of the guide-disciple relationship in Christianity, Neoplatonism, Hermetism, and Gnosticism / Richard Valantasis.
       p.   cm.—(Harvard dissertations in religion ; no. 27)
  Includes bibliographical references.
  ISBN 0-8006-7081-7
  1. Spiritual life—History of doctrines—Early church, ca. 30–600. 2. Neoplatonism. 3. Gnosticism. 4. Hermetism. 5. Semiotics. I. Title. II. Title: Spiritual guides of the 3rd century. III. Series.
  BR195.C5V34 1991
  291.6'1'09015—dc20   91-33295
                                                                  CIP

The paper used in this publication meets the minimum requirements of American National Standard for Information Sciences—Permanence of Paper for Printed Library Materials, ANSI Z329.48-1984.   ∞™

Manufactured in the U.S.A.   AF 1-7081

95   94   93   92   91   1   2   3   4   5   6   7   8   9   10

Contents

Acknowledgments

My support for this thesis has been legion. First, the sisters of the American foundation of the Society of St. Margaret in Boston, who encouraged me at the beginning of my graduate study and who continually gave meaning and context to my learning, granted me a leave of absence to complete its writing. The sisters' encouragement was a "pillar of cloud by day" to me. The Society of St. Paul in Palm Desert, California, provided a congenial place and welcome opportunity to formulate final thoughts in the warmth of their community and their sunshine. The parishioners of the Church of St. John the Evangelist, Bowdoin Street, Boston kept me (and my wife) sane through the seemingly endless revisions. My weekly dinners with Thomas M. Hoopes regularly reminded me that the search for God leads from the academy to the lives of many lay lovers of God.

George MacRae, SJ worked with me to develop the topic and to write the prospectus. Both at ETS/Weston and Harvard, George encouraged me to apply literary methods to Scriptural and Patristic sources, and at Harvard he planted a spark of love in my soul for the Nag Hammadi documents. I will always cherish the exuberant joy he expressed to me and to others when he presented the prospectus to the Committee on the Study of Religion. His early death prior to the completion of the following Nag Hammadi chapters deeply grieved me. This verbal stele is set up as a thank-offering for his life and teaching.

Margaret R. Miles also guided and inspired my graduate study. Her dual interest in methods of interpretation and early Christian texts made my soul sing. Especially after George MacRae's death, Margaret encouraged, supported, nurtured, corrected, reproved, read and re-read my project. She was my Iouel, and initiated me into the greater mysteries of feminist criticism. She is both my mentor and friend.

I would also like to thank the final readers: Helmut Koester, Bishop Demetrios Trakatellis, and Margaret Miles. Their thoughtful reading of this thesis and expansive discussion of possible subsequent avenues of investigation have mapped out a lifetime of research projects. The defense was the most pleasant of all my graduate experiences.

Finally, I wish to thank Janet Carlson, my wife. For over twenty years I have prayed daily before an icon of the Theotokos entitled ἡ ὁδηγήτρια, "The Guide," in which the Mother of God as an instructor points toward Jesus, the Savior. As I wrote this thesis I discovered anew that Janet is my guide pointing to Christ the Light, especially when I could see only darkness. She embodies for me the Theotokos, and I dedicate this book to her in thanksgiving for her ineffable love, support, assistance, and divine wisdom.

Short Titles

Information appears here for frequently used works which are cited by short title. A few short titles do not appear in this list, but in each instance full bibliography is given on the page(s) preceding such references. Abbreviations used in this volume for sources and literature from antiquity are the same as those used in *HTR* 80:2 (1987) 243–60. Some abbreviations from that list can be easily identified.

Berchman, *From Philo to Origen*
> Robert M. Berchman, *From Philo to Origen: Middle Platonism in Transition* (Brown Judaic Studies, 69; Chico: Scholars Press, 1984).

Blonsky, *On Signs*
> Marshall Blonsky, ed., *On Signs* (Baltimore: Johns Hopkins University Press, 1985).

Brisson, *Prophyre*
> Luc Brisson, et al., eds., *Porphyre: Vie de Plotin* (Histoire des Doctrines de L'Antiquité Classique 6; Paris: Libraire Philosophique J. Vrin, 1982).

Burkert, *Mystery Cults*
> Walter Burkert, *Ancient Mystery Cults* (Carl Newell Jackson Lectures, 1982; Cambridge: Harvard University Press, 1987).

Cox, *Biography*
> Patricia Cox, *Biography in Late Antiquity: A Quest for the Holy Man* (Berkeley: University of California Press, 1983).

Crouzel, *La Lettre*
> Henri Crouzel, ed., *Grégoire le Thaumaturge. Remerciement à Origene suivi de La Lettre d' Origène à Grégoire* (SC 148; Paris: Cerf, 1969).

Crouzel, "Le Remerciement"
> ————, "Le Remerciement a Origène de saint Grégoire le Thaumaturge: son contenu doctrinal," *Sciences écclesiastiques* 16 (1964).

Culler, *Pursuit of Signs*
    Jonathan Culler, *The Pursuit of Signs: Semiotics, Literature, Deconstruction* (Ithaca: Cornell University Press, 1981).

Eco, *Reader*
    Umberto Eco, *The Role of the Reader: Explorations in the Semiotics of Texts* (Bloomington: Indiana University Press, 1984).

Festugière, *Révélation*
    A. J. Festugière, *La Révélation d'Hermès Trismégiste* (3 vols.; Paris: Société d'Edition Les Belles Lettres, 1983).

Foucault, *Care of the Self*
    Michel Foucault, *The History of Sexuality*, vol. 3: *The Care of the Self* (1984; reprinted New York: Pantheon, 1986).

Foucault, *Use of Pleasure*
    _____, *The History of Sexuality*, vol. 2: *The Use of Pleasure* (1984; reprinted New York: Random House, 1986).

Keizer, *Eighth*
    Lewis S. Keizer, *The Eighth Reveals the Ninth: A New Hermetic Initiation Disclosure (Tractate 6, Nag Hammadi Codex VI)* (Seaside, CA: Academy of Arts and Humanities, 1974).

King, "Allogenes"
    Karen Leigh King, "The Quiescent Eye of the Revelation, Nag Hammadi Codex XI.3 'Allogenes,' A Critical Edition" (Ph.D. diss., Brown University, 1984).

Lambdin, *Sahidic Coptic*
    Thomas O. Lambdin, *Introduction to Sahidic Coptic* (Macon: Mercer University Press, 1983).

Layton, *Rediscovery of Gnosticism*
    Bentley Layton, ed., *The Rediscovery of Gnosticism; Proceedings of the International Conference on Gnosticism at Yale, New Haven, Connecticut March 28–31, 1978* (2 vols.; Studies in the History of Religions 41; Leiden: Brill, 1980–81).

Mahé, *Hermès*
    J.-P. Mahé, ed., *Hermès en Haute-Égypte: Les Textes hermétique de Nag Hammadi et leurs parallèlles grecs et latins* (Bibliothèque Copte de Nag Hammadi, Section "Textes" 3; 2 vols.; Québec: Les Presses de l'Université Laval, 1978–82).

Mahé, "Symboles Sexuels"
    _____, "Le Sens des Symboles Sexuels dans Quelques Textes Hermétiques et Gnostiques," in Jacques-É. Ménard, ed., *Les Textes de Nag Hammadi* (NHS 7; Leiden, Brill, 1975) 123–45.

Parrott, *NHS 11*

> Douglas M. Parrott, ed., *Nag Hammadi Codices V, 2–5 and VI with Papyrus Berolinensis 8502, 1 and 4* (NHS 11; Leiden: Brill, 1979).

Reitzenstein, *Mystery-Religions*

> Richard Reitzenstein, *Hellenistic Mystery-Religions: Their Basic Ideas and Significance* (Pittsburgh: Pickwick, 1978).

Robinson, "Three Steles"

> James M. Robinson, "The Three Steles of Seth and the Gnostics of Plotinus," in Geo Widengren, ed., *Proceedings of the International Colloquium on Gnosticism, Stockholm August 20–25, 1973* (Stockholm: Almqvist & Wiksell, 1977) 132–42.

Scopello, "Youel"

> Maddalena Scopello, "Youel et Barbelo dans le traité de l'Allogène" in Bernard Barc, ed., *Colloque International Sur Les Textes de Nag Hammadi (Québec, 22–25 août 1978)* (Bibliothèque Copte de Nag Hammadi, Section "Études" 1; Québec: Les Presses de l'Université Laval, 1981) 374–82.

Stroumsa, *Another Seed*

> G. Stroumsa, *Another Seed: Studies in Gnostic Mythology* (NHS 24; Leiden: Brill, 1984).

Tröger, "Codex VI"

> Karl-Wolfgang Tröger, "On Investigating the Hermetic Documents in Nag Hammadi Codex VI: The Present State of Research," in R. McL. Wilson, ed., *Nag Hammadi and Gnosis* (NHS 14; Leiden: Brill, 1978) 117–21.

Turner, "Threefold Path"

> John D. Turner, "The Gnostic Threefold Path to Enlightenment: The Ascent of Mind and the Descent of Wisdom," *NovT* 22 (1980) 324–51.

Turner, "Literary History"

> _____, "Sethian Gnosticism: A Literary History," in Charles W. Hedrick and Robert Hodgson, eds., *Nag Hammadi, Gnosticism, and Early Christianity* (Peabody: Hendrickson, 1986) 55–86.

1

Introduction:
Guides and Their Significance

The great Christian ascetical writers of the fourth and fifth centuries witness to a tradition of spiritual formation already ancient and venerable. One by one, Cassian, Jerome, Palladius, Athanasius return *ad fontes* to explain the great ascetical formulations by ascribing their origin to some earlier desert monastic ascetic. Athanasius,[1] for example, writing in the middle of the fourth century relates this about Anthony:

> For there were not yet so many monasteries in Egypt, and no monk at all knew of the distant desert; but all who wished to give heed to themselves practiced the discipline in solitude near their own village (ἕκαστος δὲ τῶν βουλομένων ἑαυτῷ προσέχειν οὐ μακρὰν τῆς ἰδίας κώμης καταμόνας ἠσκεῖτο). Now there was then in the next village an old man who had lived the life of a hermit from his youth up. Anthony after he had seen this man, imitated him in piety. At first he began to abide in places outside the village; then if he heard of a good man anywhere, like the prudent bee, he went forth and sought him, nor turned back to his own place until he had seen him; and he returned, having got from the good man as it were supplies for his journey in the way of virtue.

Before advancing into the desert (ca. 285) to live his own eremetical life, Anthony, the traditional originator both of monasticism and monastic asceticism, learned his asceticism primarily from an ascetic man who lived the

---

[1] Athanasius, *Vita Antonii*, 3.

solitary life. Athanasius's ideology may have prevented him from describing this man more fully. Who was he? Where did he learn his asceticism? Who was his spiritual guide? Was he a Christian?[2] Athanasius simply presents him as Anthony's first spiritual guide.

Anthony's guide stands as a sign of an older generation's spiritual formation of the succeeding one. What preceded the fourth- and fifth-century golden age of ascetical formation? Often the origins of spiritual formation and guidance are ascribed to *paideia*, from Greco-Roman educational practices:

> As the beginnings of spiritual guidance in Greco-Roman antiquity coincide with the beginnings of general education, so too the function of the spiritual guide coincides with that of the educator, insofar as we understand education (*paideia*) to include the whole of the endeavor to make a person fit for life and, consequently, the formation of a person's moral attitudes as well.[3]

This conceptualization frequently leads to a discussion on the one hand of Greco-Roman social organization and institutions of education, and on the other of the teachings of Greco-Roman philosophers about education.[4] The fourth-century Egyptian monastic foundations did not, however, mimic this classical tradition in their teachings or in their social organization. The historical model of the Greco-Roman philosophical school never replaced the desert as the origin of monastic asceticism, even for the more sophisticated and classically educated Cappadocians.[5]

The missing link between the second-century philosophical school and the

[2] Athanasius describes these early ascetic masters as working toward προσοχή, a concept which has a long Stoic and Platonic history before it entered Christianity. The ambiguity regarding the religious affiliation of Anthony's early guides cannot be easily resolved. See Pierre Hadot, *Exercices Spirituels et Philosophe Antique* (2d ed.; Paris: Etudes Augustiniennes, 1987) 19–24 for the Stoic background; and see pp. 59–74 for the Christian development.

[3] I. Hadot, "The Spiritual Guide," in A. H. Armstrong, ed., *Classical Mediterranean Spirituality: Egyptian, Greek, Roman* (New York: Crossroad, 1986) 436.

[4] For example, on the histories of education, see Henri Marrou, *A History of Education* (London: Sheed and Ward, 1956); G. W. Bowersock, *Greek Sophists in the Roman Empire* (Oxford: Clarendon, 1969); M. L. Clarke, *Higher Education in the Ancient World* (London: Routledge and Kegan Paul, 1971); Stanley F. Bonner, *Education in Ancient Rome: From the Elder Cato to the Younger Pliny* (Berkeley: University of California, 1977). These have generally supplanted Werner Jaeger, *Paideia: The Ideals of Greek Culture* (3 vols.; Oxford: Basil Blackwell, 1947–54); and idem, *Early Christianity and Greek Paideia* (Oxford: Oxford University Press, 1961).

[5] Anthony Meredith ("Asceticism—Christian and Greek," *JTS* 27 [1976] 313–32) has studied the relationship of fourth-century Christian ascetical writers (Athanasius, Basil, Gregory of Nyssa) to Hellenic ascetical writers (Porphyry, Iamblicus, Philostratus). He concluded that only Gregory of Nyssa had the more strictly philosophical vision of the ascetical life, even though Basil had modified the desert ideal of Athanasius to reflect his own culture and environment.

fourth-century Egyptian monastery may exist in one common element which runs through all the later literature such as *Apothegmata Patrum*, Cassian's *Conferences*, and Athanasius's description of Anthony's early formation: they all portray the relationship of the spiritual guide to a disciple as the beginning of ascetical formation. Within those relationships, the guides trained the disciple in a way of perceiving and relating to the mental and emotional self, the religious community, and the wider world.[6] The substance of the training revolved about the transmission of traditional material regarding the interior life. Any one of the conversations in this literature would attest to this structure.

Most studies of ascetic literature in Late Antiquity have been interested in Christianity.[7] The myth of the monk replacing the Christian martyr, and the subsequent rapid growth and expansion of monasticism, overshadowed all other Late Antique ascetical movements.[8] Monastic literatures flourished after the reign of Constantine in the heady days of Christian triumphalism in which, to Christian historians at least, paganism finally died a natural death and pagan religions were displaced by Christianity. This fourth- and fifth-century literature gives the impression that Christianity generally, and monasticism specifically, developed the only successful asceticism. Historians, since Eusebius, have had a definite Christian bias.[9]

[6] Robert Kirschner ("The Vocation of Holiness in Late Antiquity," *VC* 38 [1984] 105–24) discussed the vocation of the pagan philosopher, the Christian ascetic, and the rabbinic sage to be a holy master in Late Antiquity. Although he emphasizes in each case the importance of the relationship between the master and the disciple, he did not explore the inner workings of their relationship, so that the disciple has been reduced to observation and imitation of the holy master. The focus remained on the holy masters' traditional teaching by doctrine and example.

[7] See, e.g., the article by M. Olphe-Galliard and M. Viller, "Ascèse, Ascétisme" in M. Viller, F. Cavallera, and J. DeGuibert, eds., *Dictionnaire de Spiritualité* (Paris: Beauchesne, 1937) 1. 936–1018. For the most thorough treatment of Hellenic ascetic teaching see 941–60; the rest discusses Christian asceticism. Andrew Louth (*The Origins of the Christian Mystical Tradition From Plato to Denis* [Oxford: Clarendon, 1981]) has explored the Platonic, Philonic, and Plotinian backgrounds to the Christian mystical tradition which includes both dogmatic and ascetical elements.

For Christian asceticism, see Margaret R. Miles, *Fullness of Life: Historical Foundations for a New Asceticism* (Philadelphia: Westminster, 1981); and Robert Murray ("The Features of the Earliest Christian Asceticism" in Peter Brooks, ed., *Christian Spirituality* [London: SCM, 1975] 63–77) who treats primarily Syrian sources of early asceticism.

[8] The relationship of asceticism to martyrdom was a commonplace in Christianity, beginning with Clement of Alexandria *Stromateis* 6. See esp. Owen Chadwick's "General Introduction" in idem, ed., *Western Asceticism* (LCC; Philadelphia: Westminster, 1958) 13–31; and for the continuation of the tradition see Sebastian P. Brock and Susan Ashbrook Harvey, trans., *Holy Women of the Syrian Orient* (Transformation of the Classical Heritage 13; Berkeley: University of California, 1987).

[9] This is no more evident than in the scholarship investigating pagan cult in Late Antiquity. For a full argument about such historical bias with regard both to the definition of "true" reli-

The third-century was not so monolithically Christian.[10] The religious and ascetic movements were rich and varied with a sort of religious fluidity and intercommunion[11] that shames the more fundamental and denominated religious environment of today. The great spiritual guides described in ascetical writings at the apex of Christian triumphalism received their guidance in the previous generations at the feet of people who were most likely not always Christians and certainly not living in a Christian cultural environment.[12]

The third century focus on individuals,[13] their socially ascribed sanctity,[14] and the philosophical holy man[15] has already been studied, without, however, exploring the method by which the person was individuated, or more specifically, socially formed as an individual. The relationship of spiritual

gion and the "decline" of Roman religion, see S. R. F. Price, *Rituals and Power: The Roman Imperial Cult in Asia Minor* (Cambridge: Cambridge University Press, 1984) 1–22.

[10] This is evident from the extensive and monumental work of Robin Lane Fox, *Pagans and Christians* (New York: Knopf, 1987) which places both Hellenism and Christianity into a common world in a study which supercedes all others.

The prior bibliography for the history of the third century is vast, so only the most useful is noted. In addition see Peter Brown, "Approaches to the Religious Crises of the Third Century A.D.," in idem, *Religion and Society in the Age of Augustine* (London: Faber and Faber, 1972) 74–93. See also E. R. Dodds, *Pagan and Christian in an Age of Anxiety: Some Aspects of Religious Experience from Marcus Aurelius to Constantine* (Cambridge: Cambridge University Press, 1965). For sources and bibliography see S. A. Cook, et al., eds., *The Imperial Crisis and Recovery A.D. 193–324* (*CAH* 12; Cambridge: Cambridge University Press, 1939); and M. Cary and H. H. Scullard, *A History of Rome Down to the Reign of Constantine* (3d ed.; New York: St. Martin's, 1975) 507–58.

[11] The problem of self-definition in the religious and philosophical spheres attests to this fluidity: see esp. E. P. Sanders, ed., *Jewish and Christian Self-Definition* (3 vols.; Philadelphia: Fortress, 1980–1982) which covers the full spectrum of Hellenic, Christian, and Jewish self-definition. The breadth of religious interaction becomes evident in Helmut Koester, *Introduction to the New Testament* (2 vols.; Foundations and Facets; Philadelphia, Fortress, 1982; Berlin/New York: De Gruyter, 1983) 1. 362–89; and in A. J. Festugière, *La Révélation d'Hermès Trismégiste* (3 vols.; Paris: Société d'Edition Les Belles Lettres, 1983).

[12] This is evident from the discovery of so vast a collection of materials at Nag Hammadi. While the relationship of the Nag Hammadi documents to the Pachomian monastery at Chenoboskion remains enigmatic, the existence of the Nag Hammadi collection alone attests at least to an early religious eclecticism.

[13] Peter R. L. Brown, "A Social Context to the Religious Crisis of the Third Century A.D.," *Protocol of the Colloquy of the Center for Hermeneutical Studies in Hellenistic and Modern Culture, 14* (Berkeley: Center for Hermeneutical Studies, 1975).

[14] Peter Brown, *The Making of Late Antiquity* (Cambridge: Harvard University Press, 1978) 1–8; see also idem, "The Philosopher in Late Antiquity," *Protocol of the Colloquy for Hermeneutical Studies in Hellenistic and Modern Culture 34* (Berkeley: Center for Hermeneutical Studies, 1980) 1–16.

[15] Garth Fowden, "The Pagan Holy Man in Late Antique Society," *Journal of Hellenic Studies* 102 (1982) 33–59.

guide and disciple in spiritual formation represents the intersection of society and individual at the point of individuation. Spiritual guidance created the individual in society.

This study explores some third-century spiritual guides to discover who could become guides, how they structured their relationships with their disciples, what they considered important to transmit, and how they characterized and expressed both the structure and content in spiritual formation. This project surveys their relationship. This relational description explores also the disciple's perspective: how philosophical material or Gnostic revelation was incorporated into the spiritual life of the disciple, how the disciple gained access to the guide, how the disciple understood the guide, how the guide gained her wisdom and teaching, and what the aspirations and limits (esp. sexual) were to their relationship.

Spiritual guides[16] express cultural religious forms and form others in the religious aspirations of a society, so that they are specifically oriented to a particular culture and religion. The study of the relationship between spiritual guide and disciple,[17] then, involves the concrete structuring of a complex nexus of cultural and religious meanings in a relationship. This study aims not at creating one ideal model of spiritual formation for the third century, but at laying out a broad range of possible structures for the relationship.

Four texts have been selected to represent four major religious movements of the third century: Christianity (Gregory Thaumaturgos's *Thanksgiving Speech*), Neoplatonism (Porphyry's *On the Life of Plotinus and the Order of His Books*), Hermeticism (the Nag Hammadi treatise *Discourse on the Eighth and Ninth*), and Gnosticism (the Nag Hammadi treatise *Allogenes*).[18] These four texts provide religiously diverse material which structure the relationship of guide to disciple from within a particular religious tradition.

As these texts present their spiritual guides, however, the reader begins to become suspicious: Gregory Thaumaturgos's thanksgiving speech portrays Origen as larger than life, semidivine; Porphyry's Plotinus moves about his world undisturbed from his noetic preoccupation. Likewise the divine figures

---

[16] Of especial interest regarding spiritual guides is P. Hadot, *Exercices Spirituels*, 59–74; and regarding the classical tradition from primarily an ethical perspective see Paul Rabbow, *Seelenführung. Methodik der Exerzitien in der Antike* (Munich: Kösel, 1954).

[17] The best study of master-disciple relationships in the fourth and fifth centuries is Philip Rousseau, *Ascetics, Authority, and the Church In the Age of Jerome and Cassian* (Oxford: Oxford University Press, 1978) 19–32.

[18] Judaism and Manichaeism are not treated in this thesis. Although they are major third-century religious movements, their inclusion would have significantly lengthened this study. On educational formation in Judaism, see Shaya J. D. Cohen, "Patriarchs and Scholiarchs," *Proceedings of the American Academy for Jewish Research* 48 (1981) 57–85.

seem too deflated: Hermes Trismegistus, described as a god, sounds remarkably like a hierophant; while Iouel, a mythic figure, teaches just like any other philosopher. Each of these texts present important information regarding their spiritual guides, but their descriptions and presentations create the suspicion that the treatises deliberately cast their guides into *personae* that transcend biographical or mere descriptive interests. The reader suspects duplicity. The literary and artistic organization of the material suggests that the text organizes (whether consciously or not) the content to communicate a particular understanding of the guide. The suspicion of duplicity points to the literary character of the texts.[19]

A simple theory of communication would clarify the duplicity by locating its origin. The text represents a message sent by a writer to a reader. The writer of the text must so encode the text linguistically and literarily that the reader may understand it. This assumes a common context from which both reader and writer draw, the writer for creating and the reader for interpreting. The text of the treatise, encoded with its literary and linguistic elements, presents the message to the reader refering to the context they both understand which enables the message to make sense.[20] The contemporary reader's suspicion arises because it is difficult to identify with clarity both the message and the mutually understood context which helps that message make sense. The reader senses that part of the communicated message has not yet become overt. The duplicity signals unexplained or uninterpreted messages in the text which seduce the reader into further interpretative activity.

Semiotic analyses aim to make explicit the underlying structures (the mutually understood context) which makes communication possible. Semiotics, both as a field of linguistic analysis and as a theory of interpretation began prior to Plato and Aristotle and has continued to today. From antiquity

---

[19] This concept of duplicity is based upon the literary theory of Robert Scholes (*Semiotics and Interpretation* [New Haven: Yale University Press, 1982] 21–22) who writes: "Whenever a communicative act encourages us to sense a difference between maker and speaker, our literary competence has been activated. This is true not only in such obvious situations as when we encounter the words of characters in plays or stories, but in essays also, whenever the essayist adopts a tone or role that seems to be a deviation from some anticipated norm."

[20] This theory is Roman Jakobson's "Closing Statement: Linguistics and Poetics," in Thomas A. Sebeok, ed., *Style in Language* (Cambridge: MIT Press, 1960) 350-77; a diagram of this communication theory is found on 353. Umberto Eco (*The Role of the Reader: Explorations in the Semiotics of Texts* [Bloomington: Indiana University Press, 1984] 5–7) significantly refines the theory by including more of the various interpretative stages both in the production and encoding of the text by the sender and in the philological and interpretative activity of the receiver. A clear introduction to Jakobson's thought as a whole may be found in Terrence Hawkes, *Structuralism and Semiotics* (Berkeley: University of California Press, 1977) 76–87, esp. 83.

onwards these linguistic theories have become a basis for interpretative theory.

Ancient semiotic theory explored signification primarily in relationship to speech and logic. The complete history of ancient semiotic theory need not be rehearsed here,[21] except for a brief overview. What is important is that ancient semiotic theory already presented itself as a search for underlying meaning. Both in the theories of language and of interpretation, allegory being the primary model, the ancient exegetes treated the surface (or literal level) of the text as signs which did not "contain," but signified a discourse more sublime or noetic. At the linguistic level, more properly in ancient terminology the rhetorical or poetic level, Aristotle explored "the nature of meaning and metaphor and the relation between literal and non-literal discourse" in the context of logic and rhetoric[22] by distinguishing primarily between the ordinary or literal use of language and the metaphoric. The Stoics developed a semiotic theory in both language and analysis. The Stoic linguistic theory, differentiating between expression, content and referent, claimed that meaning and expression were only possible where a logical syntax undergirded a linguistic syntax through which signs could rationally express meanings.[23] The Stoics also developed allegory as a semiotic interpretative tool in which the literal text functioned as a complex of signs which required exposition. Allegorical theory stipulated that beneath the literal text lay four levels of meaning which the exegete made explicit in another text, the commentary.

This allegorical method flourished in the writings of Clement of Alexandria and Origen in the East and Augustine in the West.[24] Their exegetical

---

[21] Martin Irvin ("Interpretation and the Semiotics of Allegory in Clement of Alexandria, Origen, and Augustine," *Semiotica* 63 [1987] 33–71) has written the most thorough of the historical studies of semiotics in antiquity because it also includes information about *grammatike*, dialectic and rhetoric as a basis for allegorical interpretation.

A full history of ancient semiotics has yet to be written. John Deely, *Introducing Semiotic: Its History and Doctrine* (Bloomington: Indiana University Press, 1982) devotes only six pages (7–12) to the entire ancient world, while giving little more to the important semiotic theories of Porphyry and Augustine. Umberto Eco (*Semiotics and the Philosophy of Language* [Bloomington: Indiana University Press, 1986]) briefly outlines Aristotle and the Stoics without attempting a historical analysis.

[22] Irvin, "Allegory," 36. These are the texts Irvin lists for Aristotle's theories of meaning: *Peri hermeneias*; *Poetica* 20–22; *Rhetorica* 3.

[23] The Stoic linguistic theory is presented in Eco, *Semiotics*, 29–33.

[24] Irvin presents the best study of these writers. On allegory generally see "Allegory," 33–42 and 57–60; on Clement of Alexandria, see pp. 42–45; and on Origen, see pp. 45–52.

St. Augustine's sign theory developed in the late-fourth and early-fifth century is the most influential and the most sophisticated theory after Origen. He develops his sign theory primarily in *Principia dialecticae*, *De doctrina Christiana* (Book III), and *De magistro*. See Irvin, "Allegory," 52–57; Eco, *Semiotics*, 33–39; Deely, *Introducing Semiotic*, 17–18; and R. A.

methods stipulated that they search for underlying systems of meaning which were imbedded in the text. The commentaries, especially Origen's *Homiliae in canticum canticorum* and *In Johannem commentarius*, and Augustine's *Ennarationes in Psalmos*, produced the secondary text fully exposing the inner meaning.[25] The value of the text lay in its exposition, not in the literal expression. Origen, for example, would argue in his *De principiis* (4.3.288–312) that some texts have no literal or historical meaning, and that there are stumbling blocks of impossibilities embedded in the text to force a higher or more spiritual reading.

This brief overview of ancient semiotic theory demonstrates that the texts chosen to be studied in this thesis were produced in an environment in which the deeper meaning of the text would be assumed. The literary theories of antiquity encouraged semiotic analysis. Their methods, however, were not designed to reveal the inner workings of the text, but to incorporate philosophical and intellectual discourse into the interpretative act. The referent, in other words, for semiosis was not the text itself, what they would call the literal level, but the intellectual and philosophical systems of thought in their culture.

Modern semiotic studies reverse the referent. A similar orientation toward the revelatory dynamic of text has been turned upon itself: the semiotic underpinning of the text becomes the subtext, the commentary rewrites the literal meaning so that it may communicate. Ferdinand de Saussure, a linguist and the modern founder of semiotics, distinguised between the structures which underlie a language (*langue*) and the particular instance of speaking (*parole*).[26] *Langue* includes the conventions which enable a language to work; *parole* covers the speech act itself. This distinction between the concrete manifestation and the system which enables it to work pervades all structural investigation. In structural literary theory, Jonathan Culler

---

Markus, "St. Augustine on Signs," in idem, ed., *Augustine: A Collection of Critical Essays* (New York: Anchor, 1972) 61–91.

[25] Patricia Cox Miller relates Origen's interpretative orientation to Roland Barthes's *The Pleasure of the Text* in a study which, as in this thesis, correlates ancient and modern interpretative theories: " 'Pleasure of the Text, Text of Pleasure': Eros and Language in Origen's *Commentary on the Song of Songs*," *JAR* 54 (1986) 241–53.

[26] The most convenient introduction to Saussure's thought is Hawkes, *Structuralism*, 19–28; and Jonathan Culler, *Ferdinand de Saussure* (rev. ed.: Ithaca: Cornell University Press, 1986).

For semiotic theory generally see Roland Barthes, *Elements of Semiology* (Paris: Editions du Seuil, 1964; New York: Hill and Wang, 1967) esp. 13–20 for Saussure; see also, Eco, *Reader*; and idem, *Semiotics*. The most extensive theoretical presentation remains idem, *A Theory of Semiotics* (Bloomington: Indiana University Press, 1979). A helpful collection of practical (and more radical) semiotics is Marshall Blonsky, ed., *On Signs* (Baltimore: Johns Hopkins University Press, 1985).

characterizes semiotics as the method "which seeks to describe the underlying systems of distinctions and conventions that enable objects and activities to have meaning."[27] Semiotic analysis of literary works, then, begins with the textual elements that betray a cultural system. In describing Origen as a teacher, Gregory Thaumaturgos refers to a Platonic myth of ascent to salvation. This myth underlies Gregory's message, but does not fully describe how it functions within Gregory's speech, because the myth enables Gregory to describe something different. Semiotic analysis uncovers the system that makes such communication possible.

To discover such cultural systems that lie behind communication does not mean that a cause or even an antecedent has been found. Semiotics seeks simply to construct the systems which enable meaning without ascribing causality or temporality to them. Culler explains:

> Structural explanation, as it seems best to call it, relates objects or actions to an underlying system of categories and distinctions which make them what they are. In this perspective, to explain phenomena is not to discover temporal antecedents and link them in a causal chain but to specify the place and function of the phenomena in a system.[28]

The system enables the text to signify: it neither in itself causes signification, or carries any particular signification, nor does temporal antecedence determine the meaning in the text. The system simply connects elements so that communciation is possible. The text's language encodes the message which the reader must recode to understand it.

Semiotic analysis, both ancient and modern, emphasizes the role or function of the reader or receiver of the text. Whether the reader was originally a third-century philosophical student or a twentieth-century scholar, she must connect the message of the text with enough of the contextual systems to make the text's communication understandable and to fascilitate the reader's interpretation. For example, in reading the treatises from Nag Hammadi, students begin to understand them only when they have read enough to understand the sorts of references made in the text: Jewish wisdom literature, creation myths, salvation myths, Hebrew and Christian biblical references, theological debates, philosophical speculation. The more students understand these conceptual systems, the more competent they are to make sense of the text and to interpret it. The reader of any text, as she knows the contextual systems, becomes competent to understand and interpret.

---

[27] Culler, *The Pursuit of Signs: Semiotics, Literature, Deconstruction* (Ithaca: Cornell University Press, 1981) 25.

[28] Ibid., 30.

This project has two parts. In the first part (Chapters 2 through 5), each text will be analyzed semiotically. The referent for each Chapter is the spiritual guide; the text, the signifier; and the particular construction of the spiritual guide, the signified. The analysis searches for the underlying system which gives meaning to that particular presentation of the spiritual guide. The method progresses in complexity in each succeeding Chapter. The Chapter on Gregory Thaumaturgos's text will exemplify the simple description of denotation and connotation as a semiotic means of uncovering the underlying systems. The Chapter on Porphyry will explore the concept of binary opposites to understand the conflict between two related literary programs within the treatise, an analysis which explores semiotically the literary encoding. The next Chapter (on the Hermetic texts) will investigate a more complex underlying system of encoding in which both narrative presentation and discursive reflection in the texts converge to create a complex system. In the next Chapter the Gnostic treatise *Allogenes* will proceed one step further and investigate the narratological systems underlying the various revelations. Each Chapter becomes increasingly more complex in both its literary and semiotic analysis.

These four Chapters lay out four different systems, sometimes with reverberations between them, for the construction and description of the relationship of spiritual guide to disciple. Separately they characterize four choices, or four possible systems for understanding the relationship. Together they begin to describe the range of underlying systems which were available in third-century cultures for the description. The aggregate of the systems represents more than the sum of each part, because it is now possible to explore the interconnection of systems and categories that were represented in the religious arena.

The final Chapter, by way of summary, will explore the overall possibilities for third-century religious people to explain the relationship of guide to disciple. In a sense, this chapter creates the reader's competence to read and interpret the texts which have already been studied. This is not an attempt to create one ideal, but to lay out the various cultural systems that were available.

Absence is a difference which makes meaning. In this final chapter it will become clear that some of the writers of these texts made clear decisions to include or exclude material. For example, three of the four treatises give instructions regarding the production and publication of the text. What does that absence signify in the remaining text? Likewise two texts have direct sexual reference, another flatly denies the sexual dynamic, and the last ignores it. What does that signify for each one? A more complete description of the possible systems will enhance the reader' competence to interpret the texts.

The following Chapters walk, as it were, with Anthony to observe some ascetics who explored their own spiritual formation by gaining control of themselves, living on the edge of their villages, and providing others with ascetical models. The Chapters will, like visits to different practitioners, explore the divergent and rich options available to ascetics in the fourth century. Each spiritual guide represented here could have been one of Anthony's.

2

The Spiritual Guide
as Teacher and Revealer

When scholars have studied Gregory Thaumaturgos's "Thanksgiving Speech" they have usually understood it to be a treatise about Origen: their interest lay primarily in information regarding Origen, not Gregory. This has created problems in that Gregory's speech has been treated as transparent to historical reality without a thorough evaluation of the text as source. No historical text, unfortunately, is so transparent.

From a semiotic perspective, the backward perspective into historical texts requires the contemporary reader of the text according to the theory of communication to make a "'philological' effort to reconstruct [a] sender's codes."[1] This semiotic reconstruction works at two different levels: the level of the language itself (called the dictionary meaning) and the level of the conceptual formulation (called the encyclopedia meaning). The bi-level procedure investigates not only the content (signified), but also the manner of expression (the signifier) in its most complex state. The philological reconstruction cannot assume that the content (the signified) may be taken without exploration of other levels of meaning in the text.

Most historians describe their reconstructions of the past as the reconstructions of the referents: the historical person or event, the linear movement through time and tradition. Semiotics cautions historians to recognize the limits of their own methods in that these referents are historical construc-

[1] Eco, *Reader*, 5.

tions, conceptual models created by historians to impose meaning on events or people. Such has been the case with Gregory Thaumaturgos's speech. Scholars have treated the "Thanksgiving Speech" attributed to Gregory Thaumaturgos from just such limited referential perspective. Tradition regards it to have been written by Gregory, eventually a bishop of Pontus and a wonderworker, about his teacher Origen who had left Alexandria for Caesarea. The text is thus known as Gregory Thaumaturgos's *In Origenem oratio panegyrica*.[2] These identifications of the author and the subject of the oration are carried in the title of the work,[3] although without specific reference within the text itself, and form the basis for the historical tradition about the text: that Gregory Thaumaturgos[4] (ca. 213–270 CE) studied with Origen in Caesarea for the five years from 233–238 CE, and wrote his *In Origenem oratio panegyrica* in 238.[5]

Scholarship has focused on the historically referential questions raised by the text. Crouzel, the most widely published scholar on Gregory, has been interested in showing the close and integral relationship between Gregory's thought and Origen's theology.[6] Pierre Nautin, who maintains that the name

---

[2] Both Johannes Quasten (*Patrology* [Utrecht-Antwerp: Spectrum, 1953] 2. 124–25) and Berthold Altaner and Alfred Stüber (*Patrologie* [Freiburg: Herder, 1978] 211) present Gregory as the author and Origen as the teacher-subject.

[3] For a discussion of the various titles see Henri Crouzel, "Le Remerciement a Origène de saint Grégoire le Thaumaturge: son contenu doctrinal," *Sciences écclesiastiques* 16 (1964) 60, n. 3. See also his introduction to idem, ed., *Grégoire le Thaumaturge. Remerciement à Origene suivi de La Lettre d' Origène à Grégoire* (SC 148; Paris: Cerf, 1969) 38–39. The other historical sources are summarized in idem, "Grégoire le Thaumaturge" in *Dictionnaire de Spiritualité* (Paris: Beauchesne, 1967) 6. 1014–20; as well as idem, *La Lettre*, 14–22.

[4] The traditional title of the *In Origenem oratio panegyrica* bears the name of "Saint Gregory the Wonderworker (Thaumaturgou)." Eusebius (*Hist. eccl.* 6.30) refers to Gregory, a bishop of Pontus, and identifies this Gregory with Theodore, one of the illustrious students of Origen. Pierre Nautin (*Origène: Sa Vie et Son Oeuvre* [Paris: Beauchesne, 1977] 81–84) while evaluating the sources for Origen's biography concludes that the oration is written by Theodore who is distinct from the Gregory of the Letter of Origen to Gregory and also from the Gregory of the oration. He maintains (p. 86) that Eusebius knew Gregory Thaumaturgos and Athenodore, the bishops of Pontus, and that he had the oration under the name of Theodore.

[5] The text used throughout is Crouzel, *La Lettre*. He employs P. Koetchau's text (*Des Gregorios Thaumaturgos Dankrede an Origenes als Anhang der Brief des Origenes an Gregory Thaumaturgos* [Freiburg, 1894]) as corrected by A. Brinkmann "Gregors des Thaumaturgen Panegyricus auf Origenes," *Rheinisches Museum für Philologie* 56 (1901) 55–76. There is a reliable translation by S. D. F. Salmond in ANF 6. The translations in this Chapter, however, are my own.

[6] See Crouzel, *La Lettre*, 46; and idem, "Le Remerciement," 59–61. This insistence on the correlation between Gregory and Origen is made explicit, e.g., in an article on another of Gregory's works where Crouzel ("La Passion de l'Impassible: Un essai apologétique et polémique du IIIe siècle," in *L'Homme devant Dieu: Mélanges offerts au Père Henri Lubac* [Paris: Aubier, 1964] 1. 274) writes: "If the *To Theopompus* is a work by the Thaumaturge, one

of the author of the address is Theodore, has been interested in the testimony this text provides for the study of Origen's life and work.[7] Finally, Adolf Knauber looks at the teaching method and purpose of Origen's school in Caesarea.[8] There has also been a keen desire to place the text solidly either within Alexandrian Christianity (Crouzel and Nautin) or within a generalized Hellenistic background (Knauber).[9]

These historically referential questions, however, do not address the issues that the text itself has raised. Gregory's speech at its most elementary level describes his teacher: *how* he understood his teacher and gave expression to that understanding; *how* his teacher taught him and brought him to a conversion; *what* his teacher taught him and in what order.[10] Gregory also employs complex metaphors and mythologies, written at the denotative and connotative levels of the text, to articulate his teacher's significance and the meaning of their relationship. The major denotation of the guide is "teacher" while the connotative systems extend to systems of revelation, asceticism, sexuality and mythology. Revelation and revelatory formation give structure to the relationship of guide to disciple in the transmission of tradition.

Two phenomena within the text itself draw attention to the articulation about the teacher and the structuring of this relationship. First, the text names itself as a "thank you speech." The speaker identifies the genre of the work as a λόγος εὐχαριστήριος [*In Origenem oratio panegyrica* III.31, see also IV.40],[11] a thanksgiving speech to a teacher upon the completion of the course of study. The speech surveys the teacher's educational program,

---

would expect some comparability with the doctrine of his revered teacher, Origen." See also Crouzel, *Origène* (Paris: Éditions Lethielleux, 1985).

[7] Nautin, *Origène*, 80–86, 184–197, 380–382.

[8] Knauber, "Das Anliegen der Schule des Origenes zu Caesarea," *MThZ* 19 (1968) 182–203. In this category is also Ferdinand Cavallera, "Origène éducateur," *BLE* 44 (1943) 61–75; and Crouzel, "Le Remerciement," 59.

[9] For the debate on whether the author, text, and school were Christian or not, see Knauber, *Schule*; and Crouzel's response in "L'Ecole d'Origène à Césarée: Postscriptum à une edition de Grégoire le Thaumaturge," *BLE* 71 (1970) 15–27.

[10] Robin Lane Fox (*Pagans and Christians* [New York: Knopf, 1987] 517–28) treats the subject of the speech as primarily referring to Gregory Thaumaturgos and not to Origen. Fox, however, takes the biographical material literally to describe Gregory's life.

[11] For a full discussion of the genre of the work see Crouzel, *La Lettre*, 38–39. The text does not easily fit into any of the categories of epideictic speeches. The closest would be "The Leavetaking" (συντακτικός) which is described in D. A. Russell and N. G. Wilson, ed. and trans., *Menander Rhetor* (Oxford: Clarendon, 1981) 195–201; this form, however, applies mostly to departing from a city. Gregory includes some of the elements and tone of the leavetaking, but without fully aligning his speech to the genre. Fox (*Pagans and Christians*, 525) calls it a "thank you letter" even though there seems to be no epistolary element in it; earlier it is called a "panegyric" (p. 517). Its genre must, therefore, remain enigmatic.

the nature of the student's relationship with the teacher, and the teacher's method of instruction. In this way the speech explicitly addresses the nature of the student's spiritual formation in the tradition by the teacher. And this explication forms the heart of the text.

The various "voices" of the text indicate the second interior phenomenon. Personal pronouns are "textual strategies" which function as referential indexes on the subjects of the discourse.[12] There are three: an "I," a "we," and a "he/you," representing the speaker, a larger audience, and the teacher. These voices indicate that the text represents a discussion among people who are part of an inner circle, the intimates of "I" and "we."

The first narrative voice is a conscious speaker who at times is self-reflecting about his own artistry (or claimed lack of it). This voice shares some biographical information (V.48–72) which relates entirely to the speaker's education and to his providential meeting with the teacher of philosophy, but the information cannot firmly be established as either fictive detail or as historical fact.

The second narrative voice is a first-person plural whose referent is never indicated: it could be the speaker's brother (V.69), or fellow students, or the audience at the presumed presentation of the speech, or a combination of all of these. The result, however, is that the speech includes in its expression a narrative voice beyond the speaker, a voice which indicates a speaker and a more inclusive voice. This "we" is the point at which the audience at the speech-giving and "we," the historical reader, enter the text. This includes both audiences, not as an objectified "you" to whom information is given as to people excluded from the discourse, but as (albeit passive) participants in the event.

The third voice is that of the third-person-singular reference to the teacher which will be analysed in this Chapter. The teacher is presented as objectified, as a distanced referent. Occasionally he is addressed directly, but mostly the separation from him strategically mirrors the occasion of withdrawal from him as teacher.

These voices set up the dynamic of the text in the context of its self-named thanksgiving. The speech explores the nature of the relationship of these three voices by presenting its structure and by exploring both the denotations and connotations of that relationship in various cultural settings.

The spiritual guide is a teacher. The student's speech develops, through its secondary systems of signification, a particular mythological interpretation of the role and function of the teacher. In the context of describing the educational process, the speaker connotes that the teacher is part of a myth of

---

[12] Eco, *Reader*, 10–11.

translation to a divine region. By practice of migration godwards the teacher becomes divine, and returns from that divine region to pass on the benefits received from that translation. In another secondary system, the student describes his bonding to the teacher, while the teacher, as divine agent, in another connotative system plants a spark in the soul of the student and thus includes the student in the mythic structure of educational and spiritual formation. As connotative systems, both the bonding and the planting of the spark have sexual implications. Education is placed in the context of a myth of salvation through relationship with a divine agent. This mythic construction defines the role and function of the teacher as revealer.

This Chapter consists of four sections. In the first I will investigate briefly the educational biographical section of the oration for a description of the levels and types of teachers. This will entail an exploration of denotative categories. It will be seen that the student's teacher of philosophy, the culminating teacher in a series of educational situations, is singled out as divine. In the second section, I will look at the description of the subject matter of the oration: the teacher in the context of the myth of translation to and return from the divine. Here will be seen the benefits the teacher receives for his effort. This section outlines the major connotative systems of the teacher's signification. In the third section, I will describe the student-teacher relationship as a bond which ends in the planting of a salvific spark into the student's psyche. The student is converted to the teacher and to philosophy. This, together with its sexual implications, constitutes the actual form of the relationship. In the fourth section, I will describe the teacher as revealer in the student's speech and develop the concept of the spiritual guide as teacher and revealer.

The Different Teachers

There are four levels of educators[13] in the short educational biography in which the student explains how fortuitously he came to study with the teacher. This biography constitutes an exploration of the denotations of the spiritual guide. The first educators were his parents whose primary work was to rear him (V.48) and to be sure that he received the elementary education proper to a well-born child [V.56]. When he began to mature (described as the coming of reason), his mother enrolled (φοιτᾶν [V.56]) him with a rhetor, his second teacher. Discerning his ability as a rhetor, his rhetorical

---

[13] These four educators reflect the common practice of Roman education which has been described by Stanley F. Bonner, *Education in Ancient Rome From the Elder Cato to the Younger Pliny* (Berkeley: University of California Press, 1977) 3–96.

teacher arranged for the student to become a hearer (V.60) in law. The student's law teacher is his third. The student was not interested so much in law as in pleasing the teacher ("I was persuaded rather to please the man than to be a lover of the art" [V.59].). The law teacher made a statement about the student, namely that the law "would be a viaticum for him," which the student describes as an oracle delivered by a divine inspiration. The images are piled up: the law teacher "utters by inspiration" and "by some more divine inspiration." This piling of images underscores the oracular presentation. The law teacher, then, is portrayed as someone capable of delivering an oracle.

The oracle, namely, that law was a viaticum, was literally true because the student travelled on family business when he met his fourth teacher in Berytus. The spiritual meaning of the oracle was that he was not to study law, but philosophy with this man. With this teacher, the student experienced "communion" (κοινωνία [V.70]) and "the assistance of our souls toward salvation" (V.70).[14] And it is to this philosophical teacher that his guardian angel and *paidagogos*, has entrusted him.

The philosophical teacher is described in the educational biography as a "holy man" (V.63) from Alexandria whose life has providentially intersected the student's life. The student refers to him, moreover, as a "divine man" who is the guide for him in his conversion to philosophy. He writes of his conversion: "But one thing was dear and beloved to me: philosophy and the guide to her, this divine man" (VI.84). The student, then, attributes divinity, or at least a special relationship to divinity, to his last teacher.

The student presents four denotative interpretations of spiritual guides who are teachers: parents, rhetor, lawyer, and philosopher. Each one has its own specific educational orientation, performed under the guidance of the guardian angel.[15] The presence of the guardian angel draws attention: it stands as a sign of the spiritual significance of formation. The guardian angel spiritualizes educational formation by directing the significance away from the merely paedagogic. With each educational development there is, moreover, an increment of spiritualization of the teacher's function. Under his parents he attains the capacity for reason. His rhetorical teachers discern his talent, and point him to the law teacher who proclaims an oracle. The mantic function is replaced by a divine one in the philosopher, the final teacher.

---

[14] This teacher is not the only philosopher available to the student, but unlike the others, he professes to be a true teacher and one who instructs both in word and life (XI.133–36).

[15] The guardian angel (δαίμων) as teacher is not unusual in that it is raised here, in *Allogenes* 45,9–10, and in Porphyry "Life and Books" 10.15–34. See E. R. Dodds, *The Greeks and the Irrational* (Berkeley: University of California Press, 1951) 42–43 (with notes identifying Platonic references), and 289–90 (which deals with the *daemon* in Porphyry "Life and Books").

With each teacher there is also an increment of devaluation of the content of teaching in favor of a relationship with the teacher. The law teacher, not law, is the source of his attention, and when he encounters the teacher he experiences κοινωνία. The progression of teachers moves the student closer at each level to the divine teacher who is his revealer.

The exploration of the denotative categories creates a curious admixture of elements here. At its most simple denotation, the educational biography presents a sequence of educational formation from parents, to rhetoric, to law, to philosophy. That simple sequence, however, when viewed from the connotative systems produces rhetors who discern, lawyers who pronounce oracles, philosophers who are divine, and a divine figure who is a paedagogue. The simplicity of the denotative sequence vanishes in the connotative systems.

The guardian angel further complicates the process of formation, for at one level the educational formation does not take place where it appears to be (with parents, rhetor, and lawyer), but these apparent levels of formation are merely tools of the spiritual paedagogue. Their spiritual function becomes the important, and yet hidden, significance of the educational formation. The guardian angel, moreover, delivers the student to the philosophical teacher and disappears from the scene until the end when the student is about to leave the teacher. The divine figure entrusts the student to a humanly divine person for formation, and only resumes its function again when the divine philosophy teacher is no longer guiding. Providentially orchestrated, the formation remains hidden and divine: the significance of the signs hinges on their relationship to the guardian angel.

The Teacher in the Myth of Ascetical Transfer

This scrambling of significations prepares the further explanation of the philosopher. Two connotative systems interweave to portray the figure of the teacher. The first system revolves about a myth of the ascent and descent of a revealer figure. The second connotative system, derivative from the first, explores the benefits derived from that myth of ascent and thus further expands the range of significances.

This philosophical teacher, the divine man, is the subject of the oration. The student defines how the teacher is divine by describing the teacher in terms of an esoteric myth which he characterizes as a "transfer" by practice into the divine. The student suggests this mythic construction at a critical point when he introduces the subject of his oration. This is the first impression the reader/hearer receives of the teacher and thus it is an important clue to imaging the teacher. The description sets the stage for the audience's understanding of the subject and its interpretation of the teacher:

> I intend to say something about the man on the one hand who is an apparent and seeming human being (Περὶ γὰρ ἀνδρὸς διανοοῦμαί τι λέγειν, φαινομένου μὲν καὶ δοκοῦντος ἀνθρώπου), and on the other hand (for those who have the greater capacity to see [τὸ δὲ πολὺ τῆς ἕξεως τοῖς καθορᾶν δυναμένοις]) who is already transferred by a greater practice of migration toward God. (II.10)

Having set out the subject of the oration, the student also relates that his interest is not in relating the teacher's birth, rearing, or beauty, but rather :

> What are his most godlike [attributes] and whatever in him happens to be related to God, both being enclosed in this visible and mortal person (ἐγκαθειργμένον μὲν τῷ φαινομένῳ καὶ θνητῷ τῷδε), and pressing hard with as much labor as possible to become like God (ὅτι δὲ φι⟨λο⟩πονώτατα ἐξομοιοῦσθαι βιαζόμενον τῷ θεῷ). (II.13)

There are essentially five individual elements to the mythic construction of the teacher's transference. The first element delimits who is able to approach this "seeming" aspect of the teacher. Only "those who have the greater capacity to see" may appropriate this other aspect of the teacher. This presents the teacher-student relationship as esoteric: to those capable of seeing, there is another reality available.

The second element is that the subject, the teacher, is a human being who is "enclosed in a visible and mortal person." He is also, however, an apparent and seeming human being. The teacher, although enclosed in the mortal, visible body, is also one whose existence is only apparent or seeming. The student grants that his teacher is mortal, but that he also has a "docetic" quality about him.[16]

The third element relates that the teacher is "already transferred" (ἀπεσκευασμένου ἤδη). In the middle, ἀποσκευάζειν means to "pack up and depart" or, if in the passive, it is "to be transferred."[17] The image implies that the teacher has already moved, been transferred, departed, or removed himself to another arena. Presumably this forms a part of the "seeming" quality of the teacher that, although in his mortal person, he is also removed.

[16] The possible alignment of the teacher with a "docetic" figure is highly suggestive of discussions of the 2d and 3d centuries about the divinity of Jesus and his mortality. See J. N. D. Kelly *Early Christian Doctrines* (rev. ed.; New York: Harper and Row, 1978) 141.

[17] See LSJ, 217.

The transferred state is described further as a "migration which is toward the divine" (μεταναστάσεως τῆς πρὸς τὸ θεῖον). The abstract noun form of this word is rare. The verbal form means "to flee, to wander, to leave home." As a noun it means "a fugitive, a wanderer." As an abstract noun it means "migration"[18] and suggests that the teacher gradually moved from his home toward the divine. The teacher entered a process of migration—a migration not to another country but to an altered state of existence, the divine.

The fourth element describes the teacher as transferred "by a greater practice" (μείζονι παρασκευῇ). Παρασκευή has the sense of preparation, practice, arrangement, provision, training. It seems to be synonomous with *askesis*, but without the connotation of physical, athletic practice. The teacher achieves the transfer and the migration toward the divine through his own activity and practice. It is not something conferred upon the teacher by the divinity, but something that results from his labor.

The teacher, moreover, is described as "pressing hard with as much hard labor as is possible." The migration toward God and the "becoming like God" require difficult effort and perseverance. It is not a divine status given freely, but a divine status earned by hard work.

The fifth element relates that the end of pressing hard is to become like God. This godlike aspect of the teacher is the subject of the oration and the teacher's goal.[19] The teacher works in order to become godlike, and to the student this is the most important aspect of the teacher. The student presents his teacher as one who has migrated toward the divine by his hard work and one who has worked as hard as possible to become like God.

The student does not say that his teacher is God, but godlike.[20] The exuberance of the divine man who is the advocate of philosophy yields here to a more precise description of the relationship of the teacher to God. The teacher earned his divine likeness through his hard work. The divine likeness had much of the power of God to draw the student into relationship ("we were drawn to him by some greater necessity in his words": ὥσπερ ὑπό

---

[18] See *LPGL*, 854.

[19] Plotinus (*Enneads* I.2, "On Virtue") connects the godlikeness to the acquiring of virtues. Taking up an argument from Plato's *Theaetetus* that the escape from evil is to become godlike, Plotinus argues that the acquisition of certain virtues ends in becoming godlike. Our speech, however, does not restrict the godlike status to the arena of virtue, but relates it to the teacher's ascetical activity. Plotinus's argument is mirrored more closely in the section of the speech which presents the study of virtue (IX.115–26).

[20] For a discussion of the biographical difference between being a "son of God" or "God-like" see Patricia Cox, *Biography in Late Antiquity: A Quest for the Holy Man* (Berkeley: University of California Press, 1983) 17–44.

τισιν ἀνάγκαις μείζοσι τοῖς λόγοις αὐτοῦ πρὸς αὐτὸν ἑλκόμενοι [VI.78])
because there was a sort of divine power in his words ("he set us up by his
speeches, I don't know how, with a sort of divine power": ἡμᾶς
παριδρύσατο λόγοις τοῖς αὐτοῦ, οὐκ οἶδ' ὅπως, σύν τινι θείᾳ δυνάμει
[VI.80]). The teacher has the divine attractiveness: the same ability to draw
as does the divine.

These five elements combine to create a clear construction of the teacher's
relationship to God. The teacher begins as a human being who is totally
human and mortal (2). Through hard work, labor, preparation, practice (4),
the teacher "packs up and leaves" (3) his mortal state and appearance in
order to take on a more "apparent and seeming humanity" through migration toward God (3). The migration removes the humanlike aspects of birth,
beauty, and strength, and heightens the more godlike attributes of his being
(4). The teacher thus becomes like God, and like God is able to attract and
compel students/people (5). None of this, however, is readily apparent,
except to those whose ability to see enables them to apprehend (1) the divinized status of the teacher.

The student's description of the teacher relates an esoteric myth. To those
who do not have the power to see, there is nothing different about the
teacher. For those who are able to see the difference, the teacher, gradually
divinizing himself through his practice of migration, sheds humanity in order
to enter the inner communion with the divinity.[21] The images are of spatial
migration, of moving from one place to another, and these spatial images are
used metaphorically to describe the gradual interior progression of a human
being into divine status. This esoteric myth echoes the guardian angel's
paedagogic function. A hidden supernatural orientation supercedes the
apparently natural development: behind the teacher is a guardian angel
paedagogue, and behind the philosophical teacher is a divine man. Each has
greater significance and value in their supernatural orientation. These godlike statuses would only be known to the students.

Plato first develops the mythic construction of ascent to divinity, or to the
divine regions, as a means of education. In the *Symposium* (210A–212A) he
describes the youth's ascent from corporeal beauty, to conceptual beauty, to
formal beauty, and to the psychic beauty beyond form as a preparation for the
higher contemplation of laws, science, and wisdom. Such ascent not only
educates but also saves the youth by freeing him from bodily existence to
become "like the gods" (*Theaetetus* 176AB).[22] Gregory's myth, however,

---

[21] For a discussion of the concept of divinization as it appears in the speech, see Crouzel, *La Lettre*, 73–74; and idem, "Le Remerciement," 84–85.
[22] John D. Turner ("The Gnostic Threefold Path to Enlightenment: The Ascent of Mind and

does not exactly describe an ascent through ontological levels, but an ascetic "transfer" to another, more divine realm. It might be that Gregory's "practice" and Plato's graded ascents are the same, but Gregory does not make this explicit. Gregory's "transfer" seems much more bilocational than Plato's gradual ascent, and yet Gregory seems to draw upon the Platonic ascent.

This myth of ascent presents the first connotative system which explains *how* the teacher became divine. The second system evolves from the benefits of such an ascent. These benefits locate the ascent not as an escape,[23] but as the first step (albeit incomplete) in formation which equips the teacher to guide students: the teacher does not flee from the cosmos but ascends to the divinity in order to descend again as a fully mature spiritual guide. The ascent procures divinity for the teacher; the descent procures the benefits for the student. The benefits are described as prophetic revelation. The complex connotative systems (prophetic, legal, social, educational, oracular, hermeneutical) weave together the revelatory function of the teacher.

The migration godward procures for the teacher certain benefits which are passed on to the student. These three classes of benefits derive from the teacher's special relationship to the divine: they represent the fruit of the teacher's labor of migration. The first class of benefits establishes that, because of the teacher's close proximity to God, God honors the teacher as friend[24] and establishes the teacher as an advocate or mouthpiece:

> For the leader of all men, who gives promptings to the prophets who are friends of God and who suggests every prophesy and secret and divine word, honoring him thus as a friend established him as a mouthpiece. (XV.176)

There are three indications of the intimate relationship: first the indication that the teacher has an equal status as the "prophets who are friends of God" and the suggestion that such a status opens the teacher to hearing prophetic, secret, and divine discourse. In the second God honors him as a friend. It is not simply that the teacher has the title "friend of God," but that God has honored him as a friend. In the third the teacher receives the title προήγορος which means literally advocate, or someone who speaks on another's behalf. In this context it could well mean "mouthpiece."

---

the Descent of Wisdom," *NovT* 22 [1980] 332–46) explores the Platonic ascent ontologically and epistemologically.

[23] On the theme of ascent as escape see Gregory Shaw, "Apotheosis in Later Platonism: Salvation as Theurgic Embodiment," in Kent Harold Richards, ed., SBLASP (Atlanta: Scholars Press, 1987) 111–12 and 119.

[24] On the wider significance of this designation see Brown, *Making*, 54–80.

The second class of benefits relates to the description of the teacher as a hearer of God: "He was a skilled and sagacious hearer of God" (δεινὸς ὤν ἀκροατὴς θεοῦ καὶ συνετώτατος [XV.174]). The teacher becomes a hearer of God: this establishes the student-teacher relationship with the divinity, so that the teacher, learning as a student directly from God, passes on this relationship to his own student.[25] Such a conception elevates the status and importance of student-teacher to a primary means whereby God relates to others.

The teacher's "hearer" relationship to God implies an educationally intimate connection. The student attributes this connectedness to the teacher's communion with the divine spirit:

> He says these things not in any other way it seems to me than by communion with the divine spirit (κοινωνίᾳ τοῦ θείου πνεύματος), for that same power is necessary both for those who prophesy and for those who listen to the prophets. Unless the spirit of prophesying itself has bestowed upon him the intelligence of his words, he will not be able to hear the prophet. (XV.179)

The teacher's ability to learn from God rests on sharing the divine spirit. This divine spirit becomes the common denominator of the ability to speak, to hear, and to understand prophesy. At the ontic level at which the teacher functions, the shared participation in the divine spirit further indicates the intimacy of the relationship.

The third class of benefits wherein the teacher becomes an interpreter of the oracles of God clarified this intimate participation:

> This is the greatest gift which he received from God and he was able to distribute every beautiful thing from heaven: to be an interpreter of the oracles of God for humanity (ἑρμηνεὺς εἶναι τῶν τοῦ θεοῦ λόγων πρὸς ἀνθρώπους), to understand the things of God as spoken by God (συνιέναι τὰ θεοῦ ὡς θεοῦ λαλοῦντος), and to expound for humanity as they are listening (καὶ διηγεῖσθαι ἀνθρώποις ὡς ἀκούουσιν ἄνθρωποι). (XV.181)

The teacher's ability to understand God as God speaks and to teach human beings as they listen manifests the immediacy of the teacher's relationship to God. This represents a mutual and immediate participation of teacher in God, and student in teacher, so that the interpretation of the oracles of God becomes a sign of the intimate and continuing communion which the teacher shares with God. The teacher, therefore, acts as an interpreter and expounder

---

[25] The Arians (Arius and Asterius) also seem to have described the relationship of Father to Son as Teacher to Student. See Robert C. Gregg and Dennis E. Groh, *Early Arianism: A View of Salvation* (Philadelphia: Fortress, 1981) 163–64, 169–70.

of whatever is difficult in the Scriptures: ''He interpreted and clarified whatever was obscure and riddling'' (αὐτὸς ὑποφητεύων καὶ σαφηνίζων ὅ τί ποτε σκοτεινὸν καὶ αἰνιγματῶδες ἦ [XV.174]). The language here again is mantic: the teacher acts as one able to expound, as a priest who presents an oracle. The teacher, as a hermeneut, really functions as a revealer of the divine oracles, clarifying what is dark and unclear, but most importantly, relating what he hears from God in the inner sanctum of his participation in the divine being.

Friend and advocate of God, hearer of God through communion with the divine spirit, interpreter of the oracles of God—these benefits result from the teacher's ascetical transfer into the divinity. When these benefits interact with the myth of ascent and descent, they extend the range of significations. No one category explains the teacher; no one arena of activity captures the teacher's essence. The teacher functions in social (''friend of God'') and legal ''mouthpiece'' (προήγορος) categories, as well as in prophetic and oracular circles. The teacher's revelation surpasses the coeval categories and creates a different signification which at once transcends those categories and emerges from them.

The Student-Teacher Relationship

The structure of the student-teacher relationship communicates the method of transmission of the tradition. The relationship addresses the question of *what* the teacher does. In the broader arena of spiritual guides, the relationship describes how the adept directs the growth of the disciple. The answer to the question *what* does not relate to the content of the tradition: the answer is only minimally ''to teach'' because the more important bonding of student to teacher, a conversion of one to the other, precedes the teaching. The arena of the solidification of relationship becomes mythic and recreates at another level the myth of ascent and descent. This is accomplished through the constellation of connotative systems which describe the relationship: bonding, conversion, planting of a spark, Scriptural exegesis.

In the context of such a presentation of the teacher, the structure of the relationship between student and teacher takes on added importance: it is not just the relationship of human and divine in an anthropology, but the social relationship of human and divine. The divine realm enters society through a person in a relationship: the student encounters the divine in the person of the teacher. The structure of the relationship actually gives form to the means of revelation in a community.

The teacher's practice of transfer has procured for him these benefits. But how the benefits are transmitted to the student has not yet been explained.

The sixth chapter of the speech, still prior to the description both of the content and of the dialectical method of the educational system, presents the means of transmittal of such benefits as the relationship of student to teacher inaugurated in the student's conversion.

The basis of the relationship and the means of transmitting the benefits is a "binding." The teacher "used every means to bind us" (συνδήσασθαι πάντα τρόπον ἐμηχανήσατο [VI.74])—discourse, everything of beauty, and all of his powers (VI.74). These means were employed to praise the philosophical life (ἐπαινῶν μὲν φιλοσοφίαν καὶ τοὺς φιλοσοφίας ἐραστὰς [VI.75]) and to condemn ignorance (ψέγων δὲ τὴν ἀμαθίαν καὶ πάντας τοὺς ἀμαθεῖς [VI.76]). The binding had with it an element of compulsion or necessity because the teacher wielded personal power: "For he was in some way a mixture of a sweet grace and persuasiveness and a kind of compulsion" (ἦν γάρ πως καὶ ἡδείᾳ τινὶ χάριτι καὶ πειθοῖ καί τινι ἀνάγκῃ μεμιγμένος [VI.78]). The power, the compulsion and attractiveness were located in the teacher, not in philosophy. The teacher attracted and bound the student and eventually "set us up beside himself by his words, I don't know how, with a kind of divine power" [VI.80]. The bonding is at first to the teacher and then to philosophy.

The bonding constitutes, moreover, a conversion:[26] the student converts to the teacher by being bound to him through discourse and relationship. The speech presents two descriptions of this bonding/conversion. The first is the "arrow" of the teacher's discourse: "We were shot as by some sort of arrow (ὥσπερ τινὶ βέλει) by his discourse" (VI.78). The effect of the shooting with a discursive arrow was a conversion to philosophy and a powerful attraction to the teacher:

> We turned somehow and also reasoned, and we adhered to the study of philosophy, not as yet persuaded by everything, but we were not able (I don't know why) to stand apart (from him), and we were always drawn toward him as by some compulsion greater than his words. (VI.78)

---

[26] On the concept of divine figures who descend and convert see Ramsay MacMullen, "Two Types of Conversion to Early Christianity" *VC* 37 (1983) 174–92, esp. 178. A. D. Nock (*Conversion: The Old and the New in Religion from Alexander the Great to Augustine of Hippo* [Oxford: Clarendon, 1933] 167–85) argues that the only true non-Christian conversion was the pagan's conversion to philosophy; MacMullen (*Christianizing the Roman Empire [AD100–400]* [New Haven: Yale University Press, 1984]) has largely discredited this. All of these studies seem to consider conversion in the predominantly Christian sense of a turn away from a false to a true religion. The possibility of conversions to different lifestyles (as in the educational arena, to philosophy; and within Christianity, to monasticism) has not been studied: it would require a different understanding of the concept of conversion.

The attraction and conversion is more completely to the teacher because of his compelling power and his persistent invitation to philosophy. Although not completely convinced by philosophy, they could not leave the teacher because they were drawn to him as by a divine force. The teacher has become the primary force and object of the conversion; philosophy remains secondary. Through their bonding to the teacher, they begin to relate, albeit hesitatingly, to philosophy. The arrow of discourse bonds the student to teacher, of conversion to philosophy: the two are almost synonomous.

The second description, confirming the conversion more to the teacher than to philosophy, is the "dart of friendship": "For truly he even hurled the dart of friendship (φιλίας . . . κέντρον) at us" (VI.81). This dart of friendship became an intimate means of personal bonding. That bonding ends in salvation and a participation in the benefits which had been bestowed upon the teacher:

> He was not trying otherwise to circumvent us by words, but by dextrous and philanthropic and useful purpose both to save us and to establish us as participants in the good which comes from philosophy and especially in those other (benefits) which the deity bestowed upon him alone. (VI.81–82)

Once the teacher binds the student to himself, the student may participate in the benefits both of philosophy and of those which the deity bestowed upon the teacher. The bonding of student to teacher is salvific: the teacher initiates the relationship through his various powers both logical and divine in order to save the student and to enable the student to receive the benefits of the teacher's knowledge and divine skills.

So much of Gregory Thaumaturgos's description of the teacher-student interaction revolves about suggestions of sexual relations that clearly the sexual dynamic exceeds the Platonic model of education in the *Symposium*. Gregory shows no evidence of abstracting from physical relationships to noetic, because his language consistently betrays the physical aspect. At first, their relationship appears to be classically Platonic: the teacher attracts and compels the student by his beauty to begin the educative ascent. But Gregory's description never moves from that attraction. The teacher entwines the student in a compelling discourse in which he is drawn to the teacher first and only secondarily to philosophy, as though he hurled a "dart of friendship" at him. Until this point one can only presume a sexual relationship. With the "spark," however, the sexual dynamic becomes explicit, and in the scriptural exegesis Gregory justifies that sexual relationship.

Gregory explains that this bonding results in a planting of a spark in the soul:

Therefore such a spark—the love which is both towards the same holy and beloved logos which attracts everyone by his inexpressable beauty, and toward this man who is his friend and mouthpiece—being thrust into the midst of our soul was lit and burned. (VI.83)

The spark (σπινθήρ)²⁷ is identified with love (ἔρως)²⁸ toward the attractive logos and towards the logos's friend and advocate/mouthpiece. The emphasis, however, is on the planting of the spark within the soul. There is an identification of love (ἔρως) with such a spark (οἷος τις σπινθήρ): the spark and the love mutually define one another.

The thrusting of the spark into the soul has sexual connotations, not only because the image itself suggests pederasty (a pederasty in keeping with the *Symposium* and Roman practice as well),²⁹ but also because even as a Gnostic term "spark" has a sexual meaning. Aside from the medical references to "spark" as a seed or principle of life which converts blood into male semen or female milk,³⁰ the Gnostic spark is a principle of generation, especially in Sethian mythology. Michel Tardieu, in studying the metaphor of the spark, includes the generative signification,³¹ although he does not emphasize it. He refers spark to ψυχή, νοῦς, πνεῦμα, and ἔρως as an enlivening and salvific principle, and as a sign of the gnostic. The identification of spark with seed and the love in this context leaves no option: Gregory presents the relationship sexually.

The effect of the planting of the spark of love into the soul is to complete

---

²⁷ The spark (σπινθήρ) is an element in Gnostic mythology. In the *Excerpta Ex Theodoto*, e.g., the spark is the spiritual seed which the Son deposits with the Father at his death on the Cross. The spark is created by the logos and kindled by the savior in order to bestow life. It is thus a salvific principle planted in humanity and kindled by the savior. The spark plays a similar role in the mythology of the "Apocryphon of John," and Hippolytus. For a discussion of the spark in the Gnostic cosmology see Kurt Rudolph, *Gnosis: The Nature and History of Gnosticism* (New York: Harper and Row, 1983) 57, 66–67. See also Hans Jonas's discussion of Gnostic anthropology in *The Gnostic Religion* (2d ed.; Boston: Beacon, 1963) 44.

²⁸ This ἔρως is part of the Platonic educational and relational system: see the *Symposium* and the *Phaedrus*. For a full discussion see: A. H. Armstrong, "Platonic *Eros* and Christian *Agape*," *Downside Review* 79 (1961) 105–21. See also idem and R. A. Markus *Christian Faith and Greek Philosophy* (London: Darton, Longman and Todd, 1960); and Markus, "The Dialectic of Eros in Plato's Symposium," *Downside Review* 73 (1955) 219–30.

²⁹ The sexual relationship caused Plutarch problems, but he felt that it was an important part of educational formation. See Plutarch "On the Education of Children" 15–16.

³⁰ The sexual theories of Galen will be discussed in Chapter 4 below. The immediate reference within Gnosticism is to Hippolytus *Refutatio omnium haeresium* 6.13 when he discussed Simon Magus (ANF 5. 79).

³¹ Tardieu, "ΨΥΧΑΙΟΣ ΣΠΙΝΘΗΡ Histoire d'une métaphore dans la tradition platonicienne jusqu'à Eckhart," *Revue des Etudes Augustiniennes* 21 (1975) 225–55.

the conversion by making the student an alien, one who withdraws from society:[32]

> Being especially wounded by it [love] I was persuaded to have no care for all of the deeds or lessons which seemed proper to me, and among other things even my own wonderful (study of) law, nor for fatherland and household and the things present there and those from which we had departed. But for me there was one friend and beloved: philosophy and the guide to her, this divine man. (VI.84)

The spark of love leads to a total rejection of social and political ties, as well as a rejection of career and personal aspirations. The student becomes an alien bonded to philosophy and to the guide to philosophy, the divine teacher. The conversion which has taken place in the student begins the process of migration godward. The spark having been placed in the student's soul, the student's orientation focuses entirely on the divine realm, philosophy and the divine guide.

This description of the conversion is linked syntactically to a long (VI.85–92) exegetical diversion:

> But for me there was one friend and beloved, philosophy and the guide to her, this divine man; "and the soul of Jonathan was bound to David" (καὶ συνεδέθη ἡ ψυχὴ Ἰωνάθαν Δαυίδ). (VI.84–85)

The point of the diversion is twofold. First, that the binding of Jonathan to David was a binding of their ruling powers, the psyche: αὐτὰ τὰ κυριώτατα, ψυχή (VI.86). This orients the binding to the intellective, noetic aspects of human being, and thus justifies the sexual dynamic in the same way that the physical beauty is justified in the Platonic system. The second point of the diversion is to explain the relationship of the greater, more advanced guide to the lesser advanced disciple. Since the souls are free (VI.87) and since the greater has no need of the lesser but the lesser has need of the greater, it is the responsibility of the greater to establish the bonds with the lesser:

> For the greater, being independent, would not choose to be bound to its lesser, but it is necessary for the lesser, being in need of the aid which is from the better, and being bound, to be attached to the greater in order that on the one hand that which remains in itself might have the benefit of no harm from the communion with the less, and, on the other hand, that which is disorderly in itself, which is thoroughly bound and fitted to the better aspect, might without harm be subdued by the necessity of the bonds to the better. (VI.90)

---

[32] For a discussion of ἀναχώρησις, see Crouzel, *La Lettre*, 74–76.

The binding of the greater to the lesser does not diminish the independence of the greater, while it does supply the necessary assistance to the lesser. The teacher remains, thus, independent and beyond diminishment by the binding to the student, while the student bound to the greater power, is subdued without harm. The sexual nature of the relationship continues in the question of submission, a posture inappropriate to men of stature.[33]

The relationship of the student to the teacher, thus, mirrors the mythic structure that was seen in the teacher's relationship with the divine. The teacher, described as progressing godward gradually leaving behind the mortal frame and assimilating more and more to the divine, achieved a sort of divine status through his effort. The teacher becomes a powerful force in attracting others to him, a divine attraction derived from his particular relationship with the divine and from the benefits of the divine which have been peculiarly bestowed upon him. Returning to the mortal realm, the teacher binds students to himself through his discursive powers, the power of the beautiful itself, and through his achieved divine powers. This binding brings the student to a point of conversion at which time a spark is planted in the soul and is lit and burns. This implanting of the spark leads the student to become an alien by rejecting his former social and intellectual identity and by orienting himself entirely to both philosophy and the divine guide. The divine quest which was the starting point for the teacher has now, thus, been passed on to the student.

The sexual image of the spark, of love, and of the bond underlines the mythic structuring of the educational process. The role and function of the teacher is set in the context of his ascent to the divine realm and his election there. From there the teacher returns to plant the divine spark in the student: the teacher, thus, becomes the savior, the Gnostic logos, the means of salvation, the lover. The planting of the spark constitutes a conversion which sets the student onto the same mythic quest. The relationship of student to teacher provides salvation and divine benefits. The growth which takes place in the student revolves about philosophy, but the solid foundation of education is the attractive discourse and love of the teacher. The student's conversion, then, is ambiguous: is it really to philosophy at all? Or does it relate only to the divine guide, the teacher?

Such a conflation of the myth of salvation through educational ascent is very bold. The teacher is not only an agent of the divine realm, but in fact, *is* the divine realm for the student. The teacher is the savior, the connection to the logos, the divinity—and the means to that divine state has been his own asceticism and practice of migration.

---

[33] This need only be noted here; in Chapter 4 the topic will be more fully explored.

The student's exegesis of the passage "and the soul of Jonathan was knit to David" delimits the extent of that bonding and also rejects some possible interpretations. Here he provides, especially in the sexual implications of the exegesis, the theoretical and philosophical relationship inherent in the myth. His problem is that he wants to protect the autonomy, honor, and independence of the divine and of the divine-incarnate, the teacher. The superior is never diminished by being bound to the lesser, yet through the bond, benefits accrue to the lesser. In that respect, the distinction between the divine and the human, the superior and the inferior, only applies so long as the inferior is inferior. When, through the relationship with the teacher and through practice, the student progresses to the divine, the distinction no longer holds. He becomes a teacher, a savior, a bearer of the divine spark. Just as Jonathan was knit to David, and the teacher to the divine, and the student to the teacher, so will the student's future students be knit to him. The human relationship mediates the divine realm.

The relationship of student to teacher is complex. It begins in a kind of necessary or compelling entanglement of the student in the teacher's mind and society which transfers the benefits of the teacher's asceticism to the student. This takes the student out of the familiar realm: he leaves behind all to explore the new realm, the divine realm signified in the planting of the spark of love. This desire inaugurates the quest which plays out the scriptural bonding of Jonathan and David which made them equal. The myth of the relationship replays the myth of ascent in a social environment: that which the ascent myth relates about the teacher's relationship to the divine is applied to the relationship of the student to the teacher.

The Teacher As Revealer

In the peroration to the oration, the speaker shows signs of deliberately developing this mythic construction as a secondary system of meaning in the treatise. The speaker, as will be recalled, introduced the teacher's divinity and the myth of ascetic transferal when he presented the subject of his oration. The carefully constructed peroration closes the discourse by emphasizing the divinity and salvific work of the teacher, by dramatizing the bonding with the teacher, and coincidentally by portraying the sort of revelation that occurred in the relationship with the teacher. The peroration thus draws together all of the connotative systems into one final presentation.

The peroration bears the marks of careful construction, and thus it balances various themes of the portrayal of the teacher. The peroration begins with the introduction of a new metaphor for the teacher: "And to speak briefly, he was indeed a paradise to us, an imitator of the great paradise of

God" (καὶ συνελόντα εἰπεῖν παράδεισος ἡμῖν ὄντως οὗτος ἦν, μιμητὴς τοῦ μεγάλου παραδείσου τοῦ θεοῦ [XV.183]). Three analogies further articulate this metaphor: (1) Adam's expulsion from the paradise of delights (XV.184–89) in which the student is Adam and the teacher God; (2) the prodigal son who left home and found hard labor (XV.190-94); and (3) the Babylonian exile of Jews from the sacred city (XVI.195–99) where the student, being cast forth from the sacred environment, leaves behind the arena of revelation.

The peroration continues with a consolatory appeal for protection by the Savior of all now that the seeds have been planted within him. This savior will protect the educated student:

There is the savior of all, both of the half-dead and of the plundered, the guardian of all, the doctor, word, the unsleeping guard of all humanity.

Ἔστιν ὁ σωτὴρ πάντων, καὶ τῶν ἡμιθανῶν καὶ τῶν λεληστευμένων πάντων κηδεμὼν καὶ ἰατρός, λόγος, ὁ ἄγρυπνος φύλαξ πάντων ἀνθρώπων. (XVII.200)

This savior will perhaps guide the student back to the teacher again. This savior is ambiguously presented: the referent could include the guardian angel and/or the Christian Logos. The re-entrusting to the providential paedagogue neatly closes the system opened in the educational biography.

The peroration continues with a restatement of his intent to thank the teacher (XVIII.203) and asks for the teacher's prayers (XIX.204–6). This final section contrasts markedly with the appeal to the savior of all for protection because while the students were with the teacher he "saved them through the holy instruction" (σώσας μὲν παρόντας τοῖς ἱεροῖς σου μαθήμασι [XIX.204]) and now as they are departing he is requested to "save them by his prayers" (σώζων δὲ ταῖς εὐχαῖς καὶ ἀποδημήσαντας [XIX.204]).

There are, then two sorts of saviors: the savior of all, and the savior by teaching and prayer. The teacher is this latter savior. The student returns to the care of the savior of all only after he completes his study and only with the continued support of the teacher through the seeds already planted and through his prayers. This juxtaposition of saviors supports the teacher's portrayal as a divine figure as well as augmenting the understanding of education as salvation.

The three analogies of separation (from paradise, the prodigal son from his homeland, the Babylonian captivity) further emphasize the importance of the student—teacher relationship as the basis of this educational salvation. The student metaphorically describes intense feelings of separation and withdrawal from his teacher. The teacher, after all was a paradise to them—a place for converse with God, a place for revelation. By entering the relationship with the teacher, the student enters a paradise, and by withdrawing, his experience is one of explulsion from paradise, hard work, and exile.

The student summarizes the revelatory relationship that he is leaving behind in this way:

> I seem to be one of those who is expelled from a city and this sacred fatherland of mine, in which both by day and night the holy laws and hymns and songs and mystic discourses are announced, and (in which there is) light by the sun and continuously, (where) by day we conversed with the divine mysteries on our own behalf, and at night possessed by mental presentation those things which by day the soul saw and managed, and to speak altogether briefly there the inspired possession was forever. (XVI.196)

This description, with its emphasis on the revelation, the perpetual study, and the nightly mediation on the sacred mysteries, defines the revelation. The revelation which the teacher passed on was the full expression of the divine and the work of education was to reveal in study and meditation the sacred mysteries. ''And to speak altogether briefly there the inspired possession was forever.''

The peroration thus brings together the mythic, revelatory, and salvific connotative systems of signification about the teacher as revealer. The teacher is a human being who by ascetical practice becomes divine. His divinity bestows upon him greater powers of interpretation, understanding, communication, and instruction. Returning from his divinization, the teacher binds the student to himself through a religious conversion brought on by discourse and personal relationship of love. The teacher plants a spark, a love, in the psyche of the student which begins the process of education and revelation through the many areas of philosophical, natural, and ethical study. These studies are taught as sacred mysteries and are the subject of meditation. The teacher reveals the mysteries in a sort of paradise which a relationship with him constitutes. The student experiences salvation in this instruction, and when he leaves the school, it is like an expulsion from paradise, an exile. The teacher is a revealer of the divine, a revealer through whom the student is saved.

The secondary systems of signification, as complex as they may be, have combined to draw a very dramatic picture of the spiritual guide and his relationship with the disciple. The disciple, guided by an unseen divine force, is entrusted to the guide who contains divinity within himself. After contact with the adept, the disciple again pursues the unseen divine savior, but now as one enlightened, divinized. The disciple has become a guide.

3

Books as Spiritual Guide

Semiotics "seeks to describe the underlying systems of distinctions and conventions that enable objects and activities to have meaning."[1] In the last chapter these underlying distinctions and conventions were studied in relationship to secondary, connotative systems. With a treatise like "On the Life of Plotinus and the Order of His Books"[2] which stands so clearly in a literary tradition, however, the semiotic analysis must extend to a type of literary semiotic theory, as has been proposed, for example, by Jonathan Culler whose starting place for his semiotics of literature is at the intertextual level of a given text's existence:

> Since [texts] participate in a variety of systems—the conventions of literary genres, the logic of story and the teleology of emplotment, the condensations and displacements of desire, the various discourses of knowledge that are found in a culture—critics can move through texts towards an understanding of the systems and semiotic processes which make them possible.[3]

---

[1] Culler, *Pursuit of Signs*, 25.

[2] The standard text for "On the Life of Plotinus and the Order of his Books" is in the Oxford Classical Texts series: Paul Henry and Hans-Rudolf Schwyzer, eds., *Plotini Opera* (Oxford: Clarendon, 1964) 1. 1–38. See also A. H. Armstrong, trans., *Plotinus* (LCL 440; Cambridge: Harvard University Press, 1978) 1. 1–85. There are some interpretative notes in Roger Miller Jones, "Notes on Porphyry's *Life of Plotinus*" *CP* 23 (1928) 371–76.

[3] Culler, *Pursuit of Signs*, 12.

The literary text is interwoven into any number of different systems of conventions and distinctions which enable meaning to take place. The critic, by identifying these interwoven systems, begins to understand the underlying processes which make meaning possible.

The investigation, as in any structural system, of these underlying processes, begins with an identification of oppositions: "To describe the system would be to identify the oppositions which combine to differentiate the phenomena in question."[4] These oppositions, combining in the creation of differentiations, set forth the signification of the literary text:

> The general implication of this method, which has become a fundamental principle of structural and semiotic analysis, is that elements of a text do not have intrinsic meaning as autonomous entities but derive their significance from oppositions which are in turn related to other oppositions in a process of theoretically infinite semiosis.[5]

Enigmatic oppositions are at the heart of Porphyry's text "On the Life of Plotinus and the Order of his Books." Porphyry juxtaposes oppositions of a godlike philosopher upon edited texts, of philosophers who lead students by experience and philosophers who lead students by texts, of a philosopher who is noetically above the world and yet socially active at every level of society from the emperor to slaves, of a person known by his *nous* and yet graphically described in his *soma*. In this Chapter these enigmatic distinctions combine to create meanings for the treatise.

The starting point of these distinctions resides in a curious place: the title. The literary text has been known by scholars and studied through an abbreviation of its title to "The Life of Plotinus." The abbreviation has reinforced a tendency toward reading the text simply as a biography in a long tradition of hagiographical biography. It has been assumed that there is no significance to the order of the texts beyond the chronological and thematic lists included in the biography. The title, however, has a relationship both within the treatise (to the discussion of the chronological and edited order of the texts) and without (as an introduction to the edited works). The title clearly announces this: ΠΕΡΙ ΤΟΥ ΠΛΩΤΙΝΟΥ ΒΙΟΥ ΚΑΙ ΤΗΣ ΤΑΞΕΩΣ ΤΩΝ ΒΙΒΛΙΩΝ ΑΥΤΟΥ.[6] The title gathers the two focuses of the text (life and books) and

---

[4] Ibid., 28. This is written as part of an evaluation of the centrality of Lévy-Strauss's investigations as a foundation of structuralist analysis.

[5] Culler, *Pursuit of Signs*, 29.

[6] "On the Life of Plotinus and the Order of his Books"; in order to be inclusive of both textual and biographical emphases in the treatise, I shall abbreviate it as "Life and Books."

presents them in relationship to a series of texts.[7] Roland Barthes, reflecting on the literary function of the title, writes:

> The function of the title has not been well studied, at least from a structural point of view. What can be said immediately is that society, for commercial motives, needing to assimilate the text to a product, a commodity, must have *markers*: the function of the title is to mark the beginning of the text, i.e. to constitute the text as a commodity. Thus all titles have several simultaneous meanings, at least two of which are: (1) what it utters, linked to the contingency of what follows it; and (2) the announcement itself that a piece of literature is going to follow (i.e., in fact, a commodity); in other words, the title always has a double function: as utterance and as *deixis*.[8]

The utterance is that our text has two parts (life and texts) and the *deixis* is that the life and texts are related and that the title itself points not only to the text of which it is title, but also to the edited texts to which it is an introduction.

The title points to an enigmatic relationship of life and books which seems only to be resolved through the purchasing and study of the texts which follow the introductory essay. In this Chapter I shall argue that there is an enigma which sustains a reader's attention and which is not resolved in the introductory essay. The enigma, on the one hand, revolves about the accessibility of the philosopher Plotinus as a divine sage, an ontologically noetic philosopher, who has a large coterie of students. The other part of the enigma revolves about the presentation of the texts: this accessible philosopher can only be known through his texts. The spiritual director, the spiritual guide, in the final analysis, is not Plotinus, but his books. The books are the basis for spiritual formation. Since there is no relationship with Plotinus except through the books, in essence, the edited books are the only articulated means of Plotinian formation, and so Porphyry's editing of the books and the writing of the introductory essay become a marketing function of a spiritual publishing project.

---

[7] Richard Goulet ("L'oracle d'Apollon dans la Vie de Plotin," in Luc Brisson, et al., eds., *Porphyre: Vie de Plotin* [Histoire des Doctrines de L' Antiquité Classique 6; Paris: Libraire Philosophique J. Vrin, 1982] 1. 371–75) shares this perspective on the treatise in his study of the signification of the oracle.

[8] Barthes, "Textual Analysis of a Tale of Poe," in Blonsky, *On Signs*, 87.

The Structure of the Treatise

The title of Porphyry's text indicates that he assumed two different literary (and semiotic) characters:[9] that of biographer[10] and that of editor. Porphyry as biographer of a divine sage has been recently explored by Patricia Cox. She has investigated the history of biography as a literary genre, and studied Porphyry's "Life and Books" as one of the biographies of holy sages.[11] She summarized her appoach in this way: "Ancient biographies of holy men were caricatures whose aim was to evoke, and thus to reveal, the interior geography of the hero's life."[12] She concluded that there are two basic forms of the biography: the son of god, whose birth narrative attests his divine status, whose unique divine status makes him inaccessible to other people, and who works miracles; and a god*like* holy man, whose assimilation to God does not emerge from birth, whose education perfects what is already strong, who is eminently knowable by other human beings (because they are special men, but not unique) and who perform no miracles.[13] The biographies of the holy sages were of the godlike variety whose concern was "to demonstrate the extent of a man's assimilation to God, or how he was godlike."[14] The descriptive traits used to portray the level of divinity became literary motifs which the biographers employed in "various combinations of these motifs, depending upon the degree of divinity being claimed for the specific philosophers."[15]

---

[9] This is not a biographical statement about Porphyry. Culler (*Pursuit of Signs*, 38) states: "The work is a product not of a biographically defined individual about whom information could be accumulated, but of writing itself. To write a poem the author had to take on the character of poet, and it is that semiotic function of poet or writer rather than the biographical function of author which is relevant to discussion of the text."

[10] Earlier studies of the biographical material have included A. Priessnig, "Die Biographische Form der Plotinvita des Porphyrios und das Antinosleben des Athanasios," *Byzantinische Zeitschrift* 64 (1971) 1–5; and more peripherally H. J. Blumenthal, "Marinus' Life of Proclus: Neoplatonist Biography," *Byzantion* 54 (1984) 469–94. An older view discredits the perspective of the biography. See J. Bidez, "Literature and Philosophy in the Eastern Half of the Empire," in S. A. Cook, et al., eds., *The Imperial Crisis and Recovery A.D. 193–324* (*CAH* 12; Cambridge: Cambridge University Press, 1939) 629–35. "In more than one place the philosopher is looked at through the idle fancies and hallucinations of silly imaginations obsessed by the marvellous, and many a story casts a halo round his head which he himself would not have permitted" (p. 630).

[11] Cox, *Biography in Late Antiquity: A Quest for the Holy Man* (Berkeley: University of California Press, 1983).

[12] Ibid., xi.

[13] Ibid., 35–43.

[14] Ibid., 21.

[15] Ibid.

A "composite image" of the biographer's divine philosopher revolves about two primary focuses: that the divine philosopher had superior wisdom which was only improved by education and which included a gifted insight into and concern for other people;[16] and that the divine philosopher practiced asceticism which enabled him to be recognized easily (for asceticism was a form of advertising) and which revealed his interior freedom from bodily and corporeal encumbrances.[17] There is no question that Porphyry's portrayal of Plotinus falls into this categorization.

Cox's study of Porphyry's "Life and Books," which she consistently abbreviated as "Life of Plotinus," placed Porphyry, the biographer, in the biography as a prism reflecting within himself the life of Plotinus whose life he is writing. This prismic refraction projects the images with which the biography is built: the style is the method.[18] She writes:

> In Porphyry's biography, the soulfulness of Plotinus shines like a face reflected in many mirrors. What we can know about a life is its veil of images; biographical interpretation is a labyrinthine tracing and a weaving together of the tracks of soul in life.[19]

Porphyry and Plotinus mutually reflect and interpret each other. "The biography, then, is the baffled telling of a vision, a 'placing' of soul through image and type."[20] She concluded that "the entire biography is characterized by the kind of poetic thinking that allows for history a soulful depth, a hearth that shimmers forth in images."[21] Three daemonic presences, "phantasms," image forth Plotinus—each of which reflects through Porphyry to Plotinus: Socrates, Odysseus and Hestia/hearth. The "biographical method can be understood as an evocation of Plotinus's interior familiars; it is a poetic placing that calls forth the daemonic faces of the man's soulful presence."[22]

Cox's analysis of the biographical aspect of Porphyry's "Life and Books" has captured the underlying systems which enable Plotinus to be recognized and understood biographically as a divine philosopher. Her interpretation of the interplay of image and history draws out of the text the vibrancy of Porphyry's portrayal. These underlying systems of signification,

---

[16] Ibid., 21–26.
[17] Ibid., 26–30. There is actually very little discussion of asceticism in "Life and Books."
[18] Ibid., 132.
[19] Ibid., 107.
[20] Ibid., 110.
[21] Ibid., 114.
[22] Ibid., 132.

of generic intertextuality, form the basis of *one* aspect of the enigmatic presentation of Plotinus in the text.

The biographical intertextuality, however, represents only one part of the announced subject matter of the treatise. The structure of the treatise, which emerges more from a description of its content than from any literary tradition, shows the interrelationship of the announced themes. Porphyry does not announce his outline or purpose; hence, the structure must be gleaned from an analysis of the various parts of the treatise.

There are four sections which exhibit clear cohesiveness. The first is the introductory material (1–3) which presents Plotinus's attitude toward his body and his educational formation. The second is the chronological listing (4–6) of Plotinus's works. This section divides the works of Plotinus according to the works before Porphyry's arrival at the school, after Porphyry's involvement with the school, and the final treatises written after Porphyry had retired to Sicily. These first two sections of the treatise comprise the beginning six chapters.

The next two clearly cohesive sections of the work are found at the end. The final section of the treatise is the thematic outline of the treatises as they are arranged in the Enneads (24–26). This clearly parallels the chronological listing in the beginning. The section immediately prior to the listing of the Enneads (17–23) presents five evaluations of Plotinus's work: Amelius's defense, Porphyry's conversion to Plotinus and witness to his power, Longinus's scholarly evaluation, a presentation of an Oracle relating to Plotinus and finally an interpretation of the oracle by Porphyry. These five evaluations traverse a wide intellectual and religious spectrum (from scholar-academic to oracle) and introduce the thematic presentation of the Enneads. These last two sections comprise the last ten chapters of the treatise. These four sections combined, two at the beginning and two at the end, account for approximately two-thirds of the material in the treatise.

In the middle of these enveloping sections, there are three sections with more roughly thematic relationships. The first section is the description of Plotinus's educational relationships with his students (7–9): his male hearers, his writings, and his female hearers. The next section describes Plotinus's personality (10-12): his personal powers, his ability to perceive character, and his social and political interests (Platonopolis). The third section presents information about the school (13–16): its meetings, Plotinus's writing and teaching method, his relationships with good students, and the Christians and other philosophical sectarians who entered his school.

The overall outline of the treatise, then, seems to be as follows:

I. Introduction (1–3)
   A. Plotinus's attitude toward his body
   B. Plotinus's educational formation

The clearly cohesive sections (I, II, VI, and VII) form an envelope for the treatise which gives emphasis to the beginning in chronology and the end in theme. In the biographical genre, these two lisitings of the books constitute one of the Odyssean framings of the treatise. Cox writes:

> First there is the procession of the works through time, then there is their constellation by likeness. This is another Odyssean frame: two journeys, and two ways of wandering, through contemplative images that express Plotinus's literary voyage in the sea.[23]

When this Odyssean frame is gathered into its relationship to other sections of the treatise, the significance dramatically increases. Chronology and body are linked, as well as intellectual activity and the thematic arrangement. The books and their order speak as loudly as the images.[24] The treatise begins in the concrete physical realm of the body and the chronological listing of the treatises, and ends with the evaluation of the intellectual strength and intellectual order of his work. The shame and mistreatment of the body is strongly contrasted with the sympathetic and laudatory evaluations of his work at the end which culminates in the recital of an oracle and its interpretation by Porphyry. The literary movement is from the body to the mind, from *soma* through educational relationships, descriptions of personality, and the meetings of the school to the *nous*: a movement from chronological understanding of texts to noetic organization.

There are a number of significances which emerge from the structural

---

[23] Ibid., 125.

[24] J. Igal ("The Gnostics and 'The Ancient Philosophy' in Porphyry and Plotinus," in H. J. Blumenthal and R. A. Markus, eds., *Neoplatonism and Early Christian Thought: Essays in Honour of A. H. Armstrong* [London: Variorum, 1981] 138–41) has suggested that Porphyry has even adjusted the titles of the treatises in the second listing of the books to accommodate his literary and intellectual agenda.

organization of the treatise. The first is that the structuring of the treatise leads directly beyond itself into the thematic ordering. It is impossible to separate the "Life and Books" from the collection of treatises which follow: the listing of the thematic organization links the treatise to the Enneads. The reader is not intended to stop with the biography or the life, nor with simply the knowledge of the listing of the texts, but to proceed to the enneads themselves. The order of the books literally and figuratively circumscribe the biographical interest.

Next, Porphyry, as the prism, intrudes into the picture. Porphyry is a mediator of Plotinus to books and books to readers. As the editor and publisher of the books, both the collection and organization of Plotinus's books revolves about him. He refracts, constructs, builds the knowledge of Plotinus's *nous* which is captured in the books. Although they are Plotinus's books, they will only be known through Porphyry's work. Porphyry is a major figure both in the biographical account of the life and in the development of the books. One of the interests of the "Life and Books" is in fact to present the biographical link to Plotinus and the editorial superiority of Porphyry as editor of those books.

The structure of the treatise, moreover, provides an interesting interpretative framework. Aside from the direct reviews given by Longinus of Plotinus, Amelius, and Porphyry, of Amelius's review of Longinus in a letter to Porphyry, we are given information to assist the reader in understanding who Plotinus really is and how he came to write. The reader is informed that Plotinus is a divine sage, and that he was totally oriented to his *nous*: in order to understand his writings, then, we must understand these biographical phenomena. But the reader is also informed that Porphyry, Plotinus's student, friend, and editor, has packaged these noetic treatises thematically for easier consumption. The thematic organization gives the treatises their signification—at least for the reader who was not there with him.

Finally, the books are referred to in every section of the treatise except one (IV, Plotinus's personality [10-12]). The reader is provided information about everything from noetic generation, orthography, intellectual development (actually the lack of any developmental orientation on Plotinus's part). Before the chronological listing Porphyry gives the educational origin of Plotinus's thought in Ammonius's esoteric teaching. At the end Porphyry provides the divine depository for Plotinus and his *nous* and then leaves only the books in their thematic order. Plotinus is deposited in heaven, and the books (which are his repository) are deposited with the reader.

The Teachers in the Treatise

The distinctions which create meanings, however, continue beyond just the structure and biographical genre of the treatise. The discourses about life and about books continue throughout the treatise. A very natural question arises: How does Plotinus's life relate to other teachers? This is a question about the broader educational landscape and what possibilities this landscape holds. The discourse about life and books in the educational landscape develops both directly through Longinus's discussion of the philosophers of his day and indirectly through the portrayal of and importance of Ammonius. These broader distinctions raise important questions about Porphyry and the texts.

Porphyry makes a number of distinctions about the kinds of teachers in the biography. At one level, the teachers are distinguished according to those teachers whom Plotinus himself recognized as authentic philosophers (Ammonius, Amelius,[25] Porphyry) and those rejected (the teachers of Alexandria, Longinus). On another level, good teachers are those to whom Plotinus is drawn or those who are drawn to Plotinus (Amelius, Porphyry), while the poor teachers are all the others, or those whom Plotinus reclassifies (as Longinus is). The primary distinction is that Plotinus is, along with Ammonius his teacher, a noetic teacher, while all other teachers function at a different and lesser level. There are clearly two classes of teachers, among the lesser class there are three mentioned: his grammar teacher, the philosophers of Alexandria, and Longinus.

Plotinus's first teacher was his "grammar teacher" (γραμματοδιδάσκαλος [3]). We are given no other information about him, except that it was while he was under this master that he was weaned at eight years old.[26]

Twenty years later, when he was twenty-eight, Plotinus was drawn to study philosophy (ὁρμῆσαι ἐπὶ φιλοσοφίαν), so he went to hear the well-esteemed teachers of Alexandria. These teachers were presumably teachers of philosophy. Plotinus's reaction to them was interesting: "Returning from hearing them he was downcast and full of grief" (κατιέναι ἐκ τῆς ἀκροάσεως αὐτῶν κατηφῆ καὶ λύπης πλήρη). Clearly these Alexandrian philosophers were not satisfying to him. Plotinus explained his mental pain

---

[25] Porphyry claims that Plotinus calls Amelius by a more philosophically astute name; see Leonardo Taran, "Amelius-Amerius: Porphyry *Vita Plotini* 7 and Enapius *Vitae Soph.* 4.2," *AJP* 105 (1984) 476–79.

[26] See Lucien Jerphagnon, "Plotin, Épiphanie du Nous: Note sur la *Vita Plotini* comme typologie," *Diotima* 11 (1983) 111–18. He suggests (pp. 114–15), to my mind unconvincingly, that there is a numerological significance to this and the other ages that are presented because they compare to the various stages of a person's life as outlined by Hippocrates and Censorius, or because they are multiples of the number 9.

to a friend who "understanding the purpose of the psyche sent him to Ammonius" (τὸν δὲ συνέντα αὐτοῦ τῆς ψυχῆς τὸ βούλημα ἀπενέγκαι πρὸς Ἀμμώνιον). There are a number of observations about these philosophical teachers of Alexandria from Porphyry's and Plotinus's perspectives. They were considered good: they were the well-esteemed philosophers of Alexandria (τοῖς τότε κατὰ τὴν Ἀλεχάνδρειαν εὐδοκιμοῦσι συσταθέντα). They were not, however, the teachers for Plotinus: these teachers affected Plotinus by making him "downcast" and "full of grief." Something at a nonconscious level indicated their insuitability for Plotinus. His friend, however, discerned the "intent of the psyche" and sent him to Ammonius.[27] Plotinus could relate to the noetic philosopher, Ammonius, not to the other sort of philosopher, despite their high esteem. This is the first sort of distinction about the teachers of the time.

The third of these lesser teachers, Longinus, gives us a perspective on the difference between the greater and the lesser teachers. Longinus was also a student of Ammonius at Alexandria, so the difference between the greater and lesser teachers is not established on the basis of their relationship with Ammonius. Longinus, however, was *not* among those of Ammonius's students who agreed to keep his doctrines esoteric. Some distinction is proposed between those who received esoteric teaching and bound themselves not to reveal it and Longinus who simply studied with him. Plotinus claims that Longinus was a scholar and not a philosopher: by this there seems to be no *intellectual* incapacity because Plotinus does not imply that Longinus is intellectually inadequate. Plotinus does, however, assert that there is a difference of approach: what scholars do and what philosophers do are not to be confused by Plotinus's students. Porphyry, moreover, points out that Longinus, a friend and a scholar whose opinion he values by including it as an evaluation of Plotinus's work, is the most critical and thorough scholar of philosophy of his times. Longinus mirrors Porphyry as a dedicated scholar and as one oriented to books and reviews of books. But Porphyry stands within the inner circle as the one who encourages, interprets, and organizes Plotinus's books. The distinction that is being made depends, it seems, on Longinus's own classification of those teachers who communicate with their students primarily through writing, and those teachers who educate primarily

---

[27] In Neoplatonic thought, the psyche is understood as an "image of the mind" so that, in fact, the friend's discernment of the will related to the noetic part of Plotinus's life; see V.1.3. The context of the quotation further articulates the relationship of *psyche* to *nous*: "For, although it (*psyche*) is a thing of the kind which our discussion has shown it to be, it is an image of Intellect; just as a thought in its utterance is an image of the thought in soul, so soul itself is the expressed thought of Intellect, and its whole activity, and the life which it sends out to establish another reality...." (trans. Armstrong, LCL 444). See also the discussion in LSJ, s.v., ψυχή.

through guiding their students into an understanding of their doctrine. Longinus is among those who work with texts. He is not of the sort of teachers who guides their students into understanding of doctrine. This is his disadvantage. Although Longinus places Plotinus in the category of the writing teachers, Porphyry insists that writing is only secondary to Plotinus's method. Plotinus was not a good writer, nor an articulate one, but he was an excellent guide into doctrine: his *nous* guided and directed his thought so that the writing reflected the direct and relational teaching. He had many hearers, both men and women, and he was sought out by the privileged who were about to die because they knew that Plotinus would be a "holy and divine guardian" (Porphyry "Life and Books" 9.6ff). Plotinus seems almost inundated by those seeking to follow him. Porphyry presents Plotinus both as a writer and a leader, but with the emphasis on the leading aspect of his teaching.

The distinction, then, between the lower and the higher teachers is between those who teach by relationship, that is those who educationally form or guide their students, and those who teach by writing, who are primarily oriented to text. The writers are clearly the lower or lesser class, the guides are the higher.

Ammonius,[28] the first in the greater teachers, is a case in point. He is the first of the noetic teachers and a major figure in the educational information of the treatise. He is mentioned as an important part of Plotinus's educational biography (3), again in a section on Plotinus's school-meetings (14), and in the review article by Longinus (20) which Porphyry includes in his sections on the evaluations of Plotinus's work.

The most important information regarding Ammonius is given in the educational development section of the introductory section of the biography (3). Plotinus responded to Ammonius as nonconsciously as he did to the popular philosophers of Alexandria whom he rejected. While he came away from the others "downcast" and "full of grief," he came away from hearing Ammonius saying to his friend that "this is the one I've been searching for" (τοῦτον ἐζήτουν). The same sort of instinctive rejection of the other philosophers became the instinctive recognition of Ammonius.

Plotinus became Ammonius's student and "acquired such a philosophical habit of mind" (τοσαύτην ἕξιν ἐν φιλοσοφίᾳ κτήσασθαι) that he even ventured into Persian and Indian philosophies (ὡς καὶ τῆς παρὰ τοῖς Πέρσαις ἐπιτηδευομένης πεῖραν λαβεῖν σπεῦσαι καὶ τῆς παρ' Ἰνδοῖς κατορθουμένης). Ammonius's first work in relation to his students is to teach a "phi-

---

[28] See Willy Theiler, "Ammonios und Porphyrios," in *Porphyre* (Entretiens sur l'antiquité classique 12; Geneva: Fondation Hardt, 1966) 85–123.

losophical habit of mind.'' More exotic Persian and Indian philosophies could be based upon this foundation. It took eleven years to acquire this philosophical mind set (Ἕνδεκα γὰρ ὅλων ἐτῶν παραμένων τῷ Ἀμμωνίῳ συνεσχόλασε). Aside from the reference to Persian and Indian philosophies, there is no mention of the content of the educational program. The main occupation was to develop this philosophical mentality (ἕξις).

Ammonius's three students (Errenius, Origen, and Plotinus) agreed not to reveal the doctrines (μηδὲν ἐκκαλύπτειν τῶν Ἀμμωνίου δογμάτων) which were made clear in their hearing (ἃ δὴ ἐν ταῖς ἀκροάσεσιν αὐτοῖς ἀνεκεκάθαρτο). This agreement was kept more carefully by Plotinus than by Errenius and Origen who both began to publish doctrines taught by Ammonius. Plotinus did not write anything of the doctrines, but did begin to base his own lectures on those of Ammonius (ἐκ δὲ τῆς Ἀμμωνίου συνουσίας ποιούμενος τὰς διατριβάς). The preservation of Ammonius's doctrines as an esoteric trust to students certainly implies that the content of Ammonius's teaching was not for public consumption. There was some need to maintain the relationship of Ammonius's doctrine to the method of learning which Ammonius passed on to his students.

In the description of Plotinus's school-meetings (14), there is a clearer description of Ammonius's function in Plotinus's professional life. Porphyry reports that after having the commentaries either of Severus or Cronius or Numenius or Gaius, among others, Plotinus would speak his own mind (ἀλλ' ἴδιος ἦν) both in holding an unusual perspective (καὶ ἐξηλλαγμένος ἐν τῇ θεωρίᾳ) and in bringing to bear the mind of Ammonius (καὶ τὸν Ἀμμωνίου φέρων νοῦν). One component of Plotinus's unique position was his ability to bring Ammonius's *nous* to bear on the questions at hand. Ammonius's mind could be retained by his students: his doctrines kept from the public, his method of teaching forming the basis of Plotinus's classes, and his mind brought to bear on the school issues. Plotinus's aspires to become the Ammonian type of teacher.

Longinus (20), moreover, in distinguishing between those teachers primarily known for writing their doctrines for future students and those teachers known primaily for leading students in their doctrines, places Ammonius in the category of the leading teachers, the teachers who lead (προβιβάζειν) their students forward into grasping for themselves those things which are acceptable (εἰς τὴν τῶν ἀρεσκόντων ἑαυτοῖς κατάληψιν). Ammonius, then, was a teacher who taught primarily through personal training of students.

Ammonius is the ideal teacher in the biography. His teaching is done through a kind of noetic formation, a development of a philosophical mindset. The formation is based on personal relationship and is the foundation of all other learning. The mind (νοῦς) is the basis both for the relationship and the teaching, which must, therefore, be kept esoteric in order, presumably, to keep the content of the teaching connected to the method. The mind is the locus of all true philosophical activity.

The study of the various teachers in the treatise raises two issues: one about Plotinus and one about Porphyry and the books. Plotinus is ambiguously presented. Longinus's understanding of Plotinus is as a writing philosopher oriented toward posterity. Porphyry presents Plotinus as esoterically trained by Ammonius, and as a philosopher with a great following of students. The emphasis on the students not only manifests Plotinus's popularity, but also implies an esoteric orientation. Porphyry and Amelius, moreover, appear as members of an inner circle, but there is no indication that there is any sort of esoteric doctrine. They encourage him to write, and then take down, edit, and interpret what he does indeed write. They are oriented to the books, which function in Plotinus's school in the same way that the esoteric teaching functioned in Ammonius's. Ammonius shadows forth Plotinus as an ontologically noetic person. But Plotinus's *nous* is shadowed forth only by his books: his students are not committed to secrecy, but to a writing and publishing program.

Such a presentation of the philosopher implies that what the reader of the books receives is as good as Plotinus himself, and, in fact, the *nous* of Ammonius as well. The books are located in a living tradition: they are not simply being preserved for posterity. Porphyry is the curator not of scholarly treatises, like the secondary teachers, but of the books of Plotinus, the *nous* of Ammonius.

The Direct Portrayal of Plotinus

Now the question arises about Plotinus himself. Given the educational environment outlined above, and the orientation toward the books, does the portrayal of Plotinus conform to the same presentation? There are four categories of presentation: Plotinus in the body (somatic), in the mind (noetic), in the oracle (oracular), and in the books (bibliographic). These presentations are linked in the biographical structure which begins in the body and ends in an oracular apotheosis, as well as being linked in the discourse about the editing of the texts which begin in chronological order and end in thematic order. These portrayals, then, are an important system of interconnections: they comprise a semiotic system of distinctions and relations which allow the person and the books of Plotinus to make sense, even though that sense will formulate an enigma.

The Somatic Portrayal

Plotinus is never presented as a disembodied person. On the contrary, Porphyry presents Plotinus as emphatically and graphically somatic. The very first impression given of Plotinus is that "he seemed ashamed at being in a body" (ἐῴκει μὲν αἰσχυνομένῳ ὅτι ἐν σώματι εἴη) which included a refusal to recognize either his race, parents, or country of origin (1). Cox suggested that this shame about being in the body, as well as his scorn for bodily functions shadows forth Socrates and his advice to free the soul from bondage in the body.[29] It is certainly not intended to show that he had a preferred divine origin: Plotinus by being ashamed acknowledged his (to his mind) unfortunate somatic origin and, therefore, placed himself generically in the godlike rather than the son-of-God biographical tradition.

Plotinus, moreover, kept secret his own birthday so that there would be no celebration of his origin. This avoidance of birthdays is part of the generic structure of the biography: the godlike holy sages are biased against birthdays because they are viewed as a sign of somatic entanglement.[30] He did celebrate the birthdays of Plato and Socrates—their daemonic presence give greater meaning to Plotinus's origin and orientation than does the celebration of his own birthday.[31] Plotinus recognized both that he was embodied and that he could enjoy the fellowship of gods and the great teachers.[32]

Just in case the reader were apt to suppress Porphyry's insistence on Plotinus's somatic state, we are given graphic descriptions of Plotinus's lack of concern over his harsh physical problems. We are told that he suffered from a sickness of the colon but refused an enema for it (2.1–5).[33] He did not find either baths or massages necessary (2.6), so that after the death of his masseurs, he became sick with a sickness which eventually caused his death. Plotinus simply did not regard his body as something very important, and yet he was very graphically bound to it. Porphyry underscores this somatic element in Plotinus's makeup.

The emphasis on the harsh bodily realities of Plotinus's life dramatizes the intellectual and noetic aspect. The somatic Plotinus is always managed from the intellect. This is presented in two emphases. The first is that Plotinus's mind directed the treatment of his body. He refused enemas for his sickness in the colon on the basis that it was inappropriate for an elder to receive such a medical treatment (οὐκ εἶναι πρὸς τοῦ πρεσβύτου λέγων ὑπομένειν τὰς

---

[29] Cox, *Biography*, 116.

[30] Ibid., 37.

[31] This seems to be the point of two other anecdotes as well: the divine daemon companion who is the object of Plotinus's undivided attention (10.29); and his fellowship with Plato and Pythagoras after death (22.52–64). The body is not disparaged here, but connected to the divine realm.

[32] John M. Rist, "Plotinus and the *Daimonion* of Socrates," *Phoenix* 17 (1963) 13–24.

[33] This medical information also seems to have significance. On its possible connection to discernment see Philip Merlan, "Plotinus and Magic," *Isis* 44 (1953) 341–48.

τοιαύτας θεραπείας [2.2–3]). Such social considerations became the basis for his intellectual regulation of his body. There were also theological or philosophical reasons: he refused to take other medicines because they were made up of the flesh of animals (2.4–6). And finally there were educational reasons: Plotinus delayed his own death in order to deliver a final instruction to Eustochius (2.23). Such details provide the image of Plotinus's physical body always being managed and corrected by the intellectual concern or orientation which could arise in social, philosophical, or educational concerns.

The second example of the management of the body from the mind is the curious instance given at the very beginning of the biography about Plotinus's refusal to have a portrait painted of himself (1.4). Plotinus argued that the portrait is an image of an image, a derivative image of a longer lasting secondary substance (εἰδώλου εἴδωλον . . . πολυχρονιώτερον).

Plotinus's opinion, however, does not discourage his students. They go about having a portrait made. The interesting aspect of this is that the εἴκων, the physical representation, could only be produced through the intellect. Even though the concept of the portrait was rejected on the basis of a philosophical argument, Carterius drew the portrait by making mental or intellectual impressions, the "striking fantasies" (φαντασίας πληκτικωτέρας), of Plotinus while in his presence, and then take that intellectual image presented to the artist's mind (ἐκ τοῦ τῇ μνήμῃ ἐναποκειμένου ἰνδάλματος τὸ εἴκασμα) and reproduce it in the portrait of the physical impression. The mental image was corrected from the "footstep" or "track" (ἴχνος). The mind created the image which in turn created the physical portrait. This presentation affirms that the physcial, somatic image of the teacher may only be produced from the intellect.[34] The mind manages the body.

The Noetic Portrayal of Plotinus

Yet there is an even closer relationship between the *nous* and the body, closer than simply the regulatory function. In a description of Plotinus in the school-meetings there is this description: "When he was speaking, the proof of his mind was the light which illuminated as far as his face" (13). The body is the arena in which the mind is revealed: there is a revelatory link between the mind with its benefits and the body which demonstrates the

---

[34] Cox (*Biography*, 110) explains the portrait in terms of Porphyry's relationship to Plotinus: "In honoring Plotinus in this way, he was at the same time honoring the memory, and evoking the knowledge, of a face of his own soul" so that the portrait "both masks the man's 'inner realm' *and* takes us into it."

functioning of the mind. The logical proof that the mental capacity is the fact of facial illumination.

With such a description, Porphyry paints a picture of the noetic teacher whose mind is primary in regulating the body and in revealing itself in the body. It is the *nous* which distinguises Plotinus as a holy philosopher. Porphyry presents this depiction in a number of different ways.[35]

The first presentation is that of a teacher whose orientation was totally toward the *nous*. This complete noetic orientation even applied to the manual arts of teaching. In chapter 8 we are told that he loathed proofreading his own writings, that he did not form his letters clearly, nor did he care about syllabification or orthography, "but he was only concerned for the mind" (ἀλλὰ μόνον τοῦ νοῦ ἐχόμενος). It is the mind which must take precedence over all other aspects of writing. In a sense the writing arts are the somatic part of education, which are ruled by the noetic part, but which are not of themselves worth cultivating. Porphyry mirrors Plotinus's disregard for his body with his disregard for writing.[36]

This noetic orientation was manifest also in the way he thought because Porphyry presents his thinking as completed at once in his psyche.

> Since he completed in himself from beginning to end the subject for reflection, later transferring what he thought into writing, he would continue thus writing that which he had set forth in his mind (ψυχή) seeming to copy the written things as from a book. (8)

The thoughts appeared in his mind as fully formed. There is not sense of a development, or a process: they are complete thoughts completely formulated and Plotinus is presented in his writing as merely copying or translating them from one arena to another, from his psyche to his books, from within himself to his writings.

This picture of a noetic being is further emphasized in the fact that at all times, in writing as well as in conversation, the *nous* remained constantly his orientation:

> When he was both discussing something with someone and continuing in conversation, he was oriented toward his subject matter; as one who at the same

---

35 See Jerphagnon ("Épiphanie," 112) who argues that, for those initiated into true philosophy, Plotinus is an epiphany of *nous* in the cosmos, a sort of divine *nous* incarnate. This contradicts both Cox's thesis about the godlike status of the biographical aspect of "Life and Works" and my own perspective on the centrality of the books.

36 See Denis O'Brien, "Comment écrivait Plotin? Étude sur *Vie de Plotin* 8.1–4," in Brisson, *Porphyre*, 1. 329–67.

time fulfilled the necessity of conversation and (the necessity) of those things proposed for speculation, he held his thoughts without interruption. (8)

Here is a teacher so oriented toward the noetic things that nothing will interrupt the ongoing noetic work. It is as though the mind was capable of working entirely independently of the situation in which Plotinus was operating. In a sense this is a very static view: his mind was an already written book awaiting copying. The mind functions, presenting fully complete thoughts to the arena of thinking, while the teacher goes about his business both conversing and writing. Porphyry writes:

> After the one he was talking to left, neither did he repeat the things that had been written, because as I have said his sight was not strong enough for reading. (but) he would add the following things in order as if there were no time of interval intervening when he was involved in the conversation. (8)

This static quality is not meant to indicate that Plotinus was disengaged from his life and his work. We are given every indication that he was totally engaged, but we are meant to understand that his engagement did not detract from his ability to stay in tune with his noetic part. Neither conversations, nor writing could interrupt his mind: the books were already written without any interruption or intervention.

His ability to remain engaged at once in conversation or writing and with the mental work which is going on continuously at another level indicates that Porphyry views Plotinus as a self-contained mind. He writes:

> He was therefore present both to himself and at the same time to the others, and indeed, he would never slacken his attention towards himself, except perhaps in his sleep . . . and the turning toward his mind was persistent. (8)

The important point is the last phrase: ". . . and his turning toward his mind was persistent" (καὶ ἡ πρὸς τὸν νοῦν αὐτοῦ διαρκὴς ἐπιστροφή). All of his bodily functions were oriented toward the enhancement of this noetic aspect of his being. He is persistently and uninterruptedly oriented toward the *nous*, which is the origin of his books.

This constant orientation toward the mind was something unusual. It is not the way most people operated. Plotinus's household, though filled with orphans, students, and friends, was a place where Plotinus protected others from being drawn away from the mind. He was capable at all times to hold on to his contemplation (9). Even in the hectic social life of his household he always stayed oriented to his mind.

Porphyry presents the *nous* as the most vital aspect of Plotinus's life. Throughout the treatise the *nous* is the basis for Plotinus's activity. The *nous* was the basis for Plotinus's insight into and understanding of human character (11) both in the sense of discovering who stole Chione's valuable necklace, and in the sense of discerning that Porphyry's suicidal tendency was not a noetic inclination, but a melancholic disposition. In the school-meetings, moreover, not only was his face lit up by his *nous*, but also he was able to "discover and consider" the things that were brought forward for discussion (13): he was most capable (δυνατώτατος) of discovering and thinking through the issues. Such ability was manifest in his writings which were "abundantly more thoughtful than wordy" (νοήμασι πλεονάζων ἢ λέξεσι). It was not just his own *nous* that was brought to bear, but also that of Ammonius (14), even though other scholars who were even Ammonius's students did not have the *nous* to understand Plotinus (Longinus in "Life and Books" 20).

This noetic quality, the ability to function from within the *nous* and to bring the *nous* to bear on all questions (philosophical, medical, sociological, political), is the most pronounced attribute and gift of the teacher. The *nous* defines the true philosopher and teacher. It is something which the true philosopher simply has, for we are given no indication as to a means of developing *nous* or even of developing noesis. It is not trainable, or progressive, but a static quality which is beyond disturbing or interrupting in those who have it.

It is, then, an ontological state tied to the philosopher's way of living, and a given which animates and directs all the other aspects of the philosopher's life: his relationships with others, his politics, his psychological insight, his intellectual perceptiveness—all these relate to the fact that somehow this teacher has a perceptible and active *nous*.

The Oracular Portrayal

The oracular portrayal of Plotinus has two referents: on the one side, it looks to the demands of the biography of a holy philosopher for an ascetical orientation; on the other hand, it provides the editorial characterization a means of authenticating the books' divine inspiration. The oracle is placed at the end of the series of evaluations of Plotinus's work: it constitutes an evaluation of both his life and his books. It also structurally provides Porphyry with an interpretative point of departure.

The oracle is the penultimate statement:[37] it summarizes the evaluative

---

[37] There is another scholarly discourse about the place of oracles in Porphyry's thought. That diachronic discussion does not seem to have a bearing on the signification of the oracle in the "Life and Books." For further discussion, translation and evaluation see: Richard Goulet, "L'oracle d'Apollon dans la *Vie de Plotin*," in Brisson, *Porphyre*, 1. 369–412. See also John J. O'Meara, *Porphyry's Philosophy from Oracles in Eusebius's Praeparatio Evangelica and Augustine's Dialogues of Cassiciacum* (Paris: Études Augustiniennes, 1969); and idem,

sections of the treatise in providing a divine evaluation, and it introduces the thematic listing of the books. The weighty shame about the body expressed in the first chapters of the treatise is balanced by the release of the body from the world in which it has functioned to the heavenly realm where it lives with the gods and with Plato and Pythagoras. The oracle, thus, disposes of the body, placing the body in heavenly companionship after death, it leaves the books as the body's presence in the world. With Plotinus's apotheosis, the books form the end of the biography.

It is noteworthy that there is so little discussion of Plotinus's asceticism in the treatise. In 8.19 Plotinus is portrayed as reducing sleep and eating lightly in order to facilitate his contemplation. Beyond that, the oracle alone provides an ascetical orientation to an otherwise statically portrayed noetic person. In the oracle Plotinus is presented as becoming diviner, as keeping the body pure, as being under divine guidance, and of being sleepless. We understand, for the first time in the treatise, that Plotinus struggled to become the philosopher and person that he was. His ascetical struggle resulted in his companionship in heaven with the gods and the philosophic daemons.

The oracle, then, completes the expectation of the biographer's craft: god-like philosophers practiced asceticism, and although Porphyry does not want to emphasize this, he does include that element in "Life and Books." In Porphyry's interpretation of the oracle, he builds on that ascetical model. Porphyry places himself in the position of verifying and affirming the truth of the oracle, first by confirming the personal traits which the oracle presented, and then by attesting to the ascetical reality of the purity of Plotinus's soul. But Porphyry moves very quickly to the heart of the matter: the reason for this ascetical activity, which was really a noetic progression in the model of the noetic ascent of the *Symposium*, was to be united to the One.[38] This is the center of the interpretation: not only after his death but during his life Plotinus was united to the One. And here again the link is made to the books in that because of this union, what Plotinus wrote was divinely inspired: "the things that he wrote were written under their inspection and observation" (23.18–21). The union with the divine is connected to the writings: the writings, thus, are authenticated as divinely inspired.

Finally, Plotinus is placed in a heavenly realm with the great daemons. Porphyry and the oracle put Plotinus in the position to shadow forth his presence, like Socrates, Odysseus, and Hestia. The shadowing forth, however, is

---

Porphyry's Philosophy from Oracles in Augustine (Paris: Études Augustiniennes, 1959).

[38] Dominic O'Meara ("A propos d'un témoignage sur l'expérience mystic de Plotin," *Mnemosyne* 27 [1974] 238–44) suggests that this mystical union was an habitual, not occasional, state for Plotinus.

not through the students, or through relationship with the philosopher, but through the books. Plotinus now functions with respect to the books in the same way that the great daemons functioned in relationship to him.

The Bibliographic Portrayal

Much has already been said about the relationship of books to the person; it seems that the orientation toward the books is ubiquitous in the treatise. The most important aspect, not yet presented, is that Porphyry, in describing his conversion, does not come to believe in the person, but in the books. It is a most fascinating discussion of conversion through texts. Porphyry was thrown off by Plotinus's teaching method which he experienced in the classes as conversational (ὁμιλοῦντι δὲ ἐοικέναι ἐν ταῖς συνουσίαις [18.6–7]) and whose logic seemed difficult to grasp (καὶ μηδενὶ ταχέως ἐπιφαίνειν τὰς συλλογιστικὰς ἀνάγκας αὐτοῦ τὰς ἐν τῷ λόγῳ λαμβανομένας [18.7–9]). So he wrote (ἀντιγράψας) a treatise against him. Plotinus had the treatise read to him by Amelius whom he commissioned to unravel the difficulties (λῦσαι τὰς ἀπορίας). Amelius wrote a treatise in response:

> When Amelius wrote a long book about Porphyry's difficulties, and in turn when I wrote in response to his writing, then when Amelius also responded to this writing, at the third (writing), I Porphyry, scarcely understanding the things which had been said, changed my mind and wrote a recantation which I read in the class. (18)

Their entire relationship is based upon the composition of treatises in response to one another. Writing and responding in writing constitutes the explicit means of intellectual communication. It is, then, not surprising that Porphyry's conversion is to the books: "and from then on, I believed in the books of Plotinus" (κἀκαῖθεν λοιπὸν τά τε βιβλία τὰ Πλωτίνου ἐπιστεύθην). And even this conversion inspired both Plotinus and the others to write more books.

Plotinus's Social Relationships

This anecdote about Porphyry's own conversion to Plotinus's books is an important one for defining and structuring the relationship of the guide to the disciple. Even in his lifetime, Plotinus communicated with his associates through his writing: the books with which he communicated were either already formed in his mind, or written out and published, or composed by his associates under his guidance to be read to one another. The structure of the relationship revolves about the exchange and reading of books. Books form the primary means of association between Plotinus and his hearers, and the hearers with each other.

Frustration results from the search for other descriptions of the dynamic of these relationships between Plotinus and his associates. Porphyry presents no direct description of the interior dynamic of relationships: the fact that Plotinus related extensively to others takes precedence over any description of the nature of that relationship. The hollow presentations of relationship draw attention to the centrality of relating through books.

Porphyry explores Plotinus's interior life, the vibrancy of his noetic insight and contemplation, by shadowing forth his personality through the daemonic presences of Socrates, Odysseus, and Hestia. The interior relationship between Ammonius's *nous* and Plotinus's teaching and thinking expresses the relational dynamic available to Plotinus. But when Porphyry describes Plotinus's relationships with others, the dynamic disappears. Only great detail about Plotinus's extensive social relationships is given. Most of his relationships are structured as associations, presences, or following—all with a distinctly hollow tone.

Despite this lack of interest in the interior aspect of relationship, Porphyry emphasizes the structures of social interrelation. Plotinus as a philosopher functions in many different social contexts: manager of an orphanage, overseer of children's elementary education, financial manager, political advisor, legal arbiter, political visionary, military man of action, among others. This represents an extensive social involvement in which he was understood to be ''gentle'' and ''at the mercy of'' those who claimed his attention, while generally not being a political threat to others (9).

This again contrasts dramatically with Plotinus's own formation under Ammonius. Porphyry presents the interior dynamic of the esoteric training, of bringing the mind of Ammonius to bear, of embarrassment when Origen attended his lectures that he would already know what was being said.

In essence this presents us with an enigmatic figure: a philosopher who is at once noetically beyond the world, but socially active and involved in it. A philosopher who received esoteric training, but passed on, even to his closest associates, a different kind of formation. This next section will explore the nature of this enigma by analyzing the descriptions of relationships in the school, among his friends, in his home, and in the government.

The biography does contain references to the school-meetings, but none of the descriptions refers to relationship either in image, metaphor, myth, or suggestion. Plotinus is presented statically as the one who enters into the heart of the matter and grasps its implication (13). The descriptions of his person, moreover, are simply descriptions of his physical appearance. His *nous* lit up his face; he was gentle and attractive and sweated slightly when he spoke. There is no discourse about the way, the means, the impact; it is an objectified view of the master always from the outside—even when the description is of his union with the One.

This objectified view of the philosopher continues in a point of view which isolates the philosopher. Plotinus functions within himself, within his *nous*, and not out of a dynamic relationship with students; even his books seem already written in his mind. He speaks in a "rapt inspiration" (14) presenting not the traditional interpretation, but his own. He was, moreover, enormously learned in all the sciences, but preferred not to conduct research in other fields. The philosopher, thus, is involved in the tradition, but not tied to it.

The most telling information, however, regards the fact that the questions which Plotinus took up and wrote about always emerged from the discussions of the meetings. Porphyry emphasizes this throughout the treatise. Plotinus had no set agenda or sequence of issues, but only those which arose from responding to the needs of his hearers. This is an obvious Platonic reference: it is the manner of teaching of the dialogues. Yet here there is not the sense that the student is led to understanding, but that the philosopher provides the answers to those questions which cause the student difficulty. This is the situation in Porphyry's questioning of the relationship of the soul to the body, where the question must be solved and Plotinus directs Amelius to write an answer. This kind of interrelationship emphasizes the social orientation of the school, while at the same time juxtaposing this upon the centrality of the books. The questions arise in the school, the answers are formulated in the books.

The subject matter of philosophical investigation arises in the social, not the philosophical, context. The *nous* is put to work on issues that arise socially. Take, for example, the situation with Diophanes and the question of the student's submitting to sexual relations with the master. This anecdote serves a number of purposes. As Cox has pointed out, it establishes a clear linking of Plotinus to Socrates, and the student to Alchibiades.[39] This is a means of shadowing forth images of the real. Moreover, there is the related issue that a social (sociosexual) question gives opportunity for a philosophical answer in writing, an answer which Plotinus highly praises. This is paradigmatic of the orientation that philosophy arises in social context, and is answered in books.

The structure of relationships among his friends and hearers appears strictly professional, and strictly bibliographic. The relationship revolves about lectures, reading papers to one another, answering each others ques-

_____

[39] Cox, *Biography*, 118. The denial of the sexual dynamic of the relationship also carries significance. See the Conclusion in Chapter 6.

tions and editing manuscripts. Most of the hearers are described simply as associates with no other special relationship described or implied. Two of his hearers have special relationships: Zethus, the Arab, who is said to have loved him (φιλεῖν) and to have been a regular household guest; and Castricus, who adored (σεβόμενος) him. This represents a wide range of relationships from association to familiarity and love. But we are given no more of a description. There is no interest in the interior dynamic, but only in the professional and social description.

The same professional orientation is evident in his relationship with his two closest friends: Amelius and Porphyry. Amelius, a friend of over twenty-four years, relates to Plotinus primarily through the school. Amelius took notes on the classes in the early years, and took up (along with Porphyry) the critique of the sectarians after Plotinus had written his book. And Amelius wrote papers defending Plotinus to his critics and explaining Plotinus's thought to his students. No other information is given. Porphyry emphasizes the professional nature of Amelius's very long relationship to Plotinus: Amelius functions as the defender of his thought, transmitter of his lecture notes, and interpreter of his teaching.

Porphyry's presentation of his own relationship with Plotinus is no different. Porphyry flatters himself with a similar union with the One as Plotinus's and with a close and long association, but there is no personal account. It is as hollow a presentation as that of Amelius's. Porphyry, as an especial associate (μάλιστα ἕτερος), gains access to Plotinus's writings for editing.[40] Even when Plotinus comes to Porphyry to address the latter's melancholia, the anecdote is used to indicate Plotinus's perceptiveness, not to prove a relationship. Plotinus makes a declaration of analysis to Porphyry with no other level of meaning implied. Plotinus's response to Porphyry's poem on the "Sacred Marriage," and the response to Porphyry's counterargument to Diophanes both evidence the same sort of declaratory stance. In all these personal situations, Plotinus's response merely declares Porphyry's ability and giftedness, without revealing anything more. In fact, with marked contrast to Gregory's description of his conversion to the philosopher, Porphyry is converted not to the person, but to his books.

Even with his closest friends, Plotinus's relationships, though extensive, are presented without any content or substance. Porphyry presents many levels of social interrelationsips without indicating their possible significance. This same sort of mentioning extends to every level of Plotinus's relation-

---

[40] Andrew Smith (*Porphyry's Place in the Neoplatonic Tradition* [The Hague: Martinus Nijhoff, 1974] xiv) recognizes that part of the task of "Life and Books" is to establish Porphyry's place as an editor and interpreter of Plotinus.

ships, even that with the emperor Gallienus and his wife Salonia who, like Castricus, adored him, as well as with his household where any number of different relationships are presented.

What does this mean? The extensive network of relationships resist interpretation: the relationships are amassed without the sense that there is anything deeper implied. They have no interior, no dynamic: they are static. But there are so many of them. The sheer volume of relationships related in lists, or in groups of people, present a wide range of social details which say that the meaning, the significance is in the wideness of social involvement. Social diffusion, social interlocking is the heart of philosophical activity. While holding up both asceticism and withdrawal as paradigmatic, Plotinus is enigmatically portayed as a philosopher extensively involved in every level of society.

Conclusions

This Chapter began with the observation that semiotics studies the distinctions and conventions which create meaning. This was the initial observation in a literary semiotic theory. In observing Porphyry's two literary characters, as biographer and as editor of books, an enigma has emerged, an enigma which is posited in the title of the treatise and which is formulated throughout by the various distinctions which the treatise presents.

Roland Barthes has observed that the "operative value" of the positing of an enigma "is a matter of exciting the reader, of procuring clients for the narrative."[41] The positing of an enigma, in our treatise, captures the interest of the audience; it creates an interest in looking for the resolution of the enigmatic proposition. Barthes writes:

> The code of the Enigma brings together the terms through whose linkage (like a narrative sentence) an enigma is posited, posed, and after a few 'delays,' which give the narration its piquancy, the solution is unveiled.[42]

In studying the riddle, a particular instance of the literary form *aenigma*, Bentley Layton suggests that the literary form invites interpretation as "an occasion for rethinking the sense of what otherwise seems obviously impossible, a time for shift in perspective, a search for deeper meaning." The enigma constitutes an "invitation to exegesis."[43] Porphyry proposes the

---

[41] Barthes, "Textual Analysis of a Tale of Poe," in Blonsky, *On Signs*, 89.

[42] Ibid., 95.

[43] Bentley Layton, "The Riddle of the Thunder (NHC VI,2: The Function of Paradox in a Gnostic Text from Nag Hammadi," in Charles W. Hedrick and Robert Hodgson, eds., *Nag Ham-*

enigma through the mixing of the biographical genre with its expectations and modes of exposition, with that of an editorial and publishing program with its reviews, intellectual analyses, and methods of organization. The question becomes, "Where is the true Plotinus to be found?" At every point the answer to this question formulates an enigma. The "Life and Books" which posited the enigma in the title to the treatise does not, in fact, find resolution within the text at all. It remains unresolved. Barthes notes: "Every narrative obviously has an interest in delaying the solution to the enigma it posits, since this solution will toll its own death knell as a narrative."[44] Our treatise reserves resolution until the reader delves into the books which Plotinus wrote and which Porphyry has edited and to which the "Life and Books" is an introduction. The resolution in the books themselves presents a model of the spiritual guide as books.

If the positing and formulation of the enigma were to be listed in serial fashion, its centrality would be clear. The title first posits the distinction between life and books. Apparently recalling the biographical tradition, the treatise consistently holds that the person, the philosopher, is discovered not only through biography, but primarily through the books which he wrote. These books are located within the biographical tradition within the philosopher's *nous*, and they are presented as fully formulated there. The biography relates where the books were to be found.

The structure of the treatise further formulates an enigmatic opposition. It is not a serial two-part program where first is presented the biography and then is listed the order of the works. There is a mixing, a suspenseful intermingling of biographical information with editorial considerations, which point not inward to the resolution within the treatise, but outward to the enneads which follow. This seduces the readers attention: the final order of the books (chronological, or thematic) and the events of the life (presented with the death scene at the beginning and an apotheosis at the end) maintains interest in the unfolding of the oppositions. The life points to the books and the books reflect the life, and both point to the treatises which follow.

Porphyry himself formulates an aspect of the enigma. Both the life and the works find their fullest expression not in Plotinus, nor in the works themselves, but in the ordering and purifying of the books by the editor. The editor, Porphyry, is not only the prism of the biography, but he is also the focus

---

madi, Gnosticism, and Early Christianity (Peabody: Hendrickson, 1986) 44. George MacRae, ("Theology and Irony in the Fourth Gospel," in Daniel J. Harrington and Stanley B. Marrow, eds., *Studies in the New Testament and Gnosticism* [Wilmington: Glazier, 1987] 32–46) outlines the various theories of irony and applies them to John.

[44] Barthes, "Textual Analysis," 95; see also Layton, "Riddle," 43.

and center of Plotinus's books. Neither the life nor the books may be known or understood except through Porphyry.

And, of course, the curiously detailed, and yet not interiorily revealing, information about Plotinus himself formulates the enigma. Every category into which Plotinus is placed thwarts immediate comprehension. He is trained esoterically and brings the esoteric knowledge of his own teacher to bear, and yet he teaches the vast number of students who are his hearers through writing. We are informed that as a writer he fully formed his thought in his mind, and yet could not spell or write clearly. And this list, as seen above, could be expanded even more. Porphyry presents Plotinus as retaining all of the oppositions within himself: never fully comprehended in any of the categories, he remains compellingly complex. He disregards his body, a disregard mirrored in his writing and orthography. He maintains a total orientation toward the *nous* throughout his extremely active life, and yet does not need to work at writing his books because they seem fully formed in his mind. His apotheosis authenticates his writing of books, as well as pointing to the superiority of his life. And his social life is so full—and still so hollow—that we can only know Plotinus through his books.

At an intertextual level, however, the reader expects, especially following the earlier writing of Gregory Thaumaturgos, that the interior dynamic of student-teacher relationship will be exposed. These texts are speaking to one another,[45] and yet Porphyry completely frustrates any such conversation. He refuses to describe what the reader would expect to have described in such a book. He does not want to resolve the polarity of life and books, he does not want to present to the reader what the reader must turn to the books themselves, to the enneads, to find. Everything, the questions of the school, the relationships, the portrayal of the philosopher, points to the books. The resolution of all the distinctions will only come there.

This enigmatic presentation of polarities forces the reader to conclude that the spiritual guide is the books. The enigma completely frustrates any attempt at solution, so that the books and the publishing program of the enneads become the only possible means of spiritual formation. In the reading of the books, the seeker will find the wisdom and guidance of the master. It is not found in relationship with the master, or in the biography of the master, but in the books.

The books, like Plotinus himself, allow spiritual formation to happen in the normal social life of the person. Philosophical, religous formation occurs

---

[45] The debate and the rivalry of various schools and religious sects is apparent in the treatise when Plotinus's, Porphyry's, and Amelius's relationships to the sectarians is discussed (16). See also Cox, *Biography*, 136–45.

in society: the questions arise in society, among the normative events of social and political living, and the reading of the books with their guidance and solutions can be read successfully in that evironment. Porphyry has arranged it this way: the guidance which comes from the books has been conveniently organized by theme so that the questions, the formation, might happen without any intervention beyond the books themselves.

The "Life and Books" is a wonderful advertising program, a marketing device intended to catch the reader, to seduce the reader into purchasing the enneads, in order to find the spiritual direction which the reader seeks. The enigma, as unresolved as it is, forces attention to the enneads. The reader enters a relationship, not with Plotinus, nor with his editor who now recedes from the picture, but with the books which are the true spiritual guide.

This orientation towards books and their production introduces a major theme in third-century spiritual formation. Books, and the formation through books, the writing of books, and as in Gregory Thaumaturgos the interpretation of books, pervade the rest of the treatises in this study. This will become evident first in the Hermetic literature from Nag Hammadi.

4

The Sexual Encoding
of Religious Formation

In 1462 Cosimo di Medici commissioned Marsilio Ficino to translate into Latin a Greek manuscript of the *Corpus Hermeticum* which he had received from the Byzantine east. Since then, this Byzantine anthology, together with some other Greek and Latin sources,[1] has fascinated western scholars: the history of Hermetic scholarship, spanning so many years of investigation and methods of interpretation, may be written as a history of western academics.[2] The discovery of the Hermetic treatises in the Nag Hammadi Library, however, breaks this lengthy academic tradition because, until this new discovery, the scholarship was primarily based upon these Greek and Latin sources.[3] The Nag Hammadi material, the earliest manuscript witnesses to Hermetic literature, opens anew the investigation of Hermetic religions.[4]

---

[1] The critical edition of this anthology is A. D. Nock, ed., and A. J. Festugière, trans., *Corpus Hermeticum* (4 vols.; 6th ed.; Paris: Société d'Edition Les Belles Lettres, 1983). For an earlier, though largely discredited text and English translation, see Walter Scott, trans., *Hermetica: The Ancient Greek and Latin Writings which Contain Religious or Philosophic Teachings Ascribed to Hermes Trismegistus* (4 vols; Oxford, 1924–26; reprinted Boston: Shambhala, 1985).

[2] This becomes evident from reading Antonino Gonzàlez Blanco, "Hermetism. A Bibliographic Approach," ANRW 2/17.4 (1984) 2240–81. For bibliography on the Nag Hammadi treatises see David M. Scholer, *Nag Hammadi Bibliography 1948–1969* (Leiden: Brill, 1971) and its yearly supplements in *NovT*.

[3] For Arabic sources see Blanco, "Bibliographic Approach," 2252–58. Armenian materials have also been discovered; see J.-P. Mahé, "Les Définitions d'Hermès Trismégiste à Asclépius," *RevScRel* 50 (1976) 193–214.

[4] I use the plural "Hermetic religions" because there is not yet a sense, beyond the singular

Hermetic religions as a field of research do indeed need to be reworked. One scholar, after surveying the history of Hermetic scholarship, has concluded:

> There seems to be a certain exhaustion nowadays in Hermetic studies, after the extensive labours of former generations of scholars. Perhaps it is because the great, learned figures of the past have cast too long a shadow before them, and left the present generation with the feeling that there is nothing more to be done.[5]

Richard Reitzenstein[6] and A. J. Festugière[7] have dominated the discussion of the Byzantine anthology. Their questions have been the primary focus of attention: Were there Hermetic communities? Of what sort would they have been? Were the Hermetic initiations part of mystery religions? Did the Hermetic practioners use sacraments and rituals? Or were such things understood "spiritually"?[8] Was the Hermetic religion Egyptian, Hellenistic, Platonic in origin? In short the history of Hermetic scholarship in our century has been primarily interested in fitting Hermeticism into one or more of the already established academic niches of the Hellenistic era.

The Nag Hammadi documents do not necessarily fit into those categories, or at least, they offer the opportunity to look afresh at the functioning of Hermetic religions. Some contemporary scholars (Lewis S. Keizer,[9] Karl-

---

orientation toward Hermes Trismegistus, that all of these texts form *one* religion. Early Christianity in which there was diversity with a reasonably fixed kerygmatic center is not an analogous situation: most of the Hermetic documents present divergent and conflicting doctrines and practices while maintaining only a nominal center in Hermes Trismegistus. The history-of-religions school, with its presentation of the *Corpus Hermeticum* as a Bible to Hermetic communities, has been largely responsible for the presentation of Hermetism as analogous to Christianity. Contemporary scholarship grants more diversity to the texts, while still retaining the monolithic concept of a "Hermetic religion." Scholars must grant that there were many, different and often conflicting religious doctrines and practices and, thus, recognize the great plurality in the literature of the Hermetic religions.

[5] Blanco, "Bibliographic Approach," 2277.

[6] See his initial work *Poimandres: Studien zur griechisch-ägyptischen und frühchristlichen Literatur* (Leipzig: Teubner, 1904); and his subsequent *Hellenistic Mystery-Religions: Their Basic Ideas and Significance* (Pittsburgh: Pickwick, 1978).

[7] See esp. his four volume study *La Révélation d'Hermès Trismégiste* (1957; reprinted Paris: Les Belles Lettres, 1983). For a complete listing see Blanco, "Bibliographic Approach," 2274–77.

[8] See, e.g., G. Van Moorsel, *The Mysteries Hermes Trismegistus: A Phenomenologic Study in the Process of Spiritualisation in the Corpus Hermeticum and Latin Asclepius* (Utrecht: Drukkerij en Uitgerverij, 1955).

[9] *The Eighth Reveals the Ninth: A New Hermetic Initiation Disclosure (Tractate 6, Nag Hammadi Codex VI)* (Seaside, CA: Academy of Arts and Humanities, 1974).

Wolfgang Tröger[10]) have continued to treat these Coptic texts simply as new sources of information within the older academic discourse, while others (particularly Mahé)[11] have taken these new documents as an opportunity to restructure the investigation of Hermetic religions.

The Hermetic documents of the Nag Hammadi Codex 6 offer a unique opportunity for establishing a baseline for evaluating both the conceptual frame of Hermetism and the scholarly evaluation of Hermetic religions. Codex 6 contains three Hermetic tractates:[12] *Discourse on the Eighth and Ninth* (NHC 6, 6) 52.1–63.32;[13] *The Prayer of Thanksgiving* (NHC 6, 7) 63.33–65.7[14] together with a brief note *Scribal Note* (NHC 6, 7a) 65.8–14;[15] and *Asclepius 21–29* (NHC 6, 8) 65.15–78.43.[16]

The *Pr. Thanks.* and the *Asclepius* are known from other Greek and Latin

---

[10] "Die Sechste und siebte Schrift aus Nag-Hammadi-Codex VI," *ThLZ* 98 (1973) 495–503; also idem, "Die hermetische Gnosis," in idem, ed., *Gnosis und Neues Testament* (Berlin: Gerd Mohn, 1973) 97–119; idem, "On Investigating the Hermetic Documents in Nag Hammadi Codex VI: The Present State of Research," in R. McL. Wilson, ed., *Nag Hammadi and Gnosis* (NHS 14; Leiden: Brill, 1978) 117–21; and Tröger, *Mysterienglaube und Gnosis in Corpus Hermeticum XIII* (Berlin: Akademie, 1971). For a thorough evaluation of Tröger's understanding of Hermeticism, see William C. Grese, *Corpus Hermeticum XIII and Early Christian Literature* (Leiden: Brill, 1979) 50–55.

[11] I would also include the Berliner Arbeitskreis für koptische-gnostische Schriften among this more expansive group; see their, "Die Bedeutung der Texte von Nag Hammadi für die moderne Gnosisforschung," in Tröger, *Gnosis und Neues Testament*, 13–76, esp. 53–57; Mahé, "Le Sens des Symboles Sexuels dans Quelques Textes Hermétiques et Gnostiques," in Jacques-É. Ménard, ed., *Les Textes de Nag Hammadi* (NHS 7; Leiden, Brill, 1975) 123–45; idem, "La Prière d'actions de grâces du Codex VI de Nag Hammadi et Le Discours parfait," *Zeitschrift für Papyrologie und Epigraphik* 13 (1974) 40-60; idem, "Le sens et la composition du traité Hermétique, 'L'Ogdoad et L'Ennéade,' conservé dans le codex VI de Nag Hammadi," *RevScRel* 48 (1974) 55–65; and idem, "Les Définitions," 193–214.

[12] The text I use is Douglas M. Parrott, ed., *Nag Hammadi Codices V, 2–5 and VI with Papyrus Berolinensis 8502, 1 and 4* (NHS 11; Leiden: Brill, 1979). The specific editors of the Hermetic literature are Peter A. Dirkse, James Brashler, and Parrott for *Discourse on the Eighth and Ninth* (NHC 6, 6); Dirkse and Brashler for *Prayer of Thanksgiving* (NHC 6, 7); Parrott for *Scribal Note* (NHC 6, 7a); and Dirkse and Parrott for *Asclepius 21–29* (NHC 6, 8). I have also used Mahé, ed., *Hermès en Haute-Égypte: Les Textes hermétique de Nag Hammadi et leurs parallèles grecs et latins* (Bibliothèque Copte de Nag Hammadi, Section "Textes" 3; 2 vols.; Québec: Les Presses de l'Université Laval, 1978–1982). Both of these editions have consulted that of M. Krause and P. Labib, *Gnostische und hermetische Schriften aus Codex II und Codex VI* (Abhandlungen des Deutschen Archäologischen Instituts Kairo; Koptische Reihe 2; Glückstadt: Augustin, 1971). Tröger ("Codex VI," 498–502) presents a German translation without Coptic text.

[13] Parrott, *NHS 11*, 341–73.

[14] Ibid., 375–87.

[15] Ibid., 389–93.

[16] Ibid., 396–451.

texts, while the *Disc. 8–9* is a previously unknown document which may have some affinity to traditions represented in *Corpus Hermeticum* I (*Poimandres*) and XIII. The *Scribal Note* attests to the presence of other documents from which this collection is gathered:

> I have copied this one discourse of his. Indeed, very many have come to me. I have not copied them because I thought that they had come to you (pl.). And also, I hesitate to copy these for you, because, perhaps, they have (already) come to you, and the matter may burden you. Since the discourses of that one, which have come to me, are numerous. . . . (65.8–14)

The Nag Hammadi Hermetic texts then are taken from a larger pool of Hermetic texts and are intended to complete a specific person's collection. They may not be representative of Hermeticism as a whole, but they do represent one scribe's opinion of what should be gathered together for an interested consumer.[17]

Four aspects of these texts commend them as the subject of a special study: (1) The scribe's intentional choice suggests a cultural matrix of meaning: this combination of texts made sense to him, and he was convinced they would make sense to a collector. Their linking creates meaning because they signify the communication between two people about a cultural phenomenon. (2) These texts show a specific Egyptian provenance so that they represent a geographically specific Hermeticism incorporating Egyptian patterns of thought and religious practice into an Egyptian environment. Until the Nag Hammadi documents, the Egyptian provenance of Hermetic religions could only be suggested because the Greek and Latin texts have tended to suppress the Egyptian content.[18] These texts, then, portray the Hellenistic philosophical tradition against an Egyptian background, and thus they provide a corrective to an overtly Greek and Roman tradition of the *Corpus Hermeticum*.

---

[17] There has been some debate about the precise referent of the note: some argue that it refers to the immediately preceding *Pr. Thanks.*, others to the following *Asclepius*, others to both *Pr. Thanks.* and *Disc. 8–9*. For my purpose the precise referent is not so important as the fact that these texts were chosen. For a discussion of the referent see Parrott, *NHS 11*, 395–98. See Mahé, *Hermès*, 2. 459–68 for text and commentary.

[18] For the presumption of Egyptian provenance the most contemporary account is François Daumas, "Le Fonds Egyptien de L'Hermétism," in Julien Ries, ed., *Gnosticism et Monde Hellénistique: Actes du Colloque de Louvain-la-Neuve (11–14 mars 1980)* (Louvain-la-Neuve: Institut Orientalist, 1982) 3–25. See also Ph. Derchain ("L'authenticité de l'inspiration égyptienne dans le 'Corpus Hermeticum,'" *RHR* 161 [1962] 175–98) who identifies and explores four Egyptian themes (royalty, the sun, living statues, and general rites); and also B. Stricker, "The Corpus Hermeticum," *Mnemosyne* 2 (1949) 79–80. Mahé (*Hermès*, 1. 33–38; and esp. 2. 68–113) has explored the Egyptian provenance extensively.

(3) The Nag Hammadi texts are the earliest manuscript witness to the Hermetic literature. Copied sometime between 340–370 CE, they seem to reflect a manuscript date from the second half of the 3d century CE or early 4th. The Greek anthologist and the Latin translator's theological and philosophical perspective casts suspicion on the reliability of those collections, even though they have textual traditions probably extending to the 2d and 3d centuries CE. In the known texts, the Coptic tends to agree with the Greek fragments against the Latin texts as well.[19] The Nag Hammadi treatises, then, have chronological priority. (4) The *Disc. 8–9*, unknown until recently, opens the way for a study of the earliest witness to a Hermetic document. Its content and its orientation, although perhaps related to *Corpus Hermeticum* I and XIII,[20] nevertheless is unique, and thus provides an unexplored referent for Hermetic religions.

This chapter consists of three progressive arguments covering to some extent the three Hermetic documents of Codex 6. I will argue that *Disc. 8–9* presents the relationship of a spiritual guide to a disciple as modeled on a sexual relationship. This modelling reveals the sexual dynamic operative in spiritual formation. The first argument studies the *Pr. Thanks.* and demonstrates that the relationship of guide, disciple, and deity effects a transfer of power. The second documents the description of the relationship in *Asclepius*: here the "mystery" is represented as "the intercourse between the male and the female" with its attendant social implications. The third analyzes the narrative of *Disc. 8–9* to present the unfolding of that sexual description in the relationship of the guide to the disciple. The narrative of *Disc. 8–9* relates the process of spiritual formation by encoding and interpreting each stage in formation, by portraying the evolutionary development of the relationship of the guide to the disciple and both to the divine figure, and by defining the interrelationship of texts, brotherhoods, prayer, and other divine figures.

My method is semiotic: it analyzes the cultural encoding, that is, the cultural systems which enables communication to occur. The study begins by taking these treatises, their own internal narrative, and their coexistence in the Nag Hammadi library as indicative of the complex levels of communication. The careful pursuit of the narrative development of the relationship in these texts will determine both the significance of the relationship itself and the wider significance of such a relationship to Hermetic religions. This

---

[19] This is taken from Mahé's (*Hermès,* 2. 22–23) evaluation of the relationship of Greek, Latin, and Coptic sources.

[20] The bibliography for these Hermetic documents is great; of special value, however, are Grese, *Corpus Hermeticum XIII*; and Tröger, *Mysterienglaube.*

study will problematize as much as possible, making few assumptions about the wider significance of the characters and their narrative development until the narrative directs such an understanding. In the end, such a process will have shown us not merely a Hermetic initiation, nor the inner workings of a mystery religion, nor even the process of divinization of a seeker, but a surprising process of mutual divinization through the (primarily sexually described) relationship of spiritual guide to disciple.

The sexual dynamic of spiritual formation raises two major problems: sexuality[21] and gender. In his attempt "to define the regime of power-knowledge-pleasure that sustains the discourse on human sexuality," Michel Foucault[22] distinguished between the *ars erotica*, the self-reflecting esoteric art of pleasure passed on from a master to a disciple,[23] and the *scientia sexualis*, the confessional exploration of sexual acts and stimuli which produces true discourse.[24] Although the *ars erotica* is initiatory in nature, while the *scientia sexualis* is discursive, there was a degree of common material in the Christian tradition. Foucault writes:

> In the Christian confession, but especially in the direction and examination of conscience, in the search for spiritual union and the love of God, there was a whole series of methods that had much in common with an erotic art: guidance by the master along a path of initiation, the intensification of experiences extending down to their physical components, the optimaization of effects by the discourse that accompanied them.[25]

In spiritual, as well as intellectual, formation knowledge and sexuality are interrelated discourses, especially in those religious traditions which historically have practiced initiation.[26]

---

[21] See Martha Vicinus, "Sexuality and Power: A Review of Current Work in the History of Sexuality," *Feminist Studies* 8 (1982) 134–56.

[22] *The History of Sexuality*, vol. 1: *An Introduction* (1976; reprinted New York: Random House, 1980); see also idem, *The History of Sexuality*, vol. 2: *The Use of Pleasure* (1984; reprinted New York: Random House, 1986); and idem, *The History of Sexuality*, vol. 3: *The Care of the Self* (1984; reprinted New York: Pantheon, 1986).

[23] Foucault, *Introduction*, 57.

[24] Ibid., 58–73, esp. 67–68.

[25] Ibid., 70.

[26] The history-of-religions school has explored the question of initiations extensively. The following three articles from C. J. Bleeker, ed., *Initiation* (Studies in the History of Religion; Leiden: Brill, 1965) have been helpful: idem, "Initiation in Ancient Egypt," 49–58; U. Bianchi ("Initiation, Mystères, Gnose [Pour l'histoire de la mystique dans le paganisme gréco-oriental]," 154–71) who explores a phenomenological series of fecund cult, mysteries, mysteriosophy, and gnosis; and E. M. Mendelson, "Initiation and the Paradox of Power: A Sociological Approach," in Bleeker, *Initiation*, 214–21.

The presence of sexual language and referent in Gnostic and Hermetic literature has not been sufficiently explored, except by a few scholars.[27] This chapter will take the sexual discourse of these Hermetic texts as intentionally communicative: this assumes that these men expressed spiritual formation in sexual language because it best expressed the interior dynamic of their initiation.

The fact that they are all men points to the second problem, gender.[28] There are few females in these texts. Every reference to any female function relates to female biological functions: participation as the "other" in intercourse, conceiving (male) children, giving birth (primarily to brotherhoods).[29] In these texts the supression of the female has indeed become an instrument for presenting male experience as universal.[30] The usurpation of female biological functions by male spiritual guides in these texts presents, moreover, particular problems of interpretation. What does it signify that a man ("O my Father") says that he conceived and gave birth to a brotherhood? The violence of such exclusion cannot be ignored, and yet explanations (even hostile ones) are difficult to formulate. Any conclusions drawn from these texts must be carefully limited to a specific discourse between men, regarding the socialization and initiation of other men.

---

[27] There is the often quoted and very good article by Robert M. Grant, "The Mystery of Marriage in the Gospel of Philip," *VC* 15 (1961) 129–40. A later, but largely not successful, attempt to explore the sexual dynamic was made by Madeline Nold, "A Consideration of Alexandrian Christianity as a Possible Aid towards Further Understanding of Nag Hammadi Religion: A Case-in-point for a Joint Methodology," *StPatr* 14 (1976) 229–42. The most successful work, which will be analyzed later, is that of Mahé, "Symboles Sexuels," 123–45.

[28] Again the bibliography is immense. I have primarily consulted the following feminist literary theoreticians: Helena Michie, *The Word Made Flesh: Female Figures and Women's Bodies* (New York: Oxford University Press, 1987). There are four helpful essays in Elaine Showalter, ed., *The New Feminist Criticism: Essays on Women, Literature and Theory* (New York: Pantheon, 1985): idem, "The Feminist Critical Revolution," 3–17; idem, "Toward a Feminist Poetics," 125–43; Annette Kolodny, "A Map for Rereading: Gender and the Interpretation of Literary Texts," 42–62; and idem, "Dancing Through the Minefield: Some Observations on the Theory, Practice, and Politics of a Feminist Literary Criticism," 144–67. And the following essays in Elizabeth A. Flynn and Patrocinio P. Schweikert, eds., *Gender and Reading: Essays on Readers, Texts, and Contexts* (Baltimore: Johns Hopkins University Press, 1986) are of note: Mary Crawford and Roger Chaffin, "The Reader's Construction of Meaning: Cognitive Research on Gender and Comprehension," 3–30; and Patrocinio P. Schweikert, "Reading Ourselves: Toward a Feminist Theory of Reading," 31–62. Jonathan Culler (*On Deconstruction: Theory and Criticism after Structuralism* [Ithaca: Cornell University Press, 1982]) has also been helpful as an overview.

[29] On the problem of the invisibility of women and their bodies from texts, see Michie, *Word Made Flesh*, 3–11. On gender and gender typing, see Crawford and Chaffin, "Reader's Construction," 13–21.

[30] See Schweikert, "Reading Ourselves," 31–62.

Prayer of Thanksgiving and
Prayer as the Exchange of Commodities

The text of a prayer presents some interesting semiotic possibilities. Prayer is understood as the communication of a suppliant with a deity.[31] As a text a prayer becomes multivalent by its potential for interacting in environments unrelated to converse with a deity. Even though a written prayer may be so employed, it may also be used for other purposes: to act as a model for community prayer, to limit the perimeters of legitimate prayer discourse, to make a statement about the deity, or to make claims about the religious status of the people praying. The text of the prayer, thus, may be made to lie:[32] under the guise of a communication with a deity the written prayer may present a falsehood, or report incidental information, or "tell" something other than the generic concern of a prayer. This ability to "tell" indicates that written prayers are made up of signs.[33] These signs operate in an exchange between the speaker of the prayer and the divinity: they thus become a commodity in the discursive exchange.

Pr. Thanks.[34] includes two interrelated semiotic systems: the first is in the text of the prayer itself; the second is in the narrative introduction and conclusion which envelop the prayer-text. The combination of the prayer-text and the narrative envelop indicates a self-conscious manipulation of signs:

---

[31] See C. W. F. Smith, "Prayer," *IDB* 3. 857–67 for an introduction. The most comprehensive study is that of Friedrich Heiler, *Prayer: A Study in the History and Psychology of Religion* (Oxford: Oxford University Press, 1932). Prayer in the Nag Hammadi documents is treated in two essays: Eric Segelberg, "Prayer Among the Gnostics? The Evidence of Some Nag Hammadi Documents" (NHS 8; Leiden: Brill, 1977) 55–69; and George MacRae, "Prayer and Knowledge of Self in Gnosticism," in Daniel J. Harrington and Stanley B. Marrow, eds., *Studies in New Testament and Gnosticism* (Wilmington: Glazier, 1987) 218–36 (= *Tantur Yearbook* [1978–1979] 97–114).

[32] For the theory of the lie, and of lying, see Eco, *A Theory of Semiotics* (Bloomington: Indiana University, 1979) 6–7; and also idem, "Strategies of Lying," in Blonsky, *On Signs,* 3–11.

[33] Oral prayer would also make an interesting semiotic study because of its mixture of language, rhetoric, gesture, voice modulation, physical setting, and proximity to hearers, etc. The repitition of Greek vowels, commonly identified as ecstatic utterance, may be a remnant of such an oral presentation.

[34] The text is in Parrott, *NHS 11,* 378–87, as well as Mahé, *Hermès,* 1. 157–67. Both contain a synopsis of the Coptic, Latin and the Greek versions of the text. The prayer seems to be an independent piece of Hermetic literature because each version is found in a different environment. The Latin prayer is at the end of the Latin *Asclepius,* while the Greek is contained within a collection of magical texts. For a discussion see Mahé's text and article "La Prière d'actions de grâces du Codex VI de Nag Hammadi et Le Discours parfait," *Zeitschrift für Papyrologie und Epigraphik* 13 (1974) 40-60; and the discussion by Dirkse and Brashler in Parrott, *NHS 11,* 375–77.

the narrative links the prayer to the preceding treatise (*Disc. 8–9*) by giving thanks for the knowledge granted there.[35] The text communicates in three ways: (1) within the prayer-text itself; (2) in its placement in relation to other texts in Codex 6; and (3) in the interpretation of this placement by the narrative envelope of the prayer.

The Participants

The participants in the combined prayer-text and narrative envelope speak in two voices which represent three perspectives. The first voice, that of the narrative itself, functions from outside the perspective of the speaker of the prayer who is designated as "they." The introductory narrative, acting as well as a title for the prayer, relates simply: "This is the prayer which they spoke," ⲡⲁⲓ̈ ⲡⲉ ⲡϣⲗⲏⲗ ⲛ̄ⲧⲁⲩⲭⲟⲟϥ (63.33). The second voice, that of the "we" who speak in the prayer, speaks from within a relationship to the divinity who is being addressed. It is the plural voice of a community of indeterminate size. These two voices constitute the first two perspectives of the text: the third is that of the "You," the divinity who is being addressed from within the community's voice. It presents the community's portrayal of the divinity who does not speak directly either in the prayer-text or in the narrative envelope. The participants in the discourse, then, are an outsider (narrative), a community ("we"), and a god ("You").

The community[36] characterizes itself in the prayer as performing four actions: it gives thanks (63.34–35), it acknowledges the receipt of benefits from the divinity (64.4–14), it rejoices at their receipt (64.15–30), and it makes a petition (64.31–65.2). These actions indicate that the community

---

[35] Dirkse and Brashler (Parrott, *NHS 11*, 375) write: "The location of this tractate suggests that the scribe of Codex VI intended it as an appendix to the immediately preceding tractate, *Disc. 8–9*, where the knowledge for which this prayer gives thanks has been revealed."

[36] The question of Hermetic communities and mystery-community formation has a long history. Burkert (*Ancient Mystery Cults* [Carl Newell Jackson Lectures, 1982; Cambridge: Harvard University Press, 1987] 30–65) outlines a typology of three, often overlaping, social organizations: the itinerant charismatic, the clergy attached to a sanctuary, and a club. Hermetic religions tend toward the fusion of a club and a charismatic leader (who takes on the persona of Hermes Trismegistus). Tröger (*Mysterienglaube und Gnosis in Corpus Hermeticum XIII* [Berlin: Akademie, 1971] 167–69) has studied Hermetism in relationship to both mystery religions and Gnosticism, concluding that Hermetic writings appropriate the familiar terminology of the mysteries into a Gnostic community. Although Festugière (*Révélation*, 1. 81–87) would argue for a non-Gnostic, philosophical school environment, the scholarly tendency has been to view the Hermetic material as more akin to Gnosticism than either the mysteries or philosophical schools. Mahé ("Le sens," 63–64) distinguishes Hermetic from Gnostic literature. Note also that Mahé ("Symboles Sexuels," 130) claims that there are two divergent strands in Hermeticism: one opposing and one drawing near to Gnosticism.

consists of the enlightened ones who address the source of their benefits.[37]

The prayer, not directly revealing the identity of the deity to whom it is addressed, characterizes the deity from the community's perspective. In the opening section of the prayer, the figure receives thanks ("We give You thanks!" [63.34].) and homage ("Every soul and heart is lifted to You" [63.34–35].). Such designations tell more about the community than about the deity: the community was of the sort who give thanks and was united in orientation toward the deity. The only direct designation of the deity, "O Name which cannot be troubled" (63.35), describes a deity with a name beyond the community's appeal.[38] The prayer then relates that the divine figure is "honored by the name 'God', and praised by the name 'Father,'" (64.1–3). The community's bestowal of honor and praise instrumentally through names (Father and God) indicates an interchangeability in the deity's character: the community's interests create the proper name for the divinity, and the name creates the identity. The naming of the subject of the prayer as Father and God confers the divine status and character upon the figure to whom the prayer is addressed.

The subsequent characterizations of the deity exhibit even more such communal definition. At the end of the prayer the community addresses the divine figure in a list of metaphoric attributes: "O noetic light," ⲱ̅ ⲡⲟⲩⲉⲓⲛ ⲛ̅ⲛⲟ ⲏ ⲧ ⲟ ⲛ (64.23); "O life of life," ⲱ̅ ⲡⲱⲛ̄ ⲙ̅ⲡⲱⲛ̄ (64.23–24); "O womb (μήτρα) of every sowing," ⲱ ⲧⲙⲏⲧⲣⲁ ⲛ̄ⲭⲟ ⲛⲓⲙ (64.25);[39] "O womb (μήτρα) pregnant with the nature (φύσις) of the Father," ⲱ̅ ⲧⲙⲏⲧⲣⲁ ⲉⲧⲭⲡⲟ ⲍ̄ⲛ ⲧⲫⲩⲥⲓⲥ ⲙ̅ⲡⲓⲱⲧ (64.26–27); "O eternal continuance of the Father who begets," ⲱ̅ ⲡⲙⲟⲩⲛ ⲉⲃⲟⲗ ⲱ̅ⲁ ⲉⲛⲉⲍ ⲙ̅ⲡⲉⲓⲱⲧ ⲉⲧⲭⲡⲟ (64.28–29). These images characterize the divinity in three different categories: (1) philosophically as noetic light and life; (2) two descriptions of wombs (μήτρα); and (3) and one result of begetting which eternally perseveres the Father. The philosophical background and nature of Hermetic thought needs no further explanation: Festugière has explored both the

---

[37] Segelberg ("Prayer," 66) distinguishes two spiritual levels of prayers in the Nag Hammadi Hermetic writings: those who ask or petition (representing the "preliminary stage of spiritual development") and those who hymn and praise (indicating a "more advanced spiritual state"). Because this prayer gives thanks and acknowledges the divinity of the persons praying, this prayer indicates the higher category.

[38] The Papyrus Mimaut Greek text reads: "O inexpressible Name"; the Latin reads "holy and honored name." Both of these describe the deity.

[39] The coptic ⲭⲟ, as a noun, means "sowing" or "planting." See W. C. Crum, *A Coptic Dictionary* (Oxford: Clarendon, 1939) s.v. ⲭⲟ; and Thomas O. Lambdin, *Introduction to Sahidic Coptic* (Macon: Mercer University Press, 1983) 344. Mahé (*Hermès,* 1. 164) translates it "semence" ("seed"); Parrott (*NHS 11,* 384) has "creature." Because the verb ⲭⲟ ⲭⲉ- ⲭⲟ⸗ means "to sow, plant" the agricultural image should be retained.

content and the educational context.[40] The other descriptions, however, have perplexed scholars of Gnosticism and Hermeticism.

Only the medical literature of Late Antiquity similarly treats such designations as "womb" and such biological functions such as begetting as "signs." The diagnostic method of Galen of Pergamum, the second-century physician, was in fact a method of semiotic analysis in which the signifier was an event in the body and the signified a particular disease, injury, or body function.[41] Within such a semiotic framework, each part of the body had a purpose or sign-value:

> Nature had three principal aims in constructing the parts of the animal; for she made them either for the sake of life (the encephalon, heart, liver), or for a better life (the eyes, ears, and nostrils), or for the continuance of the race (the pudenda, testes, and uteri).[42]

Existing for the continuance of the race, "the work of the uteri is to receive the semen and perfect the fetus."[43] The perfection of the fetus consists in its being retained in the womb until it attain the proper size and is able to nurture itself. The usefulness (χρεία) of the womb's function (ἐνεργεία) is to enclose the fetus with its retentive faculty (ἡ καθητικὴ δύναμις) until the fetus is fully grown. When the fetus is fully grown, the "retentive faculty" rests (ἀναπαυεῖν) and the "eliminative or propulsive faculty" (ἡ ἀποκριτική τε καὶ προωστικὴ δύναμις) takes over expelling the fetus to be born.[44]

The womb is a complex sign of nurture, retention, rest, and expulsion. What, then, could be signified by such an address to the deity? "O womb of every sowing" could signify that the divinity is a universal place: the divinity retains, nurtures, rests, and, when it has grown fully, expels, every religious community, every sowing. "O womb pregnant with the nature of the Father" could signify that the deity is the community, the religious society or the safe environment in which the Father has mingled his nature to produce a fetus, a community. This interpretation would present sexual intercourse as a metaphor for the means of propagating religious orientation. The characters in such a scenario, however, are not clear: if the womb is the divinity, who, then is the Father and what is his "nature"? And finally "O eternal

---

[40] *Révélation*, III and IV.

[41] See Galen, "On the Affected Parts" (trans. Rudolph E. Siegel; New York: Karger, 1976) 4.

[42] Galen, *De usu partium*, 2.285. I have used Galen, *On the Usefulness of the Parts of the Body*. Περὶ χρείας μορίων *De usu partium* (trans. Margaret Tallmadge May; Ithaca: Cornell University Press, 1968) 2. 620.

[43] Galen, *De usu partium*, 2.293–94.

[44] Galen, *On the Natural Faculties* (trans. Arthur John Brock; LCL 71; Cambridge: Harvard University Press, 1979) 228–37.

continuance of the begetting Father'' refers to the fetus, the community, which itself has become a womb retaining those begotten by the Father. These can only be suggestions. What can be maintained, however, is that the womb referent defines a mythology in which the divinity, the other, with whom the Father (who may or may not be a divinity) has relations which create a fetus, the community.

With such an image of the deity, the community expresses its understanding that their entry into the divinity, their lifting up toward God, takes them into a womb, a constricted place in which they are nurtured until they are perfected sufficiently to nurture themselves spiritually. In assigning names to the divinity they constitute themselves as subjects of divinization and in describing the divinity as the ''eternal continuance of the father's begetting'' they characterize themselves as the agents of divinization in the cosmos.

The Exchange of Commodities

The prayer-text revolves about an exchange: the community gives thanks to Hermes for having received mind, speech, and knowledge. The prayer states:

> For to everyone and everything (comes) the fatherly kindness and affection and love, and any teaching there may be that is sweet and plain, giving us mind, discourse, (and) knowledge. (64.4–10)

Out of the paternal goodness and love come the threefold commodity of mind, discourse, and knowledge as benefits to the praying community. No content of the sign is indicated in the text, so that the exact referent of mind, speech, and knowledge remains undefined: only the signifier is listed. The signs, stated simply and abstractly, form the first in a series of three reworkings in other arenas of involvement (community activity, and subjective status of the participants).

The second listing interprets the mind, speech, and knowledge as signifiers of a capacity for action in the community:

> Giving us mind, discourse, (and) knowledge: mind, so that we may understand You, discourse, so that we may interpret You, knowledge so that we may know You. (64.8–14)

The commodities bestowed translate into three verbal actions (understanding, explaining, knowing). The referent to these signs is not the dictionary meaning of the term listed, but the function within community for which the term stands.

The third listing of the commodities moves from communal function to subjective appropriation. The three terms themselves are not listed. Instead three causes of rejoicing are presented:

> We rejoice, having been illumined by Your knowledge. We rejoice because You have shown us Yourself. We rejoice because while we were in (the) body, You have made us gods through Your knowledge. (63.15–19)

Illumination, revelation, and divinization reconstitute the commodities from their subjective and socially recognizable effect (signified by the refrain "We rejoice") as well as claiming for the speakers of the prayer a theological status as those who are illumined, those who recieve revelation, and those who are divinized while still humans.

This entire process is concretized and summarized as knowledge of the divinity: "The thanksgiving of the man who attains to You is one thing: that we know You" (64.20-22). The commodities of mind, speech, and knowledge, then, are presented as signifiers of three different arenas in a prayer context which explores the transformation that has taken place in the speaker. Mind, discourse, and knowledge signify (1) a commodity exchanged in prayer, (2) the new ability to act in community which the gnostic experiences, and (3) a special status of the gnostic in the religious life.

But the exchange of commodities does not end with those which the speaker receives. As indicated above, the divine figure receives thanks, homage, and names (undisturbed Name, God, Father). The community recognizes the divine figure as the origin of the commodities and acknowledges these benefits as the objects of desire and yearning.

And finally, the divinity is constituted as a subject of gnosis through a series of statements in direct address. At the beginning of the prayer, the divinity is addressed as "O undisturbed name" (63.36), a form of address which is continued at the end of the prayer:

> We have known You, O noetic light. O life of life, we have known You. O womb of every every sowing, we have known You. O womb pregnant with the nature of the Father, we have known You. O eternal continuance of the Father who begets, thus have we worshipped Your goodness. (64.22–30)

The listing of the divine attributes and descriptions is punctuated with the insistence that this divinity has been made and conquered as a subject by the speaker. The prayer constitutes the divinity as the subject of gnosis which the gnostic may master.

The Narrative Envelope

The narrative voice appears as intentionally interpretative: the prayer- text is introduced as an example of the prayer of the preceding tractate. The narrative places the prayer in a discursive framework of three signs: the prayer, the embrace (or possibly, the kiss), and the eating of holy and bloodless food.[45] These signs portray the outward appearance of what is taking place which is a sequence of prayer, embrace, and eating. The signs are not given a content: they stand as the suggestion of communion (the prayer), of intimacy (the embrace), and of a cultic meal (the eating).

There is also the suggestion of an order of function moving from conversation with the deity, to the intimacy of those gnostics who pray together, to the partaking of holy food. The order moves from the divinity to the meal in the context of community: it is not an order of ascent godward, but of entrance into community and its cultic meals. This community orientation permeates the *Pr. Thanks.* The prayer not only speaks in a communal voice, but also procures for the community mind, discourse, and knowledge, commodities not understood as entities in themselves, but as they translate into the community's ability to understand, explain, and know. The community both defines and participates in the divine life, while at the same time entering into a process of mutual exchange with the diety.

Asclepius, the Sexual Encoding of Relationship

Since the treatise bears no title itself, the Nag Hammadi treatise Codex VI.8 has been given the title *Asclepius 21–29* on the basis of its presumed relationship to a lost Greek original, *Logos Teleios,* which only survives in a Latin translation.[46] The Coptic text, when compared to the more periphrastic Latin,[47] is generally concluded to be an earlier witness to the Greek text.[48] Festugière has argued that the *Logos Teleios* was a mosaic of smaller, mostly independent, discourses brought together as an educational anthology;[49] while M. Krause claims that the Nag Hammadi text would represent an

---

[45] Segelberg ("Prayer," 67) argues that this indicates a developed liturgical life with some sort of sacramental acts evidencing Christian and Jewish influences. See also Birger A. Pearson, "Jewish Elements in Corpus Hermeticum I (Poimandres)," in R. Van den Broek and M. J. Vermaseren, eds., *Studies in Gnosticism and Hellenistic Religions* (Leiden: Brill, 1981) 336–48.

[46] For the Latin text see A. D. Nock, ed., and A. J. Festugière, trans., *Corpus Hermeticum* (4 vols; 6th ed.;Paris: Société d'Edition Les Belles Lettres, 1983) 2. 322–36. Parrott (*NHS 11,* 400-451) reprints the Latin text with an English translation by George MacRae. See also Mahé, *Hermès,* 2. 147–207.

[47] For an evaluation of the Latin text in relationship to the Greek, see David N. Wigtil, "Incorrect Apocalyptic: The Hermetic 'Asclepius' as an Improvement on the Greek Original," ANRW 2/17.4 (1984) 2282–97.

[48] Parrott, *NHS 11,* 396; and Mahé, *Hermès,* 2. 49–61.

[49] Festugière, *Révélation,* 2. 18–26, esp. 18.

independent discourse, functioning outside any collection of discourses.[50] Mahé thinks that the *Asclepius* is a detached piece of the larger work.[51] Independent of theories explaining the relationship of the various versions of the text, the text stands in the Nag Hammadi Library as an independent discourse which may have relationships to other versions and anthologies of discourses, but which also has an independent life.

The *Logos Teleios*, a school dialogue[52] between Asclepius and Trismegistus "probably used in a Hermetic instructional-cultic context,"[53] carries all the Hermetic themes successively almost as a summary of the master's teaching.[54] Mahé posits an evolutionary typology of Hermetic literature from the Maxim (*gnomai*), to the connecting of maxims into chapters or gnomologies, the linking of chapters together, and finally to commentaries on the linked chapters.[55] Such a typology explains the often conflicting nature of Hermetic concepts: many independent maxims with their independent annotations could be assembled into one discourse which could then function together in even larger discourses. The literary collection, annotation and embellishment of maxims represents the common scholarly practice in philosophical schools.[56] The *Asclepius* then may be described as a series of largely independent units brought together into one discourse by the needs of a particular educational program.

The anthological character of the tractate *Asclepius* is evident from listing its contents: the icon of intercourse (65.15–19), the medical interpretation of that icon (65.19–25), and the social implications of such relationships (65.26–65.38), the relationship of learning to knowledge (65.38–66.24), the anthropological basis of learning and knowledge (66.26–68.12), discourses on assorted topics of community, creation of the gods, and idols (68.13–70.2), an apocalypse (70.3–74.6),[57] ending with an individual eschatology (74.7–78.43).

Only the first three units explain the relationships within the mystery. Even they, however, seem to be independent units: there is a marked differ-

---

[50] Krause, "Der Stand der Veröffentlichung der Nag Hammadi Texte," in Ugo Bianchi, ed., *L'origini dello gnosticismo: Colloquio di Messina 13–18 Aprile 1966* (Studies in the History of Religions 12; Leiden: Brill, 1967) 61–89, esp. 81.

[51] Mahé, *Hermès*, 2. 50, 209–10.

[52] For the genre see Festugière, *Révélation*, 2. 28–50.

[53] Parrott, *NHS 11*, 396.

[54] Mahé, *Hermès*, 2. 48.

[55] Ibid., 416–36.

[56] Ibid., 422–23. He notes that the evidence for such scholarly activity is the Manual of Epictetus and Porphyry's *Ad Marcellam*.

[57] This apocalypse has attracted the most scholarly attention. See Mahé, *Hermès*, 2. 68–113; and Wigtil, "Apocalyptic," 2288–93.

ence in perspective between the iconographical and medical presentations, on the one hand, which treat intercourse as a sign, and the social implications section, on the other, which assumes the actual performance of the mystery of intercourse. All three of these units, both independently and together, explore the inner dynamic of initiation as sexual intercourse which exchanges power between the participants who must consequently guard the implications of their relationship.

Sexuality and Mysteries

The statement at the beginning of the *Asclepius* that if one wishes to see the working of the mystery one should look at the intercourse between the male and the female (65.15–19) raises two important prior questions which affect the coding of the relationship. The first has to do with the positive appraisal of sexual intercourse. In an essay exploring the Egyptian provenance and possible Pachomian connections of the Nag Hammadi library, Torgny Säve-Söderbergh listed some of the more problematic and troubling aspects of the *Asclepius* material for that environment. The first, among four, was that:

> Sexual intercourse between male and female with the purpose of giving birth to children is "the wonderful representation" . . . and a mystery, laughed at and despised by "blasphemers, atheists and impious [sic]".[58]

He concluded that

> the implications of these Hermetic texts are difficult to reconcile even with the majority of the other tractates of the library. It is still more difficult to understand their use as edifying texts for Pachomian monks.[59]

This sort of paradigmatic discomfort with the overt and direct endorsement of sexual intercourse as representative of religious initiation hinders the positive appraisal of the treatise. Sexual intercourse must, however, be treated as a sign, a code whose referent may be established from within the cultural matrix which assigns meaning to them. The referent is not to sexual activity which may be presumed to have been the same then as now[60] (because no

---

[58] Säve-Söderbergh, "The Pagan Elements in Early Christianity and Gnosticism," in Bernard Barc, ed., *Colloque International sur Les Textes de Nag Hammadi (Québec 22–25 août 1978)* (Bibliothèque Copte de Nag Hammadi, Section "Études" 1; Québec: Les Presses de l'Univeristé Laval, 1981) 75–76.

[59] Ibid., 76.

[60] For a discussion of the presumed constancy of a concept of sexuality, see Foucault, *Use of Pleasure*, 4.

event in itself carries meaning), but to a series of coded messages used to give meaning to the words in the text. The referent is not to the phenomenon, to sexual relationships between initiates and mystagogues, but to the inscribing of sexual meaning into the literary-theological agenda of a Hermetic treatise which describes a very intense and energizing relationship. Mahé, in differentiating this sexual inscribing from the Gnostic variety, concludes that the positive reception of sexuality in some Hermetic texts, including the *Asclepius*, reflects perhaps an earlier and more Egyptian provenance.[61] Heterosexual intercourse as a theological category, signifies that the same divine energy which created the world in the beginning also sustains it to the ends of the universe without any essential discontinuity between creation and procreation.[62] Sexual intercourse does not mirror the truth by inverse imaging which denies its bodily and literal meaning, but rather it directly reflects the divine life.[63] Sexuality, then, is a mystery not because it is done in secret, but because the act reveals something of the divine.[64] My approach will emphasize the sign-value and revelatory function of sexual intercourse as a means of understanding the relationship of spiritual guide and disciple in the process of mutual divinization. If the icon of sexual intercourse presents the interior workings of the complex relationships between guide, disciple, and divinity, then the description would indeed be of primary interest to Pachomian monks.

The second problem is the reference to the "mystery" (μυστήριον), a term overloaded with implications.[65] Hermetism, Gnosticism, and the mysteries have held the scholarly imagination for many years.[66] Walter Burkert, in the 1982 Carl Newell Jackson lectures at Harvard University,[67] explored the origins, social organization, development, and the descriptions of the experience of the mystery cults. Burkert explains that "there is, in fact, a downright inflation of terms such as *mysteria* and *mystikos* in Gnostic and Hermetic texts, which causes a corresponding devaluation of meaning."[68] And he concludes that "the immediate value of these [Nag Hammadi Hermetic and Gnostic] texts as a source for knowledge of pagan mysteries remains limited."[69] Burkert maintains that the search for such mystery texts

---

[61] Mahé, "Symboles Sexuels," 143–45.

[62] Ibid., 131–32.

[63] Ibid., 133.

[64] Ibid., 129–30.

[65] See Günther Bornkamm, "μυστήριον," in *TDNT* 4 (1967) 802–28.

[66] For a current evaluation, see Jacques-E. Ménard, "Mystères et Gnose," *Laval Théologiques et Philosophique* 32 (1976) 131–44.

[67] Burkert, *Mystery Cults*.

[68] Ibid., 67.

[69] Ibid., 68.

is futile. Such texts do not exist because the mystery cults dealt with the development and formation of a specific experience. There might be teachings, traditions, speeches, written sacred tales, but they were not central to the event, nor did such written materials constitute a sacred scripture.[70] Burkert's definition of the mysteries underscores their experiential basis: "Mysteries were initiation rituals of a voluntary, personal, and secret character that aimed at a change of mind through the experience of the sacred."[71] Although the experience itself worked on movement between extremes, included joining a group of the blessed in praise, prominent sexuality or abstinence from sexual activity, communal meals, "yet the texts insist that the true state of blessedness is not in this emotional resonance but in the act of 'seeing' what is divine."[72] The description of and reflection on experience presented in the *Asclepius* and in the *Disc. 8–9* are not primarily evidence for mystery cult. Rather than enter into the elusive quest for the validation and interpretation of Gnostic mysteries,[73] the Nag Hammadi Hermetic texts will be taken to refer only to Hermetic religions and one purposeful collection of tractates for an interested consumer.

The Icon of Intercourse

The most startling of the characterizations of the initiation in the *Asclepius* is the encoding of the mystery as an icon of heterosexual intercourse:

> If indeed you wish (+δὲ) to see the work of this mystery (μυστήριον), then you should see the marvellous icon (εἰκών) of the intercourse (συνουσία) which happens between the male and the female. (65.15–19)

ⲉϣⲭⲉ ⲕⲟⲩⲱϣ ⲇⲉ ⲉⲛⲁⲩ ⲉⲫⲱⲃ ⲙ̄ ⲡⲉⲧⲙⲩⲥⲧⲏⲣⲓⲟⲛ ⲁⲩⲱ ⲑⲓⲕⲱⲛ ⲛ̄ϣⲡⲏⲣⲉ
ⲛ̄ⲅⲛⲁⲩ ⲉⲣⲟⲥ ⲛ̄ⲧⲉ ⲧⲥⲩⲛⲟⲩⲥⲓⲁ ⲉϣⲁⲥϣⲱⲡⲉ ⲉⲃⲟⲗ ϩⲓⲧⲙ̄ ⲫⲟⲟⲩⲧ ⲙⲛ̄
ⲧⲥϩⲓⲙⲉ

The μυστήριον here, as Mahé has observed,[74] denotes a concrete and

---

[70] Ibid., 69–73.

[71] Ibid., 11.

[72] Ibid., 93.

[73] R. McL. Wilson ("Gnosis and the Mysteries," in R. Van den Broek and M. J. Vermaseren, eds., *Studies in Gnosticism and Hellenistic Religions* [Leiden: Brill, 1981] 456) has written: "The mysteries certainly contribute to the religious ferment of our early Roman Empire, and some of their ideas no doubt passed into Gnosticism, some of their traditions were taken over. But this is at most to speak in general terms. It is when we try to identify specific points of contact, specific influences, to determine what traditions were taken over and how they were modified, that the problems arise."

[74] Mahé, "Symboles Sexuels," 129–30.

physical act which has a theologically revelatory dimension. With the wide range of possible meanings, this depiction of "mystery" cuts across the philosophical mystery with its "mysterious teachings which elevate the soul to union with the divine,"[75] the magical mysteries with their orientation toward concrete and physical actions,[76] and the Gnostic mysteries in which only the elect understand the true meaning.[77] The physical action of the mystery here presupposes no special knowledge or interpretation to qualify it as an esoteric teaching. The mystery simply functions as a revelatory act which is done in secret.[78]

The icon (εἰκών) here is no mere portrait. Because it is presented as the subject of contemption, it should, remain "icon" and not be translated with any correlative word. Again the range of meanings is wide: literally as "artistic representation," metaphorically as "mental image" or "similitude," and, as probably here, an "embodiment," a "manifestation." All of these meanings, however, assume that the image participates in the reality portrayed iconically so that the icon "implies the illumination of its inner core and essence."[79]

The relationship of these elements (mystery, icon, intercourse) could be deceiving. The conditional phrase "if you wish to see . . . then look" clearly indicates that it is a matter of personal choice.[80] The volition, however, is oriented toward reflection and meditation, not performance. The vision reveiws the φωв, the reality or working, of the mystery: a designation which points toward the inner reality and meaning rather than the appearance. The "marvellous icon of the intercourse between the male and the female" reveals the inner dynamic of the mystery and presents the icon as a subject for meditation or contemplation, should one choose to contemplate it.

The Medical Interpretation

A medico-sexual explanation specifically defines the inner workings of sexual intercourse:

---

[75] Bornkamm, "μυστήριον," *TDNT* 4 (1967) 808.

[76] Ibid., 810.

[77] Ibid., 811–12.

[78] So Mahé, "Symboles Sexuels," 129. Here he agrees with A. D. Nock ("A New Edition of Hermetic Writings," *JEA* 11 [1925] 126–37) that it is not a sacrament. Mahé argues that the mystery refers to more than simply the fact that it was performed in secret and that it has a revelatory function.

[79] Kleinknecht, "εἰκών," *TDNT* 2 (1964) 388–90.

[80] See Mahé, "Symboles Sexuels," 131, n. 23 for the parallel conditional phraseology in *Corpus Hermeticum* V, 6; XI, 14; and XIV, 9.

For when the semen comes to the climax it leaps forth. At that time the female receives the power of the male; the male also receives the power of the female, while the semen activates this. (65.19–25)

ⲍⲟⲧⲁⲛ ⲅⲉ ⲉϥϣⲁⲛⲉⲓ ⲉⲧⲁⲕⲙⲏ ϣⲁϥϧⲱⲅⲉ ⲉⲃⲟⲗ ⲛⲅⲓ ⲡⲉⲥⲡⲉⲣⲙⲁ ·
ⲛⲧⲉⲩⲛⲟⲩ ⲉⲧⲙⲙⲁⲩ ϣⲁⲣⲉⲧⲥⲍⲓⲙⲉ ⲭⲓ ⲛⲧⲅⲟⲙ ⲙ̄ⲫⲟⲟⲩⲧ · ⲫⲟⲟⲩⲧ ⲍⲱϣϥ
ϣⲁϥⲭⲓ ⲛⲧⲅⲟⲙ ⲛⲧⲥϥⲍⲓⲙⲉ ⲉⲣⲟϥ · ⲍⲱⲥ ⲉⲣⲉⲡⲥⲡⲉⲣⲙⲁ ⲣ̄ⲉⲛⲉⲣⲅⲉⲓ ⲙ̄ⲡⲁⲧ.

The representation of the initiation occurs at the climax when there is an exchange of power activated by the semen. The exchange of powers (ⲧⲅⲟⲙ) is mutual: the woman receiving power from the man; the man receiving from the woman. It is not indicated which of the semen, male or female, activates the climax.

Late Antique medical theory held that intercourse was the movement provided by Nature for the mixing of stronger and weaker semens for the generation of animals.[81] Both the male and the female had the exactly same bodily instruments, the only difference being that the woman's parts are within and the man's outside. The woman's penis, colder and less perfect because it was not strong enough to protrude, produced a weaker semen than the man's.[82] The advantage of these differences was that the woman's colder penis did not burn as much nutriment so that the excess of the nutriment could be transfered to the nurture of a fetus.[83] Nature provided for the movement of intercourse by coupling "a very great pleasure . . . with the exercise of the generative parts and a raging desire."[84] This capacity for pleasure and the intense longing to experience it provided for the continuance of the race even if the animals were too foolish or ignorant to act wisely enough to provide it for themselves. Generation occurs when the semen falls into a suitable place: the movement creates the humors in the male which transforms the blood from red blood into white semen and prepares it for expulsion.[85] During coitus the tensing of every part ensures that the semen is generated in both the male and the female and that they are directed to the proper place for generation.[86]

The *Asclepius*'s presentation of the means of intercourse deviates from the received Greek and Roman medical theory. Although the medical theory describes an exchange of unequal potency, the reference in *Asclepius* does not: it simply states that there is an exchange of power through intercourse

---

81 Galen, *De usu partium*, 2.302–3.
82 Ibid., 296.
83 Ibid., 300.
84 Ibid., 313.
85 Ibid., 315–16.
86 Ibid., 319.

with the female and the male receiving the power from each other. This is made explicit later in the treatise when it says: "For each of them gives its (part in) begetting" (65.31)—ⲡⲟⲩⲁ ⲅⲁⲣ ⲡⲟⲩⲁ ⲙ̄ⲙⲟⲟⲩ ϥ̄ϯ ⲙ̄ⲡⲉϥϫⲡⲟ. This departure from tradition, however, has important gender implications.[87] From the perspective of Late Antique medicine, intercourse provided for the mingling of the stronger, male semen with the weaker, female semen *in the womb*. In order for the exchange in the *Asclepius* to be mutual both partners would need to pass semen to the other, an act which only males were equipped to perform. Since the woman's penis and potency was seen to be weaker and deficient, females could not accomplish this sort of mutual exchange described here. Females had no physical mechanism to transmit semen outside their bodies. Only males with their protruding penises could transmit semen, so that here only males could mutually exchange semen. The exchange, then, must be between two males, a reflection of an exclusively male orientation.

Even though one of the partners is named "female," the process that is presented portrays a social isomorphism mostly identified with the male in Greek society. Only men, fully invested with their social power, participate in the mysteries. There are no women present, only female functions. Such a situation, however, would place one of the members of the initiation into the role of being submissive, penetrated. Foucault has indicated that sexual relations reflect social relations with the social hierarchy of dominant over dominated, commander and complier, relating a correlative social status:

> And this suggests that in sexual behavior there was one role that was intrinsically honorable and valorized without question: the one that consisted in being active, in dominating, in penetrating, in asserting one's superiority.[88]

To protect the initiate from social inferiority, a concern also in the whole realm of sexual relations in Greek and Roman society,[89] the meaning and interior dynamic of sexual intercoure was redefined: the "signifier" (συνουσία) signified no longer the mingling of unequal partners, but the semen activating an exchange of strong powers among men. Only men, with their full and equal social power, participate in the mysteries with the result that the exchange that happens there is first socially mutual and second a relationship that only takes place among men.

The mutual exchange of power by (male) individuals at the climax mirrors

---

[87] Mahé frequently remarks on the fact that it is an equal exchange between the sexes. See "Symboles Sexuels," 129 and 136; and *Hermès*, 2. 211.

[88] Foucault, *Use of Pleasure*, 215.

[89] See ibid., 229–46; and idem, *Care of the Self*, 187–233.

the communal exchange of commodities in the *Pr. Thanks.* The inner dynamic of this wonderful mystery portrays the very point at which all the preparatory work climax in the receiving of power from the other. The exchange, emerging from an innate desire and pleasure, engenders life and continues the existence of the theological species. For the Hermetic initiate the icon reveals what occurs during initiation. After a long preparation of longing and desire with the guide (presumably human because the description is of human intercourse and not of a *hieros gamos*[90]), an exchange of power activated by the stronger guide, occurs. The power continues the life of both, creating the life-giving relationship which propagates the life of the gnostic.

The icon and its description include no real female presence.[91] In the prayer, the deity, partially described as womb and fetus, remains outside the community. In the *Asclepius*, intercourse between the male and the female, even though described medically, remains iconic of a relationship between two socially equal males operating in an exclusively male environment.

The Social Implications

These first two pericopae of the *Asclepius* work well together: the first presents the opportunity for meditation on the icon and the second reveals the significance of the icon. Both betray the same male-oriented perspective with no reference to women or to the actual performance of the mystery. In the next pericope, the narrator explains the social implications of intercourse. This shift in the subject from "icon" to "mystery of intercourse" has been overlooked by most interpreters with the result that the icon, its medical explanation, and the social implications have been conflated to refer to one mystery of intercourse. Since most have assumed that the subjects of the intercourse include the divine Hermes Trismegistus, the intercourse has been described as a *hieros gamos* and frequently compared with the nuptual chamber of *Gos. Phil.* 64.31–33. Their interest has been focussed on the question of whether the intercourse in *Asclepius* is metaphorical or actual. Even Mahé,[92] whose typology has led me to separate them, conflates them, but

---

[90] For the distinction between the use of γάμος and κοινωνία in *Gospel of Philip* (NHC 2, 3), as opposed to *Disc. 8–9*'s use of συνουσία, see Mahé, "Symboles Sexuels," 130. See also Burkert, *Mystery Cults,* 68; and Grant, *Mystery,* 137–39.

[91] Helena Michie (*The Word Made Flesh: Female Figures and Women's Bodies* [New York: Oxford University Press, 1987] 59–64) describes a metaphorization of the female body in a Victorian poem. Here, however, unlike that metaphorization, the intent is to conceal the fact that every female sign has as its signified, a male. Michie (p. 8) would call this "a historically aggravated instance of the violent and marked separation of signifier and signified."

[92] *Hermès,* 2. 212.

argues that the "mystery of intercourse" is an "image of an image," that is, that it is an iconic representation of an intercourse which mirrors cosmic realities. The intercourse described is human intercourse, without any mention of a divinity; and this intercourse is discussed in two different ways, one as icon, and the other as an act. The subject of the discourse, however, has shifted from the representation of the reality to its actual performance by a male and a female:

> Therefore the mystery of the intercourse must be done secretly, so that the two natures[93] (φύσις) will not be disgraced before the many who do not experience that reality. For each one of them gives his (part in) begetting. For, those who are not acquainted with this reality, if it should happen before them, (find it) ridiculous and unbelievable. And moreover, they are holy mysteries of discourse and acts, because not only are they not heard, but also they are not seen. (65.26–38)

The social implications emerge not from the contemplation of the icon, but from the actual practice of the mystery of intercourse. Since it is open to misunderstanding, the intercourse must be performed secretly. The mystery is not optional or volitional: each one must contribute to begetting. Such differing details distinguish this pericope from the previous two.

The pericope presents social groups: those knowledgeable practitioners of the mystery, and those ignorant who find it "ridiculous and unbelievable." The secrecy protects the practitioners of the mystery from disgrace before the misunderstanding ignorant. The wise understand the mystery to be both discursive and practical. Its hidden nature as unheard discourse and unseen action, attests to its holiness. This experience and knowledge is not universal, but only for the experienced, the gnostics. Until then, the knowledge and the experience remain beyond belief and comprehension.

The defensive tone of the passage, in contrast to the more explanatory tone of the previous two pericopae, indicates sensitivity to the potential for misunderstanding. The text betrays interest, however, in the necessity for mutual contribution, a contribution sufficiently important to risk ridicule and disbelief. Sexual intercourse both symbolizes the exchange as an iconic representation and actualizes it through intercourse. The practitioners of the

---

[93] There are grammatical problems with this phrase which result in multiple possibilities. M. Krause and P. Labib (*Gnostische und hermetische Schriften aus Codex II und Codex VI* [Abhandlungen des Deutschen Archäologischen Instituts Kairo; Koptische Reihe 2; Glückstadt: Augustin, 1971] 188) translate it as "natural pair" (das natürliche Paar). Mahé (*Hermès*, 2. 211) argues that it means not "natural pair," but "the two natures," hence (as in Parrott, *NHS 11*, 403) translating it as "two sexes." It seems best to keep the Greek word φύσις, so I have translated "two natures."

mystery are the elite group who know both the discourse and the actions, the sign and the things signified.

The *Pr. Thanks.* delineated the exchange of power at the corporate level, and the *Asclepius* delineated that exchange at the personal level of socially equal men entering an initiatory relationship. They are describing aspects of the same relationship and interaction. In the narrative of the *Disc. 8–9* that relationship receives fuller elaboration.

Discourse on the Eighth and Ninth, a Narrative of Mutual Empowerment

The exchange of power has been a constant theme of these Nag Hammadi Hermetic documents. The multivalent exchanges between the praying community and the deity who was partially described in anatomical terms prepared for the sexual presentation of the mystery in the pericopae from the *Asclepius*. Again, the sexual encoding has focussed on the mutual exchange of power, at first in the mutual receiving of power from the male and the female at the climax in intercourse, and later in the requirement for mutual contribution to engendering in the sexual mystery. In the *Disc. 8–9* the narrative plots this exchange of power in an initiation. Both the sexual presentation and the development of the relationship as a commodity for exchange remain under the surface of the narrative, but recede from prominence, so that the narrative may develop the relationship with a full and rich signification.

Disc. 8–9 is a Hermetic educational discourse[94] whose content reflects more a mythological orientation than a philosophical and school environment.[95] Mahé, on the basis of similar anonymity in other *Corpus Hermeticum* treatises, names the characters as Tat, although not so named in *Disc. 8–9*, and Hermes Trismegistus. He observes that "despite their divine names, all of these characters behave as simple mortals."[96] Since in the *Pr. Thanks.* the community quite deliberately bestows names upon the deity, the similar

---

[94] So Mahé, *Hermès*, 1. 31. Tröger ("Codex VI," 497; and "On Investigating," 120) specifies that it is a dialogue in a Gnostic Hermetic community. Keizer (*Eighth*, 3), however, claims that the genre is a "mystery liturgy" connected with the Hermetic liturgies of *Corpus Hermeticum* I, 24–26 and *Corpus Hermeticum* XIII. The existence of such a genre seems unlikely; see Burkert, *Mystery Cults*, 69–71.

[95] Mahé (*Hermès*, 1. 25–26) concludes that in comparison to *Corpus Hermeticum* XIII and the other Hermetic documents that the three Nag Hammadi Hemetic tractates are much more mythic than speculative and show much less an educational orientation.

[96] Ibid., 4.

bestowal of names probably has narrative significance in the context of the description of the initiation in *Disc. 8–9*. The "Father" and his "Son" conduct the dialogue and at significant times, the son confers other names upon the father.

The narration of *Disc. 8–9*, showing little interest in philosophical debate or doctrine, describes an interior experience instead.[97] The description of the experience, along with discussions about and personal responses to it, creates this unique initiatory narrative. The very first sentence of the dialogue signals the initiatory theme: "O my Father, yesterday you promised me that you would bring my mind into the eighth and afterward into the ninth" (52.2–6). This initiation, the most advanced of the Hermetic initiations,[98] describes the process of Hermetic initiation and presents the codes employed to give meaning to that process.

The dialogical narrative presents an intricate, but clearly well-constructed,[99] series of questions and answers, responses, prayers, discourses, namings, and reflections to guide the reader through the progressive stages. In light of the relational emphasis in the prayer and the sexual iconography, it can be expected that the narration will portray this initiation as a mutual experience of empowerment and exchange among men.

The larger narrative structure of *Disc. 8–9* manifests such mutuality between guide and initiate. The guide and the initiate serially receive power and they pray, an experience which leads to the production of one text to ratify their experience. The initiation consists of six stages:

I. The Preparation (52.1–55.22)
II. The Prayer (55.23–57.25)
III. The Embrace and Empowerment of the Guide (57.26–58.22)
IV. The Discourse about the Silent Hymn (58.22–59.14)
V. The Son's Initiation (59.15–61.17)
VI. The Production of a Text (61.18–63.32)

---

[97] Mahé, "Le sens et la composition du traité Hermétique, 'L'Ogdoad et L'Ennéade,' conservé dans le codex VI de Nag Hammadi," *RevScRel* 48 (1974) 55–65. Mahé (pp. 63–65) applies Festugière's observation about *Corpus Hermeticum* XIII, that it is not a theoretical teaching, but an interior experience, to the *Disc. 8–9*, and concludes that it is not the teaching or the speaking that is central, but the ability to live it out that is at the heart of the treatise.

This article also explores the relationship between the *Disc. 8–9* and the other Hermetic tractates especially the *Corpus Hermeticum* XIII. It is not within the purview of this study to relate the Nag Hammadi documents to the other Hermetic tractates.

[98] Mahé, *Hermès*, 1. 46–47, 134.

[99] Mahé ("Le sens," 57) documents the careful and clear symmetrical order of the entire document which he finds unusual among the Hermetic tractates.

In its largest outline, the narrative presents both the exchange of commodities mentioned in the prayer and the icon of intercourse (the embrace which leads to the reception of power by both resulting in the engendering of a text).

Stage I. The Preparation (52.1–55.22)

Medical theory stressed that the desire and longing for pleasure which led to intercourse was Nature's way of insuring the continuance of the species. Every part of the body, and every function of the part, worked together harmoniously toward this end. The first stage of the initiation, the preparation, lays out similarly the longing and desire for initiation, defines its end, and sets the activity in motion. This is set out in three primary discourses: on the initiatory process itself, on the communal brotherhood, and on the meaning of prayer in the brotherhood. Each one of these discourses builds on the previous one to assemble the various codes which set the stage for the initiation.

The dialogue opens with the initiate's desire and longing:

> O my father, yesterday you promised [me] [that you would bring] my mind into the eighth and afterward into the ninth. You said that this is the order of the tradition. (52.2–7)

The desire is for initiation into the eighth and ninth by the guide in the traditional manner (52.2–7).[100] The guide confirms the process: "O my Son, on the one hand this is the order, and on the other, the promise was in accordance with humanity" (52.7–10). The father's promise mirrors the son's desire: it is a covenanted relationship. The covenant, however, is not between a divinity and a human, but between human beings. The tradition reflects both the order and the humanity of the initiation.

Then the guide responds to the initiate's request by describing the initiatory process:

> For I told you when I initiated the promise, I said: "If you remember each one of the steps." After I had received the spirit through the power, I set forth the action for you. For the intelligence exists in you; in me (it is) as though the power were pregnant. (52.10-18)

The elements of this description indicate that the fulfillment of the desire requires (1) that the initiate recall all of the previous educational steps, (2) that the guide receive the spirit through the power, (3) that he activate the intelligence that already exists in the initiate, an intelligence which (4) he

---

[100] On some possible, but not likely, parallels to the "promise" see Keizer, *Eighth*, 31–33.

experiences as a pregnant power within him. The guide's description recapitulates the medico-sexual explanation of the icon. The guide's pneuma, like the semen, activates the process in which two parallel powers are united: the initiate's indwelling intelligence materialized in the recalling of the stages, and the guide's spirit which he receives as a pregnant power. Since the guide activates the process, the guide functions as the stronger semen (the male) in the intercourse, with the initiate as the female. Since the signification of intercourse has been redefined, the guide and the initiate are understood to be equal and mutually exchanging partners.

The guide, however, takes on biologically female roles as well. In a male role, he activates the initiation. In the female role, however, he experiences his empowerment as pregnancy and birthing:

> For when I conceived from the fountain that flowed to me, I gave birth. O my Father, every word which you have spoken to me is right But I am amazed at this statement which you have just said. For you have said: "The power within me." He said: "I gave birth to it as children are born." (52.18–27)

This usurpation of female biological function as a gender role for the spiritual father surprises even the son, whose questioning results only in a further emphasis of his taking on of female functions. The intentional exclusion of the female establishes that the community is comprised only of males, some of whom have the androgynous role of both engendering the community and of birthing it.[101] The sexual relationships are complex: the Father conceives from the "fountain that flows" to him, which in turn gives birth as a power within him, which in turn activates the engendering of the process for the initiate. A complex sexual encoding clearly underlies the discourse.

The preparation continues with the second introductory discourse (52.27–53.27) concerning the brotherhood established by the guide's birth-giving. This defines the final social condition of the initiate. The generation of the brotherhood at once indicates the fecundity of the guide and introduces the initiate into his new community: "They have all come into existence from the same father"; the father "has called each generation"; and every generation "came about in a birth like these sons." It is incumbent, then, for the new initiate to "be acquainted with" his "brothers" and "to esteem them rightly and suitably." The initiation culminates with the initiate's entry into the community, the brotherhood. The guide's role is crucial, because every activity depends upon him: he calls, he engenders, he gives birth, he names.

---

[101] On the mythological androgyny see Mahé, "Symboles Sexuels," 137–38.

The father characterizes the brotherhood by emphasizing their regenerative role: "O my son, they are spiritual ones, for they exist as an energy that strengthen other souls. Therefore, I say that they are immortal" (53.17–21). The brotherhood operates as a spiritual force for the regeneration of other souls: they mirror the operation of the guide to the initiate among other people, in the wider community. Their immortality, their transcending the human boundary, relates to their social function of "strengthening" others. The process of initiation establishes a spiritual community with a mission to strengthen others. The initiation creates a community as a biproduct: the goal, or intent, as stated above, remains the engendering of intelligent understanding.

A pun in the text further defines the preparatory discussion of the final cause. The word ϫⲱⲱⲙⲉ, translated above as "brothers," may also mean "books." The initiate introduces the topic of the brothers by saying: "O my Father, then I have many brothers, if I am accounted among the offspring (or books)" (ⲁⲣⲁ ⲱ ⲡⲁⲉⲓⲱⲧ ⲟⲩⲛ̄ⲧⲁⲓ̈ ⲍⲁⲍ ⲛ̄ⲥⲟⲛ ⲉϣϫⲉ ⲥⲉⲛⲁⲁⲡⲧ̄ ⲙⲛ̄ ⲛ̄ϫⲱⲱⲙⲉ [52.27–29]). This ambiguity between the community and the production of books introduces into the discourse at an early point an ambiguity which seems intended, because the final product of the initiation is the production of the text and entry into a blessed fellowship.[102]

With the desire expressed, the process delineated, and the final cause expressed, the third introductory discourse (53.28–55.22) sets the stage for the initiation itself by subordinating education to prayer. Regarding his education, the initiate acknowledges that he had made progress because he has reached a level of maturity through the books (54.13–18). The guide suggests that the initiate recognize this gradual maturity by comparing his current status with that of his early years: "O my son, compare yourself to your youth" (54.10-11). While the son confesses that his understanding has been limited to the content of the books ("I do not understand anything except the beauty that came to me in the books"), the guide identifies this book learning with the "beauty of the soul" which is the "edification through the stages" preliminary to initiation (54.25–28). And the initiate indicates that he has mastered this educational formation: "O my father, I have understood each one of the books (ⲛ̄ϫⲁⲙⲉ)," (54.30-32). This discussion makes clear that the educational aspect of the initiation is successfully completed, but not the end of the process. It remains incomplete, insufficient.

Prayer completes education in the initiation. When the initiate requests

---

102 For a full discussion of the pun, see Keizer, *Eighth*, 30-31; Mahé, *Hermès*, 1. 42–43.

that the guide begin the discourse on the eighth and the ninth (53.24–27), the guide responds by discussing prayer:

> Let us pray, O my son, to the father of the universe with your brothers who are my sons that he may give the spirit in order that I may speak. (53.27–31)[103]

ΜΑΡΝϢΛΗΛ ⲱ̄ ΠΑϢΗΡΕ ΛΠΕΙⲱΤ ⲘⲠΤΗΡϤ̄ ⲘⲚ ΝΕΚⲤΝΗΟΥ ΕΤΕ ΝΑ ϢΗΡΕ
ΝΕ· ⲬΕΚΛΛⲤ ΕϤⲀϯ ⲘⲠⲠⲚⲀ̄ <ϢⲀ>ⲚϯϢⲀⲬⲈ.

The discourse begins in the communal prayer. The educational formation leads to the initiate's inclusion in the communal prayer. When the initiate indicates the level of his maturity, the master tells him: "O my son, when you understand the truth of your speaking, you will find your brothers who are my sons praying with you" (54.18–22). And finally, the request for the gift of entrance into the eighth and ninth comes in the midst of a prayer from the master. Although the initiate had requested the discourse to begin, the master delayed the response to speak of prayer, and he suggests that in the context of prayer the request for entry into the eighth and ninth is proper:

> O my son, it is fitting that we should pray to god in our entire mind with our full heart and soul, and to request of him that the gift of the eighth reach us, and that each one receive from him that which is his. Yours, then, is to understand; my own is to be able to speak the discourse from the fountain which flows to me. (55.10-22)

As in *Pr. Thanks.* the prayer functions to exchange commodities. The intent of the prayer, given here, is to provide that the community enter the eighth, that the initiate receive understanding and the the guide receive the ability to discourse from the "fountain that flows" to him. This last referent locates the discursive power in the sexual dynamic mythologized in the very beginning of the preparatory section. The exchange here, however, relates primarily to the guide and the initiate: "I will receive from you the power from the discourse which you will deliver. In the manner in which we were both told, let us pray" (55.6–10). The preparatory material has brought the narrative to the point that prayer is to begin. It has ordered all the previous education stages by subordinating them to prayer; it has related prayer to the

---

[103] I am following the reconstruction of Mahé (*Hermès*, 1. 66) <ϢⲀ>ⲚϯϢⲀⲬⲈ. The context seems to call more for an ability to speak rather than for a spirit of eloquence. The unreconstructed phrase Ⲛϯ ϢⲀⲬⲈ which Brashler and Parrott (*NHS 11*, 350) read as a genitive could simply be translated "the spirit of (Ⲛ) speech (ϢⲀⲬⲈ) giving (ϯ)" or, paraphrastically, a "spirit of discourse."

exchange of commodities; and it has described and explained the initiatory process in the language of sexual intercourse.

Stage II. The Prayer (55.23–57.25)

The prayer[104] inaugurates the experience of initiation in a progressive movement from the intense focus on the deity, to the entrance into the deity, and finally concluding in a petitionary sequence exploring the implications of such entry into the deity. The prayer itself has three parts: an address to the deity (55.24–56.17), an ecstatic utterance (56.17–22), and petitions from the guide and initiate to the divinity (56.22–57.25). Each one of these parts has a corresponding function: the address defines the divinity philosophically; the ecstatic utterance connects the divinity with the praying community—while the petitions describe the exchange of power. The three parts of the prayer reflect the progressive movement toward the divine.

The address defines the divinity functionally. Each of the attributes presents not an ontological status, but the action of the divinity. The divinity is the one "who rules over the kingdom of power" (55.24–26). In equally active definition, he prays: "This is the one whose discourse occurs in a birth of light, and his words are immortal, eternal, unchanging" (55.26–30). And in a more philosophical vein, he prays: "This is the one whose will gives birth to life forms everywhere" and "His nature gives form to substance" (55.30-33). It should be noted that, again, all of these aspects of divinity have the female biological function of birthing.

This definition of the deity bears the marks of being a later addition: there is a change of voice which gives the appearance of narrative editorializing. Aside from the first direct address to the divinity ("I call upon you who rules over the kingdom of power" [55.24–26]), the entire prayer refers to the divinity in the third-person singular. The speaker of the prayer describes the divinity as other, outside, not immediate. This is one of three places in the treatise where a narrative voice intrudes, breaking the otherwise consistent dialogical form of direct address. I would conclude that it is a later addition which defines the divinity philosophically. The text, moreover, makes sense without the addition, reading: "Let us pray, O my Father, 'I call upon thee who rulest over the kingdom of power' and then follows the ecstatic utterance."

Following this address, the vowel sequence connects those praying with the divinity. In studying the alphabetical language in magical papyrii,

---

[104] Tröger ("Codex VI," 121) notes that the Nag Hammadi Hermetic documents have significantly advanced knowledge of Hermetic prayer and worship.

Patricia Cox Miller suggests that the *Disc. 8–9* "links the substance of God with the substance of humans through the vowels." The vowels signify the intersection of the human and divine realms by invoking the divinity while at the same time "sound(ing) the depths of one's own primal reality."[105] The magical language of prayer here signifies the collapsing of any barriers between the two realms: the participants enter the divine realm without leaving the human. With this prayer, the participants leave the realm of transparent meaning, and enter a hidden, secret[106] world which mirrors the hiddeness of the mystery of sexual intercourse.

The petitions to the deity which follow the ecstatic utterance betray the multivalent dimensions of prayer semiosis which was evidenced in *Pr. Thanks.* The first petition requests power to describe the vision: "Lord, give us wisdom from your power that reaches to us, so that we may describe for ourselves the vision of the eighth and the ninth" (56.22–26). This request indicates that the vision of the eighth and the ninth has already been granted to them in the ecstatic utterance, since they are requesting the ability to describe it, not to experience it. The participants validate their vision of the ogdoad and the ennead by claiming for themselves an already advanced status:

> We have already reached the seventh, since we are pious and walk in your law. And we always accomplish you wishes. For we have walked in (your way, and we have) renounced . . . so that your (vision) might come. (56.27–57.3)

Within the context of the prayer, the participants claim that the vision of the eighth and the ninth granted in ecstasy builds on their previous religious formation.

The petitions (57.2–10) continue in earnest requesting "the truth of the icon," the ability "through the spirit to see the form of the icon which is the one that has no deficiency" and for the divinity to "acknowledge the spirit that is in" them. The exact content of the icons cannot be established, beyond their request. The deity, on the other hand, receives praises as the source of the universal soul, the unbegotten origin of the begotten one, the one who births the self-begotten and all-existent begotten things. These

---

[105] Miller, "In Praise of Nonsense," in A. H. Armstrong, ed., *Classical Mediterranean Spirituality: Egyptian, Greek, Roman* (World Spirituality 15; New York: Crossroad, 1986) 484.

[106] Miller (ibid., 487) writes that alphabetical language "is an enchanted language that reflects a dimension of reality that is normally hidden. The 'inside,' 'other side,' or even 'underside' of ordinary reality is best spoken in a poetic language that scrambles ordinary words and shows their imaginal potential . . . such linguistic play *is* difficult to understand, and that is precisely the point. . . . Language is phantasmal, nor transparent to whatever 'reality' might be."

praises culminate in the highest gift: "Receive a discursive (λογικὴ) sacrifice (θυσία) from us which we send to you with all our heart and soul (ψυχή) and strength" (57.18–23). The petitions show that through the ecstatic utterance the boundaries between the guide and the initiate on the one hand and the deity on the other are meaningless. The discursive sacrifice,[107] begun in the education of the stages through the seventh, ends in the praise and discussion from within the deity.

The movement of the prayer from description of God, to union, to the sorting out of the implications of such union, inaugurates the initiation. The narrative introduces the vision as part of the ecstatic prayer language, a theme which will become part of the initiate's own formation later.

Stage III. The Embrace and the Guide's Empowerment (57.26–58.22)

The prayer's vision seems to have been given both to the father and the son. After the union which grants the vision in the prayer, the narrative of the initiation presents the guide requesting to embrace the initiate. The experience of prayer culminates in an embrace. The text is clear about the embrace: ΜΑΡΝ̄Ρ̄ΑСΠΑΖΕ Ν̄ΝΕΝ ΕΡΗΟΥ Ω̄ ΠΑϢΗΡΕ ΖΝ̄ ΟΥΜΕ (57.26–27). The ΖΝ̄ ΟΥΜΕ is an adverbial expression with two options for translation: "Let us embrace, O my son, truly (really)," or "Let us embrace lovingly (or affectionately)." In either case, the embrace is a gestural sign of interaction, touching, real contact initiated by the guide—a sign which gives no evidence of being figurative or metaphoric.[108]

The events following upon the gestural sign "embrace" define its signification. The embrace empowers the guide. After the embrace, the guide exclaims: "Rejoice about this, for already from them the power which is light is coming to us!" (57.28–30). Through the embrace, the guide receives the light power from beyond himself which enables him to see: "For I see, I see depths about which it is impossible to speak!" (57.31–32). The embrace activates the guide's empowerment and vision, a phenomenon which fits neatly into the category of activation which is presented in the *Asclepius.*

The embrace, with its sexual implications, signifies the interactive aspect of the initiation. Through involvement with the initiate, the guide himself is brought to life, empowerment, vision. Like the description of the divinity,

---

[107] Mahé (*Hermès*, 1. 55–56) guides this argument. Mahé believes that such a literal "sacrifice of discourse" was a regular part of Hermetic worship, quite sacramental in its effect.

[108] For the comparison of this kiss with the sacramental kiss in Valentianism, see Mahé, *Hermès*, 1. 56–59; and, with less fruitfulness, Keizer, *Eighth*, 34–35. With the sort of encoding that is taking place in *Disc. 8–9* I do not find any sort of sacramental orientation to the embrace.

the guide is not presented as ontologically superior, but as one who functions socially, in relationship. The sexual comparison of the mystery points to the dynamic that spiritual formation, like sexual relations, can only occur when the energizing or excitement is activated by the embraces of the other. The presence of the other (in actuality or in image) stimulates the activity which fosters growth and which culminates in the exchange of power.

The guide's activation, however, relates to the vision granted in the prayer: the guide describes the new universe which he sees (57.33–58.28). The initiate is still on the side and has not yet received his power. The guide excitedly asks: "How shall I speak to you, o my son?" and "How shall I speak of the whole of creation?" (57.33—58.4). The response of the guide is that he will describe the universe anew from the perspective of the mind (νοῦς):[109] "I am mind and I see the other mind that moves the soul" (ⲁⲛⲟⲕ ⲡⲉ [ⲡⲛⲟ]ⲩ[ⲥ ⲁⲩⲱ] ϯⲛⲁⲩ ⲉⲕⲉⲛⲟⲩⲥ ⲡⲉⲧⲕ[ⲓⲙ] ⲉⲧⲯⲩⲭⲏ [58.4–6]). The mind may be within the guide as well as continuing to move other souls: mind is not the exclusive perogative of the guide.

The guide,[110] after seeing "the one that moves me from me from a pure forgetfulness" (58.6–7), says: "You give me power! I see myself! I want to speak" (58.7–9). The new universe is signified and articulated as the guide's experience of his own empowerment, his vision of himself, and the desire to enter into discourse. The energizing of the guide continues in his identification with the mind of the universe ("I have said, O my son, that I am Mind (νοῦς)" (58.14–15). The guide's empowerment signifies that he has "found the beginning of the power which is above every power, the one that has no beginning" (58.10-13). His vision is of a "fountain bubbling with life," an image earlier associated with the empowerment to discourse. And finally, his speaking recognizes the insufficiency of language: "I have seen! Discourse is not able to reveal this!" (58.16–17).

The guide's own enlivening ends with a riddle presented to the initiate: "For, all of the eighth, O my son, with the souls and the angels that are in it, make hymns in silence. But I, mind, understand" (58.17–22). The guide claims to understand the enigma of the silent hymn, and the activity of the eighth into which the initiate wishes to be introduced revolves about the enigma. The eighth is a silent hymning which is understood only when the guide becomes mind to understand it. The enigma of a silent hymn is

---

[109] The striking similarity here between this guide, the teacher in Gregory's "Thanksgiving Speech," and the portrait section of Porphyry's "Life and Books" indicates that this noetic element functions across religious traditions.

[110] I am following both Mahé, *Hermès*, 1; and Parrott, *NHS 11*, 359 in ascribing this line to the guide and not to the initiate as Tröger ("Codex VI") does. I would have expected some sort of direct address, "O my Father," to indicate a change in speaker at so dramatic a moment.

twofold: is it silent if it can be heard in the mind? and can it be a hymn if there is no sound? The guide understands the enigma because he is mind, he has been empowered, he has received a vision, and he has entered into the discourse, however insufficient it is in relationship to full experience. The enigma is the stepping stone for the initiate into the eighth.

Stage IV. The Discourse about the Silent Hymn (58.22–59.14)

The silent hymn does not follow from the discussion. The revelation that the eighth is a silent hymn leads to further interaction between the initiate and the guide. Three things draw the initiate into the silent hymn of the eighth: the enigma, the guide's state, and the initiate's own desire. The enigma hooks the initiate into the eighth by asking "What is the manner of making hymns through it (silence)?" (58.22–23). The guide, since his empowerment, envisionment, and discourse, seems to have changed. The guide seems no longer accessible, present to the initiate who states: "You have become such that you cannot be spoken to" (58.23–24).[111] The guide seems to have entered another state, beyond discourse. And this activates the initiate's desire: "O My Father, I want to make hymns to you while I am silent" (58.25–26). And the guide responds cryptically: "Well then sing it, for I am Mind" (58.26–27).

The guide's self-designation as "Mind" sets off a series of designations attributed to the guide by the initiate. The initiate, picking up on the "Mind" identifies the guide with Hermes: "I understand Mind, Hermes who is not able to be interpreted since he keeps within himself. And I rejoice, O my father, that I see you laughing" (58.28–30). The initiate calls the guide "Hermes" and "O my father": as Hermes he is uninterpretable, as father he is laughing. The word ⲥⲱⲃⲉ as a transitive verb means "to laugh, to sport."[112] The name Hermes and the verb "to interpret" was, from ancient times, a commonplace pun.[113] In this context, however, the naming takes on a definite meaning in that it indicates both when and how interpretation is possible. The pun inserted at this point in the narrative indicates that meaning, interpretation is not possible with those who "keep to themselves": only those who have entered into relationship, who have literally "gone out of themselves" are capable of interpreting reality. The sporting, or laughing guide acknowledges that he, as guide, is capable of even more than Hermes

---

[111] Parrott (*NHS 11*, 360) has translated this as a question. I agree with Mahé (*Hermès*, 1. 66) that it is an indicative statement. Mahé translates: "Te voici au point qu'on ne pourra plus te parler."

[112] Lambdin, *Sahidic Coptic*, 274.

[113] Beginning with Plato's *Cratylus* (408AB). See Miller, "Nonsense," 488, 492.

himself who, without the relationship with the guide, cannot become communicative. Meaning and interpretation may only result from initiation into the relationship.

The identification of the guide with Hermes includes the sort of cosmic and philosophical definitions that were attributed to the divinity in the prayer. The initiate defines the Nous-Father-Hermes as:

> And the universe rejoices because no creature will be in want of your life. For you are the lord of the citizens everywhere. Your providence protects. I name you father, the aion of the aions, the great divine spirit. And by a spirit he gives rain upon everyone. What do you say to me, O my father, Hermes? (58.32–59.11)

The cosmic and philosophical god has been collapsed into the person of the guide. The *nous* connects the guide, through his empowerment, to the divinity and then, for the initiate, becomes the point for complete identification of the divinity with the guide by a sort of transference of natures and attributes.

The injunction to secrecy at the end of this section confirms that complete identification: "Concerning these things, O my son, I am not saying anything. For it is fitting before god that we remain silent about what is hidden" (59.11–14). Like the hiddeness of sexual intercourse, these identifications are to be kept quiet.

Stage V. The Son's Initiation (59.15–61.17)

The narrative progression finally describes the son's initiation. This is a continuation of the dialogue between the guide and the initiate since the main characters remain the initiate, the guide, and a brief narrative voice while the referential characters are described as the souls and angels of the eighth, the powers of the ninth, and the divinity who is the powerful creator of spiritual beings. The narrative sequence is important because the order of the experience presents the order of the initiation. All that has preceded has set the stage for this event.

The initiate names the guide again, thereby defining again the significance of the guide and reorienting himself to the significance of his own initiation. He states:

> O Trismegistus, do not let my soul (ψυχή) become a widow (χήρα) of the great divine contemplation; for you have power over everything as teacher[114] of every place. (59.15–19)[115]

---

[114] The coptic ⲥⲁⲍ, deriving from the verb ⲥⲍⲁⲓ meaning "to write," means "scribe, writer; teacher, master; master craftsman" (Lambdin, *Sahidic Coptic*, 277).

[115] Parrott (*NHS 11*, 363) translate the Greek word χήρα metaphorically, "let not my soul be deprived." Mahé (*Hermès*, 1) retains the literal meaning: "Do not let my soul become a widow

The guide is Trismegistus, the universal power, and the universal teacher which are all recognizably divine figures. In relationship to this inflated figure, the initiate expresses both desire for contemplation and fear of a permanent separation through death. They are mixed emotions. The soul as "widow" implies a past relationship, including sexual relationship, which could end through the initiation for which the initiate longs. The fact that the initiate is "widow" underscores the guide's male gender role as propagator and leader. Both the desire and the fear increase as the guide takes on greater and more divine attributes.

That the initiation still takes place within the confines of the dialogue between the guide and the initiate is made clear in the instructions given by the guide: "Return to praising, O my son, and sing it while you are silent. Ask what you want in silence" (59.19–22). The guide continues the familiar relationship in the familiar language of father and son. The enigmatic "silent singing" is resumed.

An intrusive narrative voice provides the space for the initiation itself to happen. In the midst of a dialogue, a narrator relates that the initiate does indeed praise in silence: "When he had stopped praising, he cried out," (59.23–24). The narrative does not indicate the duration of the silence, nor present any other information regarding the circumstances or meaning. It is significant, however, that the narrator is a voice from outside the guide-initiate relationship and thus may signify external powers entering into their relationship. At any rate the narrative opens the space for the actual initiation.

The initiate then announces his enlightenment. This announcement gathers up various themes of the dialogue. First, the titles of the guide are again reordered. The guide is now "Father, Trismegistus." The initiate affirms the insufficiency of language ("What shall I say?") as did the guide at his energizing. Both the guide and the initiate have received the illumination ("We have received the light.") and the initiate claims for himself the very same vision that has occurred earlier in the guide: "I myself see one and the same vision within you" (59.26–28). Here the overlapping of identities begins anew: as the guide is to the mind, to Hermes, to Trismegistus, so is the initiate to the guide. The tradition has been passed on. And finally, the initiate describes the vision of the eighth and the ninth, and the vision of the divinity:

---

of contemplation." I translate literally with Mahé. I concur with Parrott (*NHS 11*) that the reference to "the great divine contemplation" (reading the ο νοειον as an adjective; see Lambdin, *Sahidic Coptic*, 254) rather than amending the text as Mahé, *Hermès*, 1, "(qui) est divine."

I see the eighth with the souls which are in it and the angels making hymns to the ninth and its powers. And I see him who has the power of them all who creates those who are in the spirit. (59.19–60.1)

That which is described is beyond the relationship and is related to the guide.

The initiate's experience gathers up the initiatory themes. The illumination happens in a narrated silence. When the initiate speaks he does not speak to the angels, powers, or divinities which he has seen in the vision, but he speaks to the guide. The arena of illumination is silence, a free space, in the midst of a tangible and concrete dialogue with the guide. The relationship builds to the creation of that silence. Even though external divine forces enter into the relationship and the description is accomplished through the external narrative voice, the primary relationship is not obscured.

With the experience completed, the guide presents further instruction. Each one of the instructions clearly indicates that there is a clear line of demarcation between that which has preceded and the current situation: such words as "from this time" and "from now on" draw attention to the new status of the initiate while the instruction underscores that new status. The guide first suggests that following the illumination there be a period of silence with some kind of gesture: "It is useful starting from [this time] that we are silent in an inclination (προπετής)"[116] (60.1–2). This would presumably allow for a period of reflection or readjustment to the new status. Then the guide suggests that the initiation remain secret: "Do now speak about the vision from now on" (60.3–4). And finally, the guide suggests that it is appropriate to sing such hymns for the rest of the initiates life: "It is proper to make hymns to the father until the day of dismissing the body" (60.4–6). The initiation permanently changes the status of the initiate.

The question of the hymn to be sung becomes the subject of a discourse between the guide and the initiate, a hymn of praise by the initiate, and an ecstatic utterance. The initiate begins the discourse by articulating the desire to sing the same hymn as the guide: "What you sing, O my father, I want also to sing" (60.8). The guide's response at once identifies his own activity, directs the initiate to emulate that activity, and authenticates the completion of the initiation: "I am making a hymn within myself. As you rest yourself, continue in praise, for you have found that for which you were searching" (60.9–10). The initiate acknowledges that his mind is full and asks if it is appropriate to make hymns in that condition: "But is it proper, O my father, to praise since I am full in my mind?" (60.11–13). The guide again links

---

[116] I am translating with Krause. I agree with the editors that the Greek προπετής refers to some sort of gesture and that it belongs with the current sentence, but I would prefer a more literal rendering than their "reverent posture."

the initiatory process to textuality: "What is proper is your praise that you will sing to God that it will be written in this imperishable book" (60.13–16). The purpose of singing the hymn resides in the production of text.

From this point onward, the initiate sings his own hymns and is, at the end, instructed only regarding the textual evidence. The hymn which the initiate sings summarizes his understanding of the experience of initiation. The hymn now is addressed to the divinity who is described as "Lord":

> I will sing the praise which is in my mind, as I pray to the end of the universe, and to the beginning of the beginning, the human's quest, the immortal discovery, the begetter of light and truth, the sower of the discourse, the love of immortal life. No hidden discourse will be able to speak concerning you, Lord. Therefore my mind desires to make hymns to you daily. I am the organ of your spirit: the mind is your plectrum; and your counsel plucks me. I see myself. I have received power from you, for your love has touched us. (60.17–61.2)

The initiate has been enlighted ("I see myself."), empowered ("I have received power from you. . . ."), and formed a community with the guide through the divinity's love (". . . for your love has touched us").

This latter "us" now makes the identification of guide and initiate complete. The initiate, as a guide, steps into the place of his own spiritual guide. The initiate, again in a dialogue with the guide, acknowledges his empowerment and enlightened state, conflating the guide with the divinity in a recognition of the divine status of the guide and the newly divinized status of the initiate:

> Oh grace! After these things I give thanks by making hymns to you. For I have received life from you, when you made me wise. I praise you. I call your name which is hidden within me. ⲁ̅ ⲱ̅ ⲉ̅ ⲉ̅ ⲱ̅ ⲏⲏⲏ ⲱ̅ⲱ̅ⲱ̅ ⲓ̅ⲓ̅ⲓ̅ ⲱ̅ⲱ̅ⲱ̅ⲱ̅ ⲟ̅ⲟ̅ⲟ̅ⲟ̅ⲟ̅ ⲱ̅ⲱ̅ⲱ̅ⲱ̅ⲱ̅ ⲩ̅ⲩ̅ⲩ̅ⲩ̅ⲩ̅ⲩ̅ ⲱ̅ You are the one who exists with the spirit. I make hymns to you divinely. (61.3–17)[117]

This ecstatic utterance parallels that of the guide at his empowerment at the beginning of the process.

Stage VI. The Production of a Text (61.18–63.32)

The dialogue between the guide and the initiate ends with a discussion about the production of a text, a discussion of the appending of an oath to the text, and to the wording of the oath itself.

---

[117] I am translating with Mahé: "I address my hymn to you in a divine state." Mahé (Hermès, 1. 124) recognizes this as a divinization of the initiate: "The new initiate is divinized seeing that he has become similar to the divine powers which chant within him."

Very specific information is given regarding the production of the text. The guide directs the initiate to translate the experience into a book with the title *The Eighth Reveals the Ninth*: "O my son, write this book in hieroglyphic characters for the Diospolis temple" (61.18–21). Further instructions include provision for the inscription on turquoise steles (61.26 and 29), descriptions of the stone decoration with eight guardians including frog-faced males and cat-faced females (62.1–9), the square milk-stone base of the stele (62.10-15), as well as detailed specifications for the time of placing the text in the temple (62.16–22).

It is not unusual to find provisions for placing a revelation in the temple.[118] It is unusual, however, to find here that the production of a text receives such prominent attention. The narration which has preceded has put the experience above the text, and its bookish learning. One statement may provide an insight: the Mind, presented as that which the guide has become during his enlivening and further presented as the goal of the educational formation, supervises both the relationship and the production of the text: "For Mind himself has become overseer of these things. Therefore I order that this account be carved on stone, and that you put it in my sanctuary" (61.3–62.4). The supervisor of the account (both of the initiation and of the production of the text) is the Mind: it is significantly not the divinity (Hermes, or Trismegistus), nor is it the newly divinized initiate.

The provision, moreover, for an ornate and colorful stele written in hieroglyphics presents a double and contradictory message. The first is that the stele is placed in the temple so that it may be seen, albeit in a presumably restricted environment. The stele stands as a public witness to the fact of an initiation. The hieroglyphics, however, imply a restricted access: it is written in the sacred language of the temples, not in the common language of the people. What stands as a public witness carries the message also of exclusive and esoteric knowledge through the relationship with the guide. The carved stele, then, represents the potentiality for illumination, for the potential contact with the divinity, and for the need for the initimacy of the guide to interpret and activate the symbols contained on it.

The discussion of the oath[119] limits the use of the knowledge which the stele represents. The negative function of the oath is to protect the book from perverted misreadings and the abusive use of language which would use the

---

[118] The Egyptian nature of these intstructions is striking, see parallel texts and analysis in Mahé, *Hermès*, 1. 33–38.

[119] On the oath, see Keizer, *Eighth*, 45. I do not agree that such an oath is more historical than literary because the historical basis is virtually impossible to uncover, and the literary is all that is available.

book for any other purpose than the "opposing of the acts of fate": "And write an oath in the book, lest those who read the book hold the language (ὀνομασία) for wickedness, and not to oppose the acts of Fate" (62.22–26). The potent language (ὀνομασία) must be used properly. Those who use it properly in this way "will walk in line with the law of God, not having transgressed at all, but purely asking God for wisdom and knowledge" (66.28–33). This description sets up the moral and spiritual purity of life necessary for the initiation.

This moral and spiritual purity contrasts, however, with the description of the two classes of illumination. The first class is those who are illuminated directly; the second class, those who will be initiated into illumination through education: "And the one who is not begotten first by god, comes to be by the general and guiding discourses" (62.33–63.3). This is precisely what has been narrated in the dialogue through the various discourses. The educational route to illumination, however, returns to the beginning of the discourse with its discussion of the states. Through the stages the prospective initiate will advance to immortality: "But in stages he advances and enters into the way of immortality. And in this way he enters into the understanding of the eighth which reveals the ninth" (63.9–14). This replicates the initial preliminary discourses of the dialogue. There is, however, a telling disclaimer which precedes this description. In refering to the one who must take the educational route to enlightenment, it is said:

> He whose conscience is pure within him because he is not doing anything shameful and because he does not consent to it will not be able to read the things written in this book. (63.4–9)

The sexual code is reintroduced by the linking of the pure conscience with the *denial* of shameful activity and the *denial* of consent. To be initiated through education only appears to pollute the conscience, whereas in reality through initiation the initiate's purity is maintained because the activity is not shameful and because the initiate does not give his consent. The formulation allows the point of sexuality at once to be made and to be stripped of its negative implications in the context of educational formation.

With the actual oath, the dialogue ends. The starting point and the ending point are experientially the same. Text led the initiate to experience, and through the experience, to the text enshrined, a sign of the potentiality of illumination through the relationship with the guide which looks like the intercourse between the male and the female, but which does not in fact pollute the conscience.

Conclusions

The initiatory narrative of *Disc. 8–9*, in relation to the other Hermetic texts of the Nag Hammadi library, presents the relationship of guide to initiate and the initiation process sexually. The sexual encoding, however, refers not to the standard Late Antique medical discourses, but rather, with the treatises' conscious translation of that information, it refers to a mutual exchange between equal and socially powerful men. The community is entirely of men: women are shadowy figures and men perform, or at least claim for their own performance, the biological and gender functions of women.

The sexual presentation of the process follows the inner workings of the altered version of the inner dynamic of intercourse. The guide stimulates the desire in the initiate in the initial, preparatory stages where the promises and its implications are explored and the brotherhood is presented. As the semen activates coitus, so in a prayer the visionary spirit is bestowed upon both in a union with the divinity. Through an embrace, the guide becomes empowered and begins to sing a silent hymn. The passing of the power between the guide and the initiate begins in the dialogue about prayer. Then the son receives the power from the guide and is initiated so that he too may sing a silent hymn and pray. As the product of intercourse is an engendered new life, so is the production of the text the fruit of their labor.

The process transfers power in a number of ways. Power comes to the guide like a flowing fountain. Names are given to the guide, beginning with Father, then Hermes, and then Trismegistus as a sign of the progressive deification which the guide undergoes in the initiation. The prayer language unites the guide and the initiate with the deity and bestows visions upon them. And, of course, the son receives the power from the father. The passing on of tradition, like the icon of the intercourse, becomes a multivalent and multifaceted process of mutual exchange among socially equal men.

The mutuality, however, is surprising. Both Gregory Thaumaturgos's portrayal of the teacher as mythically ascendant and Porphyry's description of Plotinus as noetically superior to all others, betray a hierarchically ordered relationship between the spiritual guide and the initiate. Despite the different arenas in which such a hierarchy is expressed, the guide remains above the student in intelligence, religiosity, knowledge, perfection, and social status. The initiate climbs to the place of the guide.

In the *Disc. 8–9*, with its redefinition of the signified of which "intercourse" is the signifier, the hierarchy collapses. The text presents their relationship as mutual, and only secondarily related to a higher or divine realm which in itself is collapsed into the relationship. The narrative description, the description of the dynamic of their mutual formation in Hermetic religion, shows the progress of their interrelated empowerment, their mutual visions, and their consequent divinization in the exchange of power.

And finally, the text, the final product of their relationship and the fetus created by the intercourse, is the only part of the *Disc. 8–9*'s narrative that is enshrined as divine. Reitzenstein[120] had formulated the concept of a "literary mystery" in which the deity instructs the initiate directly in the vision which, through the reading, evokes the experience in the initiate's imagination. The divinity, in such a scheme, resided in the text, and in reading the text, the divinity was released to form, or initiate, an experience in the reader. In a sense this is what is happening in the *Disc. 8–9*. Since the narrative of the initiation describes a mutual relationship between equals, the text of the treatise, preserved in a divine language and symbology, becomes the divine Hermes, enshrined in the temple with all the marks of numinosity. The "reading mystery" represents the divinity, just as Reitzenstein suggested, but that divine text mirrors a profound mutuality among the men of the Hermetic community. From the extant treatises in the *Corpus Hermeticum*, delivered to Marcilio Ficino to translate, that small Egyptian fetus was indeed perfected, born, matured, and generated a large family of texts enshrining the divine Hermes. The mystery, however, was really enacted, not in the text, or even in the reading of the text, but in the empowering of the men of the Hermetic community.

---

[120] *Mystery Religions*, 62–64.

5

Three Narratives
from Three Spiritual Guides

The narrative of the *Disc. 8–9* consisted of a dialogue between a spiritual guide and a disciple with only a minimal narrative structure. Such a dialogical literary artifice creates the illusion of immediate and uninterpreted interaction, so that a reader of the text "overhears" and "responds" as though to an actual conversation. The speakers never actually reveal exactly what is going on between them, so the interpreter of their conversation must provide a structure to account for the development and progression of their conversation, which in the case of *Disc. 8–9* consisted of the mutual exchange of benefits between two entitled males in a Hermetic community.

Allogenes (NHC 11, 3), a philosophically oriented Sethian text of the third century, however, provides abundant narrative structure. It has three narrators in various conversations and relationships with one another. Such a strong and developed series of narrators complicates the search for meaning in the events related in the text. The narrative text has become much more complex, and the meaning of the text more obtuse.

Allogenes' many characters enhance the complexity: Allogenes, Iouel, the Powers of the Luminaries, and Messos comprise the narrative characters. These main characters mention a host of other secondary characters whose activities and significances advance the primary character's narrative: the Triple Power, the Aeon of Barbelo, the Invisible Spirit, Protophanes, Kalyptos, Harmedon. With so many characters interacting in so many different ways with each other, it is easy to confuse primary with secondary levels of the texts.

The complex relationship of characters and narratives within *Allogenes* has yet to be delineated in any study, and thus the full significance of its content has not been explored. Aside from an (as yet) unpublished critical edition,[1] *Allogenes* has received little attention in comparison to the research on other Nag Hammadi treatises. What little attention devoted to it has been oriented toward two issues: (1) *Allogenes* as one of the texts designated as Sethian by the mythological content and by resonances with other texts in the group;[2] (2) *Allogenes* as a later Sethian text interacting with Platonic philosophical literature and moving toward monism.[3] These scholars have interpreted *Allogenes* either from its relationship to other Nag Hammadi documents or from the interaction of the revelatory content with Platonism.

If, however, *Allogenes* is approached on its own, outside the philosophical discourse, the narrative structure presents a wealth of material on a totally different topic. The subject of the treatise proves not to be the content of philosophical debate embedded in Iouel's and the Powers of the Luminaries' revelations, but the integration of this philosophical and ascetical material into Allogenes' experience. *Allogenes* does not primarily discuss philosophy, but spiritual formation.

There are in fact three spiritual guides, all with their own narrative. The first is Iouel, a female figure who presents Allogenes with some creative and

---

[1] Karen Leigh King, "The Quiescent Eye of the Revelation, Nag Hammadi Codex XI.3 'Allogenes,' A Critical Edition" (Ph.D. diss., Brown University, 1984). I have used her text and notes for the Coptic basis of my own translation, often taking a lead from her translation. Since I began working with the text before I had access to King's edition, my text sometimes reflects other readings. None of the divergences are hermeneutically significant enough to indicate in notes.

[2] This has primarily been the work of Hans-Martin Schenke "Das sethianische System nach Nag-Hammadi-Handschriften," in P. Nagel, ed., *Studia Coptica* (Berliner Byzantinische Arbeiten 45; Berlin: Akademie, 1974) 165–73; and subsequently explored in idem, "The Phenomenon and Significance of Gnostic Sethianism," in Bentley Layton, ed., *The Rediscovery of Gnosticism; Proceedings of the International Conference on Gnosticism at Yale, New Haven, Connecticut March 28–31, 1978* (2 vols.; Studies in the History of Religions 41; Leiden: Brill, 1980-81) 2. 588–616. In addition, the important study of the literary history by John D. Turner, "Sethian Gnosticism: A Literary History," in Charles W. Hedrick and Robert Hodgson, eds., *Nag Hammadi, Gnosticism, and Early Christianity* (Peabody: Hendrickson, 1986) 55–86. Also G. Stroumsa, *Another Seed: Studies in Gnostic Mythology* (NHS 24; Leiden: Brill, 1984).

[3] On the negative side of this debate see A. H. Armstrong, "Gnosis and Greek Philosophy" in Barbara Aland, ed., *Gnosis: Festschrift für Hans Jonas* (Göttingen: Vandenhoeck & Ruprecht, 1978) 87–124. Armstrong has been superceded by Turner, "Threefold Path," 324–51; Birger A. Pearson, "The Tractate Marsanes (NHC X) and the Platonic Tradition," in Aland, *Gnosis*, 373–84; Pearson, "Gnosticism as Platonism with Special Reference to Marsanes (NHC X,1)," *HTR* 77 (1984) 55–72; and James M. Robinson, "The Three Steles of Seth and the Gnostics of Plotinus," in Geo Widengren, ed., *Proceedings of the International Colloquium on Gnosticism, Stockholm August 20–25, 1973* (Stockholm: Almqvist & Wiksell, 1977) 132–42.

new philosophical speculations concerning the Triple Power. This is the only direct evidence of a female spiritual guide from the third century. Iouel gives this philosophical information while directly orchestrating Allogenes' formation.

The second spiritual guide is a group, the Powers of the Luminaries of the Aeon of Barbelo, who guide Allogenes from a philosophical to an ascetical type of spiritual formation. This also represents a different perspective: not the formation of an individual *in* community, but the formation of an individual *by* a community. The content, moreover, of their formation seems to include the philosophical material from Iouel's revelation, while redirecting Allogenes' use of that material in a spiritual withdrawal and rest.

The third guide is Allogenes himself, after whom the treatise is named, who presents the substance of the other two guides and his own commentary to Messos his spiritual son. Actually there are four perspectives because Allogenes is both a character and the narrator of the text: he has a presence as a recipient of others' formation and as a presenter of the events, both of which carry meaning.

Each one of these spiritual guides has a different perspective on philosophy and asceticism. They each interpret the other's material, and they interpret the material which they have received from other traditions. Iouel, for example, recreates Middle Platonic categories of Being to include the material on the Triple Power.[4] The Powers of the Luminaries transfer this information into a process of withdrawal to Vitality and Existence and the ascetical achievement of silence. Allogenes, on the other hand, clarifies and systematizes both of these materials for Messos.

A number of textual factors point to the Allogenes-Messos narrative as the primary one: the title of the treatise, Allogenes' central role in Iouel's and the Powers of the Luminaries' narratives, and Allogenes' explicit commitment to present material to Messos. *Allogenes'* primary narrative structure relates to Allogenes and Messos. All of the other conversations are secondary because they have been incorporated into the material which Allogenes, the narrator and spiritual guide, presents to Messos. Most of the purely philosophical material emerges from this secondary level of the narrative. Allogenes, the character and receiver of this philosophical material, reworks this material for another purpose, to present it to Messos.

---

[4] It is beyond the scope of this study to identify philosophical correlations between *Allogenes* and Middle Platonism or Neoplatonism. I am, however, struck by the concurrence of interests and categories with Middle Platonism: *Allogenes'* philosophical issues reverberate with Middle Platonism of Philo, Clement of Alexandria and Origen. See Robert M. Berchman, *From Philo to Origen: Middle Platonism in Transition* (Brown Judaic Studies, 69; Chico: Scholars Press, 1984).

This narrative approach does not mean simply that Allogenes, the character, must be understood as a figure. Most scholars recognize the unusual significance of having such a person emerge to tell a story.[5] Allogenes, does more than function as a character in a dialogue between Iouel and the Powers of the Luminaries: to see this alone is to miss the rich complexity of the treatise.

This Chapter will investigate the embarrassment of narrative riches in *Allogenes*. It will enhance the complexity of the text first by laying out the narrative structure of the treatise, then by isolating each one of these spiritual guides and their narratives: first the female Iouel, then the group Powers of the Luminaries, and finally the narrator Allogenes. Each of them presents a different system of spiritual formation in an interlocking narrative of other systems; and each one presents a different interpretation of the content of that formation.

The Narrative Structure of *Allogenes*

The text of *Allogenes* seems to demand a literary analysis:[6] the characters relate to one another in dialogue and narrative; they respond to one another; there are emotions, reactions, descriptions of events. Although more than half of the content is philosophical material, the figure of Allogenes stands as a focal point both for the receiving of revelation and for presenting reactions to that revelation. An outline of the contents of the treatise underscores its literary complexity. The letters (B through J) indicate instruction and directions given to Allogenes by others. The numbers (1 through 10) designate Allogenes' response to that instruction and the description of his own experience.

A. A 5+ line lacuna which either could introduce the first embedded text, or contain a short narrative statement. It probably needed to be a short narrative sentence identifying Allogenes, and the speaker of the first revelation.

B. 45.6d–49.37. Iouel's first and most complex revelatory section.

1. 49.38–50.21: Allogenes' first narrative.

C. 50.22–51.38 Iouel's dialogue with Allogenes and revelation of the Aeon of Barbelo.

---

[5] Schenke, "Phenomenon," 589.

[6] The only attempt has been by King ("Allogenes," 53–57) in her discussion of the genre. King recognizes the cohesive narrative structure as essential to the definition of its genre, but the actual literary study was beyond the purview of her study. Turner, ("Literary History") presents the development of Sethian literature, but does not conduct literary analyses of particular texts.

2. 52.6–52.15: Allogenes' second narrative.
D. 52.16–53.31: Iouel's dialogue and the revelation of the Triple Power.
3. 53.32–38+: Allogenes' third narrative.
E-1. +54.6–26a: Iouel's invocation.
4. 56.26b–27: Short narrative
E-2. 56.28–55.11: Iouel's invocation continued.
5. 55.12–18: Allogenes' fifth narrative.
F. 55.19–30: Iouel's fifth speech regarding unknown knowledge.
6. 55.31–34: Allogenes' sixth narrative.
G. 55.35–57.23: Iouel's final speech characterizing Allogenes' experience.
7. 57.24–59.9: Allogenes' narrative of his hundred-year preparation, and his ascent to revelation.
H. 59.10–60.12a: The Powers of the Luminaries first revelation on withdrawal, stability, and unknown knowing.
8. 60.12b–61.24: Allogenes' eighth narrative relating his withdrawals.
I. 61.25–67.19a: The Powers of the Luminaries' second revelation including the negative theology.
9. 67.19b–68.16a: A narrative of indeterminate authorship.
J. 68.16b–23: Instructions to Allogenes regarding the production of a text.
10. 68.24–69.20: Allogenes' concluding narrative to Messos.

The interaction between the direction from others and Allogenes' material is not a dialogue, as in *Disc. 8–9*, but narrative: they speak to one another relating instruction which is essentially exterior to their relationship. Iouel, for example, tells Allogenes about the Triple Power and the Powers of the Luminaries tell Allogenes about the primary revelation. The speeches are instructional narratives which include some dialogical interaction.

Even this description, however, does not account for every perspective in the text because it does not provide for Messos, Allogenes' disciple. By drawing attention to other possible perspectives on the material, Messos's presence thwarts an interpretation of the text solely oriented to Allogenes' instruction: revealers speak to Allogenes who responds to his instruction with emotion, reaction, and activity; Allogenes, in turn, relates this material to Messos who is charged with preserving and proclaiming it (69.14–19). With Messos as a character within the narrative structure, the focus of *Allogenes* shifts from the discussion of mythologoumena and philosophy to the use and interpretation of such knowledge by individuals (Allogenes *or* Messos) and by communities (Allogenes *and* Messos, the text, the proclamation). The outline of the content given above, however, does not account for this shift in perspective: to understand it is to study the narrative structure of the treatise.

Mieke Bal, who has developed a systematic theory of narrative as a tool for analyzing narrative texts, distinguishes three theoretical layers in a narrative text: text, story, and fabula.[7] Bal explains:

> That a text can be divided into three layers is a theoretical supposition based upon a process of reasoning. Only the text layer, embodied in the sign system of language, is directly accessible. The researcher distinguishes different layers of a text in order to account for particular effects which the text has upon its readers.[8]

The presence of Messos as a perspective on the text forces the shift from analysis of the content of the revelations, to an investigation of the effect and use of such contents within the narrative. Beyond the content of Iouel's and the Powers of the Luminaries' instruction to Allogenes, and the content of Allogenes' response as well, the analysis must extend to include Messos's perspective on all three sources of instruction. This entails differentiating the theoretical layers of the narrative.

Bal defines the fabula as a "series of logically and chronologically related events that are caused or experienced by actors."[9] The fabula reconstructs the logical sequence of events which occur in the narrative text[10] by isolating four elements: the events which transpire, the actors who participate in the event, the time which includes both the chronology and duration of the events, and the locations in which the events take place.[11]

The fabula of *Allogenes* involves three primary characters: Allogenes, Iouel, and the Powers of the Luminaries of the Aeon of Barbelo. A period of one hundred years separates two periods of revelation to Allogenes: before the hundred years, Iouel presents Allogenes with a variety of instructions; after the hundred years, Allogenes has visions for himself and receives

---

[7] Mieke Bal, *Narratology: Introduction to the Theory of Narrative* (Toronto: University of Toronto, 1985) 6. Eco (*Reader*, 3–43) has also explored narrative theory.

[8] Bal, *Narratology*, 6. This process of analysis does not significantly differ from the search for the literary or conceptual prehistory of a New Testament or early Christian text, although its terminology is different. The greatest difference lies in the fact that Bal does not present the conceptual prehistory as either chronologically prior to the literary text or as a literary precursor. The differentiations between text, story, and fabula merely help to understand the final written product, not necessarily the historical development of literary traditions.

[9] Ibid., 5. See also Eco, *Reader*, 27: "The fabula is the basic story stuff, the logic of actions or the syntax of characters, the time-oriented course of events."

[10] The search, e.g., for the mythologoumena of Sethian Gnosticism may be said to be a construction of a fabula, a mythical construct which underlies the potential stories, parts of which are included in the actual narrative texts in the Sethian group. The difference here is that the fabula is being constructed to account for a religious system (as in Schenke, "System") of mythologems based upon a number of texts.

[11] Bal, *Narratology*, 11–47.

further instruction from the illustrators of the Aeon of Barbelo. There is no reference to place.

The abstracted sequence of events for this narrative could be reconstructed in this way:

1. Iouel and the Powers of the Luminaries have (or have received) knowledge concerning the highest levels of being.
2. Iouel chooses to instruct Allogenes about these levels of being.
3. Allogenes receives Iouel's instruction and waits a hundred years.
4. After a hundred years, Allogenes is enlightened and receives further instruction by the Powers of the Luminaries.
5. Allogenes receives this instruction and performs the tasks which the Powers of the Luminaries recommend.
6. The Powers of the Luminaries (or some indeterminate character) request that Allogenes write a book about his experience.
7. Allogenes writes the book.
8. Allogenes later chooses to tell Messos about his experiences.

This is the chronology of events which the text presumes.

The way these elements of the fabula are organized constitutes the story.[12] The story orders the material of the fabula in a particular way through the manipulation of these five elements: the sequence of events (which may differ from the fabula) is determined, the rhythm or pace of presentation, the transformation of actors into identifiable and particular characters, the transformation of location into particular places, and the choice of the various perspectives from which material may be viewed.[13] The elements of the fabula, are, in other words, rhetorically organized to produce a certain effect:

> These elements are organized in a certain way into a story. Their arrangement in relation to one another is such that they can produce the effect desired, be this convincing, moving, disgusting, or aesthetic.[14]

The story begins to account for some of the complexity of *Allogenes*, because in this layer Messos becomes a major figure. His presence scrambles the events of the fabula by pushing every event further into the past.

This projection further into the past becomes clearer when the story is told. The last event of the fabula has become the first event of the story: Allogenes has decided to instruct Iouel by relating to him his own spiritual

---

[12] Eco (*Reader*, 27) states that the plot "is the story as actually told, along with all its deviations, digressions, flashbacks, and the whole of the verbal devices."

[13] Bal, *Narratology*, 49–118.

[14] Ibid., 7.

formation by Iouel and the Powers of the Luminaries. Allogenes tells Messos about the occasion when he heard a revelation and became capable of distinguishing between the exalted and the unknowable things. He tells Messos that Iouel appeared to him then and spoke to him. Allogenes tells Messos that he fled. After he turned inward, he saw the light within, and became divine. Iouel anointed (or touched) him and spoke to him again. The power appeared to Allogenes as silence and stillness. Allogenes described Iouel's response to the power and her praises. Allogenes heard the praise and saw the glories of the perfect ones. Iouel spoke to him again. Allogenes prayed for a revelation. Iouel spoke to him again, before she separated from him.

Allogenes prepared himself for a hundred years. A hundred years passed. At the end of the hundred years, Allogenes received an eternal hope. He saw Autogenes, Harmedon Protophanes, Aeon of Barbelo, the Spirit, and the All. Allogenes was disrobed, and taken by the light to a holy place, to view the things of which he had heard and praised. Allogenes stood upon his own knowledge and turned toward the knowledge of the All, the Aeon of Barbelo.

The Powers of the Luminaries of the Aeon of Barbelo revealed to him the power to discern about his life in the world. Allogenes heard as things were being spoken, became silent, and heard the blessedness of self- knowledge. Allogenes withdrew upward to Vitality, then to Existence, where he received a primary revelation in ignorance of the Unknown One. Allogenes was confirmed in his revelation. The powers of the Luminaries spoke to him again and ended with the instructions to write a book. They departed from Allogenes. Allogenes wrote the book as directed.

At the level of the story the most important two aspects are the inclusion of the character Messos as a focal point which makes all of Allogenes' narrative the recitation of past events, and the introduction of embedded philosophical and mythological texts as speeches from Youel and the powers of the Luminaries of the Aeon of Barbelo.

The entire thrust of the fabula is ordered by a reference to "my son, Messos." It is not so much that Iouel presents mythological or philosophical narratives to Allogenes, but that Iouel's presentations pass through Allogenes to another point, to Messos. In other words, Allogenes receives information from Iouel and the powers, he interprets that information, and passes both the material and the interpretation on to Messos who stands outside the arena of the fabula. Messos, in fact, is not even in the story except as a point of reference, a depository for Allogenes' narrative, at the beginning and again at the end of the treatise.

Allogenes has a two-fold function: he is both the narrator in the first person to Messos, the person functioning in the present, and a character in the story, functioning in the past. He both describes what he as a character felt and thought, and what he did. Messos, on the other hand, is not developed in the least: since we are only told that he is Allogenes' "son," we know only that he is male, and at some level immature. The contrast between the more developed character of Allogenes and the flat characterization of Messos is significant.

At one level of the story Messos stands as recipient of all the narrative material. At the other end, Youel and the illustrators of the Aeon of Barbelo present speeches which in themselves are narratives of cosmic or noetic fabula. These speeches, presented by characters who seem to stand outside the events they are describing, are embedded texts in that they do not relate to the primary narrative (Allogenes to Messos) but to one of the other actors (Iouel, the illustrators).[15] From Messos's perspective, these narratives by Iouel and the illustrators are twice removed. To Allogenes the character, they are immediate experience; to Allogenes the narrator, they are the substance out of which the charcterization and response to the experience may be developed for presentation to Messos.

The story includes other characters as well. Iouel and Allogenes characterize the Triple Power, the Aeon of Barbelo, Autogenes, Protophanes (Harmedon), Kalyptos, and the Invisible Spirit. They are not actors in the story, but secondary characters who are described by the primary actors in the fabula. These secondary characters participate in Allogenes' primary narrative and in the secondary narratives of the revealers. They are not directly related to the narrative.

When this story is put into language, it becomes the narrative text. Bal writes:

> A fabula that has been ordered into a story is still not a text. A narrative text is a story that is told in language; that is, it is converted into language signs. As was evident from the definition of a narrative text, these signs are produced by an agent who relates.[16]

At the textual level of the narrative all of the philological and literary elements of the story come into play: the narrator; external, non-narrative comments which introduce other, more argumentative and ideological statements into the text; various types of description; direct address, indirect address; other embedded texts obliquely or directly related to the fabula and story, among many others.

At the level of the narrative text, Allogenes becomes less a figure and more a real character. His emotional responses and his experiences mould the material into a very particular model of spiritual guidance. In the narra-

---

[15] See ibid., 142–46.
[16] Ibid., 7–8.

tive text, Allogenes becomes the superior spiritual guide who integrates into his own experience the philosophical and ascetical activity and who clearly and definitely presents that material to others, signified, in this case, both by the production of a text and an exhortation to Messos. Allogenes' guidance supercedes all the others and becomes a definitive statement and judgment of the philosophical formation by Iouel and the ascetical formation by the Powers of the Luminaries.

Allogenes' narrative text is much more complex at the literary level than has been suspected. This has important implications for the encoding of the relationship of spiritual guide to disciple. There are a number of different narrative levels at which this encoding is taking place: within the instructional material itself, to Allogenes from the other guides, within Allogenes, and to Messos. To stop only at the instruction given to Allogenes as a character is to miss the rich meaning in the set of relationships that are presented. There are many guides to whom Allogenes is disciple. Allogenes in turn becomes guide to Messos and to a text. In becoming a guide himself, Allogenes supercedes the previous instruction. These, then, should be delineated first.

Iouel as Spiritual Guide

The most prominent spiritual guide in *Allogenes* is the female figure Iouel. In a recent study of Iouel and Barbelo, Maddalena Scopello has observed that Iouel, accompanying Allogenes, the character, on the first part of what she presumes to be a "celestial voyage" (*voyage au ciel*), performs three functions: she progressively teaches Allogenes the divine mysteries; she prays; but mostly gives Allogenes revelations about Barbelo, the virgin male child.[17] Scopello suggests that Iouel and Barbelo, another female figure in the Sethian system,[18] have similar attributes and functions because Iouel is Barbelo's extra-aeonic projection ("sa projection hors de l'éon"). As a

---

[17] Scopello, "Youel et Barbelo dans le traité de l'Allogène" in Bernard Barc, ed., *Colloque International Sur Les Textes de Nag Hammadi (Québec, 22–25 août 1978)* (Bibliothèque Copte de Nag Hammai, Section "Études" 1; Québec: Les Presses de l'Université Laval, 1981) 374–76. In this article she also pursues some possible Intertestamental, Medieval, and Cabbalistic identifications of Youel with Yaoel and the Tetragrammaton and Shekina which she maintains could indicate that the figure of Youel develops both within Judaism and Gnosticism.

[18] Concerning Barbelo, Stroumsa (*Another Seed*, 61) writes: "Barbelo is one of the main female figures in the Gnostic pantheon, where she usually represents the feminine aspects of the Father." See also John H. Sieber, "The Barbelo Aeon as Sophia in *Zostrianos* and Related Tractates," in Layton, *Rediscovery of Gnosticism*, 788–95.

teaching double to Barbelo, Iouel facilitates the contact with the initiate and his instruction.[19]

The narrative text of *Allogenes* encourages by its complex content the identifications of triads and characters, but the suggestion that Iouel is simply Barbelo's double does not appear in this narrative.[20] She may be a part of a Sethian mythological *fabula*, but that cannot be established on the basis of this text.

Iouel, however, as a spiritual guide, meets Allogenes in his own environment. Allogenes' only ascent follows Iouel's instruction and separation from him, so that Iouel's interaction with him takes place where Allogenes lives. In meeting him Iouel performs three functions (listed in reverse order of importance): she invokes angelic beings; she reveals the noetic realm of which Barbelo is only one segment; and, primarily, she characterizes Allogenes both as her disciple and as an agent of experience. Iouel functions as an important, but secondary, element within the primary narrative text of Allogenes' instructions to Messos.

Iouel has six lengthy interactions with Allogenes in the first part of Allogenes' formation. The lacuna at the beginning of the treatise occurs at the point at which the first speaker would normally have been identified. Since, however, Allogenes, at the end of his first narrative section, relates that ''then Iouel, the one to whom all the glories pertain, spoke to me again'' (50.18–20), the first lengthy revelatory speech may be attributed to her.[21] In this speech, Iouel lays out many of the topics which have import to Allogenes' development.

Iouel's first speech is very complex and confusing. The narrative does not flow smoothly, partly because the introductory material is missing from the very beginning of the text, and partly because the subject matter revolves about concretized or personified philosophical concepts. Narratological theory will help unpack this situation.

It will be clearer if the conclusion regarding this speech is stated first. Iouel presents Allogenes with the substance of a philosophical lesson she had

---

[19] Scopello, ''Youel,'' 375.

[20] Scopello (ibid.) correctly identifies the nature of Iouel's relationship with the character Allogenes without, however, exploring the narrative interrelationships of the other characters. Perhaps because she identifies both the fabula and the story as relating a celestial journey she assumes the need for a spiritual guide below the aeons.

[21] King (''Allogenes,'' 35, 65) argues that because the penultimate section is of unknown voice, this section probably also belongs to another character. She recognizes that it might also be Iouel's, even though she herself chooses to frame the document in a kind of epistolary envelope.

previously taught to perfect noetic beings. The fabula of her narrative would be this:

1. Iouel has an insight regarding the Triple Power and his relationship to other noetic beings.
2. She incorporates this insight into her noology.
3. She teaches her newly revised noology to a community of noetic perfect beings.
4. Later she describes this teaching experience to Allogenes.

The pronouns in the sections help clarify this: "you" is Allogenes to whom Iouel is speaking; "they" are the perfects ones who are connected with the mind (= gnostics?); "he" generally is the Triple Power, unless it is specified to be someone else.

The story that the narrative text relates, then, might be summarized in this way. Iouel tells Allogenes about an experience she had in teaching a group of gnostics about an insight she had regarding the Triple Power and his relationship to other beings. She tells him not only what she said to them, but also what she said about the Triple Power, and how they might come to understand him. In the end, this process frightened Allogenes.

It is important to separate, as the account of the fabula and story do, the content of the teaching, the noology which Iouel taught, and the various uses Iouel makes of that teaching situation. The core of her speech is the noology; the next layer is the noology presented to perfect beings; and the final layer is the description of that presentation to Allogenes. At this outermost layer, Iouel's narrative becomes a part of Allogenes' narrative and takes on a different life.

With this narrative structure in mind, the fragmentary beginning of the treatise begins to make sense:

> . . . since they exist as perfect ones and all of them are situated in a place, being joined to the intellect. The guardian whom I sent taught you. And it is the (fem.) power which is in you that extended herself as discourse often. (45.6–12)

This introduction distinguishes between three critical elements: the community of the perfect ones, Allogenes' own method of instruction, and the interior dynamic of Allogenes' instruction. The community consists of existent perfect beings who live together in conformity to the *nous*. Iouel sent the guardian to teach Allogenes by means of the extension of an interior power into discourse. Iouel teaches through two means: sending a guardian, and implanting a discursive power.

After this introduction, Allogenes ("you") is not addressed until Iouel begins her second speech to him (beginning with 50.22). The rest of her speech relates her instruction to the community regarding the Triple Power.

Her instruction begins with a being derivative from the Triple Power, the "male virginal youth":[22]

> He is from within the Triple Power, that one of all of those who exist truly, the unmeasured one, the eternal light of the wisdom which she (wisdom) revealed, the male, virgin child, the first of the aeons, the one who is from within the single aeon of three powers, the thrice powered one who exists truly. For when he was united, he went forth and when he was extended, he became perfect. (45.13–24)

Iouel describes the male virgin child: truly existent, unmeasured, wisdom's eternal light, revealed by wisdom, the first aeon. Iouel also presents the male virgin child's relationship to other beings: from the Triple Power, and from the single aeon of three powers. Then Iouel intimates the interior dynamic of the male virgin child's formation: he was united, went forth, extended, and perfected. The language parallels the implantation of the power within Allogenes which is extended to discourse. This cannot be accidental because the introduction itself mirrors all of the elements of the phenomenon: the community of perfect beings, united to the *nous*, Allogenes with the power extending to discourse. Iouel's noology, thus, presents much more than mere philosophical speculation: it formulates and systematizes the method of instruction.

The continuation of this description of the male virgin youth's relationships with other beings underscores the confluence of noology with educational formation. After relating the male virgin youth's self-knowledge, knowledge of the Invisible Perfect Spirit, his relationship to Kalyptos, Protophanes, Armedon, and Autogenes, Iouel presents his derivation from a female figure (whose identity, unfortunately cannot be determined):

> When she knew her own existence and when she took her stand, she produced this (masc.) one who saw all those who exist individually in the manner in which he himself exists. And when they become what he is, they will see the divine thrice-male, the (fem.) power which is higher than god. She is the thought of all those who exist in a place. (46.11–22)

The interplay of revelation with processes of becoming divine manifests this confluence. This female figure "Thought" ostensibly refers back to the

---

[22] Stroumsa (*Another Seed*, 77–80) identifies this child with Seth, the savior son of Adam. He describes the Late Antique "child-as-savior" motif and the evolution of the theme in Gnostic literature.

community of those who exist in a place joined to the *nous*. When they become as the male, they too will have visions of the "power higher than god."

One final example will further illustrate this dual purpose of revelation and education on a theme of great importance to the entire treatise, negative theology. Iouel expresses the limitation of communal knowledge even by the perfect ones:

> It is not impossible for them to receive a revelation of these things if they come together. Since it is an impossibility for these individuals to reach the All which is set in the place which is exalted to the perfect, they receive from it (fem.) the first thought not like existent things, but indeed he gives existence and the hidden one of existence [or reality]. He provides for himself everything. For that one himself will come into being, if he understands himself. (48.6–19)

As a philosophical teacher, Iouel holds out the possibility for understanding the noology and its implications, while at the same time strictly limiting the actual learning. In a sense, she deconstructs her own system in the negative theology. She explains why this happens:

> For this is the one who is set above as cause and source, and an immaterial material, and a numberless number and a formless form, and a shapeless shape, an impotent one with power, and a nonsubstantial substance, and a < . . . > and an inactive activity, and he is a provider of provisions and a divinity of divinity. But whenever they receive, they receive from the first life and an undivided activity a foundation of the first (fem.) (energy) of the one who exists truly. But a second activity [lacuna 4+ lines] he possesses blessedness and goodness. For whenever they understand him as the ferryman of the limitlessess of the invisible spirit who is placed within him, she will turn herself toward him in order that she might understand who he is that is within him and how he exists. (48.19–49.14)

The content describes the being who is beyond all the categories of existence: material, number, form, shape, power, substance, and energy.[23] But Iouel explains carefully what "they," presumably the perfect ones being instructed, actually receive. They derive from the first life, the undivided activity, the foundation of energy. The community's educational formation brings them to the source of their life, but not to a full understanding. In this way, the community must understand the Triple Power as a "ferryman" to

[23] See Berchman, *From Philo to Origen*, 35–42, 63–68, 121–23.

limitless place of the invisible spirit where understanding is only vaguely shadowed forth.

From Iouel's perspective, the negative theology limits the uses of her philosophical instruction by limiting the extent of its ability to signify. Her philosophical discourse is not an indefinite power to "extend herself as discourse." At some point the categories must be transcended, or reversed. The image of the ferryman mirrors the interplay of the limited with the unlimited. The purpose of the understanding here is for a return, or a turning toward that knowledge as an interior phenomenon. The negative theology undergirds the experiential nature of Iouel's philosophical instruction.

Iouel's speech is very full and deserves close exegesis, but it suffices to show the various narrative levels and their interaction both with the content of the discussion and the formulation of the program of spiritual formation. Iouel connects the upper realm of noetic beings with the formational program of other beings, including both the perfect ones and Allogenes, by conflating the knowledge and the use of that knowledge in a process of formation. This is the mark of her educational style.

This style of mixed philosophical revelation and formation process continues in Iouel's subsequent interaction with Allogenes. These interactions, however, are much clearer because the speeches alternate more explicitly between dialogue and revelation. Iouel's material becomes much more simplified and responsive to Allogenes in the next few stages. After Allogenes responds, Iouel, in her second major speech (50.22–51–33), characterizes Allogenes as a person and then presents a fuller account of the Aeon of Barbelo. Then, in the third speech (52.16–53.31) she characterizes him as a disciple, and presents more information on the Triple Power. After an extended invocation of angelic beings (54.5–55.11), she presents Allogenes with the explanation of ignorant knowledge (55.19–30) and characterizes Allogenes' experience of spiritual formation in her final speech (55.35–57.23). Each of these characterizations follow upon Allogenes' response to her guidance.

Iouel, thus, defines Allogenes' identity from her perspective as a spiritual guide: Iouel portrays Allogenes as person, as disciple, and then as an agent receiving formation. Allogenes is chosen, entitled, and destined:

> Not everyone usually listens to these things except the great powers alone. O Allogenes, the Father of the All, the eternal one, clothed you with a great power before you had come to this place, so that you would understand those things which are difficult to distinguish from other distinctions, and those things which are unknown among the multitude. And that you will be saved up to the one who is yours, that one who was first to save and the one who does not need to be saved. [lacuna 5+ lines] . . . to you a form and a revelation. The invisible

triple powered spirit stands outside, a knowledge [which is] undivided, bodiless, eternal. (50.21–51.11)

Allogenes did not choose his own fate. His natural propensity for listening derives from an empowerment by the Father of All so that Allogenes might make distinctions[24] and be saved. Iouel indicates that Allogenes' election includes the formative process of learning to think in order to approach salvation. Allogenes, thus, at least from Iouel's perspective is not a typical gnostic, by nature different and retracing himself to his divine nature, rather he is teachable, someone given power to be formed.

Iouel mirrors Allogenes' teachable status in the Aeon of Barbelo who is presented at once as similarly formed by others and as a savior:

> As within all the aeons, the Aeon of Barbelo exists. He possess also the impression and the form of the truly existing, the image of the Hidden One. And he possesses the noetic account of these, he bears the male, noetic first appearing one (Protophanes) as an image, and he works in the individuals, either by a craft, or by a science or by a special nature. He possesses the divine self-generated one (Autogenes) as an image, and he understands each one of these. He works successively and individually, continuing to rectify the sins which are from within nature. He possesses the divine thrice-male for the salvation of them all (who possess together with) the invisible spirit. This perfect child is a word from within a plan. And this foundation. . . . (51.12–37)

Scopello, in her discussion of Iouel, too quickly identified Barbelo with Iouel.[25] Iouel actually discusses the Aeon of Barbelo who objectifies an aspect of formation. He, the Aeon of Barbelo, has attributes derived from the *typos* and *eidos* of truly existent beings; he works academically, or formationally, by craft, science, or special gift, *in order to correct nature*. Barbelo saves the natural order by his work: he, as saved savior, models the role of Allogenes in relationship to Messos.

Iouel's characterization of Allogenes as a disciple, after he has claimed to have become divine (52, 12–13), makes only two points. Allogenes' formation is perfect, or complete, and he is worthy to hear revelations:

> Since your instruction has become perfect and you understand the good that is within you, Hear concerning the thrice-power, those things which you will guard in great silence and great secrecy, because these things are not spoken to

---

[24] This process parallels that of the Middle Platonic process of *diairesis* in which identity, difference, and similarity are employed to achieve true knowledge of the levels of being. See Berchman, *From Philo to Origen*, 64–68.

[25] Scopello, "Youel," 375.

everyone, except to those who are worthy, to those who are able to hear. Nor is it fitting to speak them to a generation uninstructed concerning the All which is higher than the perfect. (52.16–29)

His perfect instruction and his knowledge of his internal goodness, an implied tautology, entitle Allogenes to receive further secret revelations. Iouel entrusts these revelations to Allogenes with instructions indicating their insuitability for the uninstructed. The key to the reception of revelations is the completion of the instruction when the disciple recognizes his interior goodness. Iouel then reveals the Triple Power who is beyond comprehension, but known as Mentality, Activity, and Thought of the Aeon of Barbelo.

Iouel's portrayal of Allogenes as a person and as a disciple prepares the way for the final characterization. The first two have related mostly to what others (the Father of All, Iouel) have done for Allogenes; now Iouel reveals to Allogenes what his experience as a disciple will be. It both points to the future and recapitulates what has apparently already been Allogenes' experience.

Iouel constitutes Allogenes as the subject of formation in an overview of the formative process which is initiated in a search for the inner good:

If you seek in a total seeking, then you will know the good which is within you. Then you will know yourself (as) one who exists with the god who preexists truly. (56.15–21)

The intensive search results in Allogenes' knowledge of himself as good and as one coexistent with a preexistent God. This affirmation of personal value and divine identification, however, merely prepares Allogenes for the next phase: it is not the conclusion of the formative process.

The search leads to revelation which follows after an extended chronological interlude:

For after one hundred years, it will happen to you, namely, a revelation of that one by means of Salamex and Selmen and the powers of the illuminators of the aeon of Barbelo. (56, 21–27)

Clearly the sense is that the preliminary self-knowledge and divine identification must take root over a long period of time, whether an actual or symbolic hundred years cannot be ascertained. Selamex, Selmen, and the illustrators provide the revelation at the proper time.

The trajectory of self-knowledge to revelation describes the exterior progression for Allogenes. Iouel then, by laying out the implications of this exterior process, presents the interior dynamic. In the first place, Allogenes' formation does not change his human status: "It is fitting for you to know it (masc.) first so that you will not suffer the loss of your kind'' (56.28–30). Iouel describes the transformation not so much as a change of kind, but as a completion, a fulfillment:

> Then, whenever you receive (one of) his thoughts , then you will be completed by the discourse toward the completion. And then you will become divine and you will become perfect. (56.31–36)

The interior progression moves from reflection, to completion, divinization, and perfection. The revelation from the illustrators takes hold of the mind, stimulates a mental discourse which in some way completes or fulfills the process. This mental and discursive completion divinizes and perfects the disciple Allogenes.

Allogenes' divinization and perfection culminates in a superior understanding because he has left the arena of those who are comprehended: ''And then the one who comprehends and knows becomes greater than the one who is himself comprehended and known'' (57.11–15). Iouel emphasizes that Allogenes' formation and his superior comprehension does not change his human status because, even though his divinization, perfection, and superior understanding would identify Allogenes with a higher realm of existence, the incorporeal natures do not form partnerships with superior beings who cannot in any way be localized (57.16–23).

Iouel's narrative portrays herself as a teacher of philosophy at many different levels: she teaches noetic relationships to perfect beings, she helps them to understand what she teaches, and she instructs Allogenes. Iouel teaches both substantively and experientially. Her instruction integrates both conceptual fields and the experience of understanding those concepts. The focus of her instruction, however, revolves about the comprehension of philosophy.

Such an intense heuristic focus influences the content of her instruction. She teaches primarily about three personified philosophical functions: the Triple Power, the male virgin child, and the Aeon of Barbelo. The search for the connections between *Allogenes* and the other Sethian documents has blurred the relatively limited scope of her teaching, because each one of figures or concepts has been related to the occurrence of that same figure in *Zostrianos* or *The Three Steles of Seth*.[26] And likewise the identification of the triad of Existence, Life, and Mind in this treatise to that of Plotinus and Porphyry has deflected from the role of this triad in *Allogenes*.[27] The

---

[26] Robinson, ''Three Steles,'' 132–42.

[27] See both Robinson, ibid.; and Turner, ''Threefold Path.'' The striking correlation, despite the presence of the Neoplatonic triad is with the Middle Platonic issues. Both language and

difficulty with both of these approaches is that they deal only with the signs, the outward signifier, in each of the sets of documents, without carefully delineating what is signified. The meaning of these personified philosophical figures and of these philosophical states remains connected to what is signified in each particular textual setting. The identification of interpretative elements has happened prematurely. In the case of *Allogenes*, the signifier and the signified are tied to a narrative structure. It is not just the content of the speeches that will give the meaning, but also the particular narrative layer or narrative text in which that content takes place.

This specificity of content within the narrative structure becomes evident in a comparison of Iouel's content with Allogenes' summary. As indicated above, Iouel gathers her instruction into expositions of three primary philosophical personifications: the Triple Power, the virgin male child, and the Aeon of Barbelo. The virgin male child and the Triple Power are explained in her first major speech; the Aeon of Barbelo in the second, and the Triple Power again in the third and fifth. Her instruction begins in the exposition of the virgin male child as derivative from the Triple Power. Iouel then subsumes under this child's information regarding his various attributes or possessions: Kalyptos, Protophanes, Autogenes, Existence, the truly existent ones, Armedon, as well as saying that this child became a feminine aeon Thought. Similarly Iouel teaches about the Triple Power. At first the definitions of the Triple Power include that he is a single aeon of three powers, perfect, blessed, One, unnameable, the fountain and foundation of all other beings, the provider, the one known in negative theology, the ferryman, the cause of salvation, to list the most important. At the end of her first speech Iouel introduces the concept of the Triple Power also mirroring the three-in-one combination of Mentality, Life, and Existence.

> He is life and understanding and the one who exists. For then he is that one who possesses his life constantly, and the mentality and the life, since the life possess nonsubstantiality and understanding. The mentality possesses the life and the existence. And these three are one, even though they are three as individuals. (49.26–37)

In her third speech, Iouel further develops this triad beginning in goodness and blessedness and moving toward the indivisibly one combination of Mentality, Activity, and Thought. The conceptual frame is not exactly the same. Iouel works her content to advance her narrative. The second reformulation

---

categories of thought reverberate extensively with Clement of Alexandria, Origen, Moderatus, and others; for introduction, see Berchman, *From Philo to Origen*, 55–164.

of the triad relates to the context of Allogenes' instruction because the triad now defines for Allogenes the unity of the various levels of existence:

> But he is known in this way, because of the third silence of the Mentality, and the second undivided Activity which is revealed in the first Thought which is the aeon of Barbelo, together with the indivisible one in the divisible likeness, and the Triple power and the nonsubstantial Existence. (53.22–31)

The categories of the triad, the reverse sequence of third, second, first, as well as the further explanations of the Triple Power in relation to divisibility all argue for a deliberate reworking of the material in a new narrative environment. The same sort of interlocking narrative development occurs with the Aeon of Barbelo who is identified as the image of the hidden one (Kalyptos) and the account of the noetic one, Protophanes, and as the one who works in the individuals, Autogenes, and the Invisible Spirit. Iouel's instruction deliberately gathers together the particulars under three general headings. The assembly of the content of her teaching, however, aims not toward the systematic exposition of those relationships, but toward the process of educational formation.

Allogenes' summary of his vision following Iouel's departure, however, organizes the same material differently:

> I saw the good, self-generated god with the savior who is the three-male, perfect child, and the goodness of that one, the first-appearing Harmedon, the perfect mind and the blessedness of the Hidden one (Kalyptos), together with the first origin of the blessedness, the aeon of Barbelo, full of divinity, and the first origin of the one without origin, the triple powered, invisible spirit, the All which is higher than the perfect. (58.12–26)

He lists all of the characters without indicating their relationship and without mentioning the triad of Mentality, Life and Existence whose use will become the substance of the Powers of the Luminaries' ascetical formation.

Iouel's heuristic interest structures her presentation of the content of the instruction. Her philosophy is not, like Porphyry's presentation of Plotinus, fully formed in her head needing only an opportunity to pour it forth. The circumstances of teaching influence the content of teaching. Iouel's method structures the material to formulate a particular experience or understanding in her disciple, Allogenes, by providing him with the occasion for his own assimilation of material, and by pointing him in the direction of his own subsequent formation.

As might be concluded from the discussion of Porphyry, Iouel stands at the opposite pole from Plotinus. Iouel is the first documented instance of a female teacher's method of guidance and content of instruction in the third century, a method which centers carefully on the process of formation.[28] Such a process of formation takes precedence over the mastery of philosophical content.

The Powers of the Luminaries as Spiritual Guide

Allogenes receives spiritual formation from another source, the Illustrators or Powers of the Luminaries (φωστῆρες) of the Aeon of Barbelo. Iouel has prepared Allogenes for this segment of his formation. She has mentioned one important aspect of the content of the Powers of the Luminaries' revelation when she tells Allogenes just before she characterizes his spiritual formation by her that he will know the Triple Power in an ignorant knowing:

> Allogenes, in an ignorant knowledge, you will know that the triple power exists before the time of the glories. They do not exist with those who exist. They do not exist in one place with those who exist. These are the ones who exist truly, but all of these exist as divinity and blessedness and Existence and nonsubstantiality and a nonexistent Existence. (55.19–30)

From Iouel's perspective, the Powers of the Luminaries, hierarchically situated below the Triple Power and chronologically subsequent to him, are nonetheless above existent things. Iouel categorizes them as truly existent beings, as having the attributes of divinity, blessedness, existence, while existing nonsubtantially and nonexistently. Iouel portrays the Powers of the Luminaries in philosophical categories which resonate with the formulations of Middle Platonism. Iouel tells Allogenes, however, that he will understand this philosophical material, not as a student or philosopher, but "in an

---

[28] There is one important implication of this method. Generally, the assumption has been that Sethians moved from mythology to philosophy, both taxonomically and chronologically, with the interaction with philosophical movements culminating Sethian development; see Turner, "Literary History," 56–69. This is based upon the assumption that "in the history of religion the objective representation is typically in the form of myth, and it generally precedes the mystical stage, which may appear as an internalized version of the same motif" (Hans Jonas, "Myth and Mysticism: A Study of Objectification and Interiorization in Religious Thought," *JR* 49 [1969] 315). If, however, Iouel's material has both mythological and philosophical integrity within a process of spiritual formation, then perhaps the mythology and the mythological verbalization of philosophy represents a choice for the most concrete and usable form of information. In Iouel's teaching environment, the concretized and mythologized cosmic and philosophical functions assist her to teach her disciples, because they are easier to grasp, and to comprehend rationally. Mythology becomes embodied philosophy, and its use becomes a teaching method: it is not necessarily chronologically prior, nor does it represent an earlier or less intellectually sophisticated stage of knowledge.

ignorant knowledge.'' Allogenes will understand these Powers of the Luminaries and their teaching, through a negation of knowledge.

Iouel's characterization differs significantly from the Powers of the Luminaries' actual narrative of formation. Elements, such as the philosophical orientation and the process of reversal, do take place, but not as Iouel predicts, and with a different emphasis.

Iouel also has prepared Allogenes for this phase of his formation by situating her formation prior to the formation of Allogenes by the Powers of the Luminaries. In her description of Allogenes' formation process, she supervises Allogenes' search, self-discovery, and identification with the divinity prior to the hundred-year period. The Powers of the Luminaries control the revelations following this interlude.

All of Iouel's information regarding the Powers of the Luminaries and Allogenes' relationship with them links her work with that of the subsequent revelations. Because Iouel mentions the Powers of the Luminaries, the events preceding and following the hundred-year interlude take on the appearance of two aspects of the same process. In fact, the Powers of the Luminaries' material has a different orientation, language, and basis than Iouel's. Allogenes' narrative text links two diverse traditions of information into one.

The difference from Iouel's formation becomes apparent from the Powers of the Luminaries' first speech to Allogenes. The Powers of the Luminaries characterize Allogenes as a subject for formation: ''Allogenes, look at your blessedness in the manner which exists in silence, that in which you know yourself within as you are'' (59.9–12). Rather than Iouel's interior goodness, the Powers of the Luminaries address Allogenes' interior blessedness, an attribute which Iouel ascribed to the Triple Power (47.16). The Powers of the Luminaries attribute to Allogenes a silent self-knowledge of blessedness which redefines the content of the spiritual formation. The Powers of the Luminaries direct Allogenes inward and thereby define the content of his formation as that which happens within him. That interior formation does not involve an assimilation of philosophical instruction, but rather the manipulation of interior states of being.

The manipulation of interior states becomes manifest in the Powers of the Luminaries' next instruction. The self-knowledge of interior, silent blessedness prepares Allogenes for performing a series of withdrawals. Two themes, withdrawal and ''standing'' characterize the sort of formation advocated by the Powers of the Luminaries:

Perform a withdrawal (ἀναχωρεῖν) up to the Vitality, seeking yourself, that (Vitality) which you will see moving. And when it is impossible for you to stand, do not fear anything, but if you wish to stand, withdraw (ἀναχωρεῖν) up to the Existence (ὕπαρξις), and you will find it standing and resting itself according to the image of the one who rests himself truly and he embraces all of these things in a silence and an inactivity. (59.13–26)

The Powers of the Luminaries describe a series of spiritual stages and what Allogenes could expect from each one. The first stage is Vitality, recognized by its movement. The second stage is Existence, or Subsistence. The "standing and resting" replace the movement characteristic of Vitality. This stage images within Allogenes' spiritual life a personification of a Resting One who "embraces" all movement in silence and inactivity. The stages to which Allogenes is invited reflect some higher divine personifications whose identity, or characteristics, Allogenes is encouraged to take on.

The Powers of the Luminaries designate the process of movement from Vitality to Existence as "withdrawal," (ἀναχώρησις), a process which becomes a self-activated ascesis.[29] Michael A. Williams describes this process as "an intriguing account of the withdrawal (ἀναχώρησις) of the figure called Allogenes through a succession of levels or conditions, culminating in a level referred to as "Existence" (ὕπαρξις)."[30] It is not an ascent,[31] but a withdrawal. The withdrawal is upward and inward for Allogenes: the arena for Allogenes' activity relates to his interior state because he is directed first to look inward, and only then to withdraw. The process does not necessarily imply an ascent to a hierarchically higher, more noetic place, but a withdrawal to a level of his own existence where he can find stability and rest. The Powers of the Luminaries set the ascetical task for Allogenes to take his stand in Vitality and Existence through withdrawal. The Powers of the Luminaries do not guarantee Allogenes success in standing: they instruct him that, should he not be able to stand, that he should not fear, but persevere in withdrawing to the next stage, Existence. Allogenes must really desire to

---

[29] Turner ("Threefold Path," 332) calls this a "self-performable technique"; he further designates it as a "by-now-traditional technique of self-performable contemplative mystical ascent and beyond this realm of pure being, which had its roots in Plato's *Symposium*" (idem, "Literary History," 59).

[30] Williams, "Stability as a Soteriological Theme in Gnosticism," in Layton, *Rediscovering Gnosticism*, 2. 819–29.

[31] This "withdrawal" is frequently interpreted as an ascent, mostly because of the conflation of these stages with the revelations on the holy place (58.26–35). See Turner, "Threefold Path," 329, 331–32; idem, "Literary History," 79–80; Robinson, "Three Steles," 135–36; Schenke, "The Phenomenon and Significance of Gnostic Sethianism," in Layton, *Rediscovery of Gnosticism*, 599; and Scopello, "Youel," 374. Only Williams ("Stability," 818–22; and *Immoveable Race: A Gnostic Designation and the Theme of Stability in Late Antiquity* [Leiden: Brill, 1985] 80, 86) maintains the literal withdrawal designated in the text. It does not seem possible to identify the withdrawal either linguistically or metaphorically with an ascent.

stand: standing is more difficult than withdrawing, because withdrawing assists Allogenes to stand. The Powers of the Luminaries instruct Allogenes in a difficult process of formation.

The second major theme of the Powers of the Luminaries is that instruction involves "standing." The Powers of the Luminaries tell Allogenes to take his stand (Coptic ⲁⲍⲉⲣⲁⲧ⸗, probably translating the Greek ἑστάναι).[32] Williams offers two important parallels to Allogenes' "stand": first, "Plotinus's references to the experience of 'standing at rest' in contemplation of, or in mystical union with, the One" in Ennead V.5 and VI.9 where an individual person withdraws mystically to the Transcendant,[33] and in Philo's account "of how wise men achieve stability when they draw near to the stability of God" in *De posteritate Caini*, 22–23, 27–28.[34] Williams finds in these three models, including *Allogenes*, "an underlying model for the retreat of the wise man to a condition of participation in the stability of the Transcendant—a condition in which knowledge of the Transcendant is received."[35] The Powers of the Luminaries' instruction to Allogenes to withdraw becomes an ascetical practice aimed at creating within the individual stability and rest. The "taking a stand" is much more difficult, then, because it requires remaining in the withdrawn state, resting at a different center of Allogenes' existence.[36]

The Powers of the Luminaries connect withdrawal and stability to vision. Their formational instruction progresses to a primary revelation:

> And when you receive a revelation of this one, by a first revelation of the unknowable one, that one that should you know him, you must be ignorant of him. And when you become fearful of that place, withdraw (ἀναχωρεῖν) backward because of the activities (ἐνέργεια). And when you have become perfect (τέλειος) in that place (τόπος) still yourself. (59.26–37)

---

[32] Williams, "Stability," 821.

[33] Ibid., 822–23.

[34] Ibid., 824–26.

[35] Ibid., 826.

[36] Williams's longer study (*Immoveable Race*) does not specifically study *Allogenes*. In it, however, he analyzes many aspects of "standing" in the religious thought of Late Antiquity; the Platonic concept of stability in the noetic realm (pp. 74–82); Jewish and Christian apocalyptic "standing before God" (pp. 82–85); the spiritual heroes' literal standing in imitation of a noetic stability (pp. 85–86) including monastic standing (pp. 86–92) and the accounts of Socrates' standing still in contemplation (pp. 92–96). Williams concludes that "all these bear witness to a common presupposition that orientation toward or the establishment of some relation to that which transcends this world tends to effect some form of physical motionlessness" (p. 96), a process which is ascetical (pp. 99–100).

The Powers of the Luminaries' revelation, from Iouel's perspective, is a revelation in a revelation: Iouel sets up the Powers of the Luminaries to give a revelation, who in their revelation describe a further primary revelation of an unknowable One. This primary revelation, which can only be known in the reverse of knowing, in unknowing and ignorance, again subordinates Allogenes' withdrawal to Vitality and Existence to something higher. When Allogenes reaches this stage, according to the Powers of the Luminaries, he has two choices: one is to become perfect and to still himself in this ignorant knowledge; the other is to fear the place. This fear, since it is an activity, necessitates a reverse withdrawal.

The Powers of the Luminaries present fear, and the overcoming of fear, as Allogenes' primary ascetical task. Fear, within the polarities set up in the Powers of the Luminaries' narrative, destroys standing, stability, the higher good. Allogenes must move through fear to a standing and stillness which reveals the one known in ignorance. The power to stand emerges from collectedness:

> And do not be greatly dispersed, so that you will have power to stand. Neither wish to be active lest you fall completely from the inactivity of the unknown one which is within you. Do not know him, for that is an impossibility, but by a thought which is light, when you know him, be ignorant of him. (60.2–12)

The Powers of the Luminaries instruct Allogenes in collecting himself, not dissipating his energy, learning not to desire activity, because all such things draw him away from the unknown one within him, the one to be known in ignorance. It is impossible to know this interior unity with any sort of activity, even intellectual: only recollected stillness, understood as a sort of passive ignorance, mirrors the one known in ignorance.

Within the narrative structure of *Allogenes*, the Powers of the Luminaries' negative theological revelation is the apex: *Allogenes* gives the primacy of quantity to Iouel, but the primacy of literary placement to the Powers of the Luminaries. The description of the One known through a primary revelation presents not only the highest revelation of god, but also the ideal pattern for the gnostic. Allogenes both seeks and finds the primary revelation, and discovers at the same time the model for his own gnostic life which he is to duplicate or mirror within himself.

In a sense, the language of "searching" is inappropriate: the image of the One revealed in the primary revelation is beyond activity and passivity, beyond searching and being found. Allogenes, mirroring this, is instructed:

> Cease hindering the inactivity which exists within you by searching for incomprehensible things, rather hear about him in the manner as is possible through a primary revelation and a revealtion. (61.25–32)

The primary revelation replaces the search as the means to the intended rest and tranquility. The asceticism has become the cessation of activity and inactivity. After laying out the ascetical task, the Powers of the Luminaries begin to instruct Allogenes in the philosophical implications of his withdrawal and stability. This lengthy instruction resumes a theme which was minor in Iouel's instruction, the Platonic triad of Mind-Life-Existence, and significantly expands on it. The content of their instruction, although derivative from Iouel's, develops a different aspect, but more importantly, in a different environment.

The Powers of the Luminaries' teaching, however, takes a decidedly negative turn. Whereas Iouel's negative theology functioned as a stumbling block to guide Allogenes into a positive experience, the Powers of the Luminaries' teaching involves a more negative withdrawal from the categories. Their revelation mirrors Allogenes experience in that the image of the divine figure gives concrete reality to the ideal set up for Allogenes. Like the goal toward which Allogenes strives, the one known in a primary revelation lives and functions beyond the categories:[37]

> For he exists as a something in the manner of existent things, or that exists and will come into being, or he acts, or he knows, without possessing Mind, nor Life, nor Existence incomprehensibly. And he exists as something together with those things which exist which he possesses. (61.32–62.2)

The One revealed appears to exist, or at least to have existence, and yet also functions beyond the Platonic triad of Mind, Life, or Existence. The are attributes to his existence, but they are not within the realm of existence. The divinity at once sets the categories and destroys them, or reverses them.

This divinity in the categories, yet beyond them, also manifests the same stability in other relations. He does not suffer diminishment, desire, giving or taking—phenomena which reflect that he does not have any need for the Platonic categories:

> Neither is he left over in any way, as though he gives anything that is assayed, or purified, or he receives or he gives. Nor is he diminished in any way either through his own desire, or by giving or receiving, or receiving through another. Neither does he have any desire from himself nor through another's agency, (desire) does not usually befall him. But neither does he give anything through himself lest he become diminished in another way. Therefore neither does he need Mind or Life, nor even anything at all. He is better than the All in the privation and the unknowability which he possesses, that is the Existence which

---

[37] See Berchman, *From Philo to Origen*, 63–68.

does not come into being. Since he possesses a silence and a stillness, lest he be diminished by those who are not usually diminished. (62.2–27)

His primary attributes are silence and stillness, which protect him from any diminishment which might arise from interaction with others or through desire. The primary revelation of being at rest and silent reflects Allogenes' experience. Williams has suggested that the function of stability in monasticism and its presence in the description of the standing and contemplating Socrates might have become "a communal practice of standing"—a practice reflected also in *Allogenes*.[38] Certainly the Powers of the Luminaries attempt here to conform Allogenes to the noetic pattern *and* to describe the noetic pattern in language which resonates with Allogenes' experience.

The negative theological revelation, a section of which is found in the *Apocryphon of John*, stunningly summarizes the ultimate goal. It could at once be a description of the true gnostic and of the One revealed in the primary revelation:

> He is neither a divinity, nor a blessedness nor perfection but he is something unknowable. He is not that which he possesses, but he is another one who is more exquisite than blessedness and divinity and perfection. For neither is he not perfect, but he is another thing that is more exquisite, nor is he not boundless, nor is he bounded by any other one, but he is a thing which is more exquisite. He is not corporeal; He is not incorporeal. He is not great. He is not small. He is not numbered. He is not a creature, neither is he something that exists. This is the one whom it is possible for one to know him, but he is another who is more exquisite, the one whom it is impossible for another to know him. He is a primary revelation and a knowledge of himself who alone understands himself. (62.27–63.14)

This description, returning to the categories of divinity and perfection in addition to blessedness, describes not only the divinity, but the fully formed Allogenes. The negative theology applies not only to the higher realms of the divine figures, but also to the spiritually formative realm of Allogenes and Messos.

The rest of the Powers of the Luminaries' revelation relates to this description of the divinity. At its core, it is totally different from Iouel's: the triple male and the invisible spirit are only mentioned twice; the Platonic threefold path receives attention only in relation to Existence. The focus, in other words has shifted to language depicting a divine figure who is at rest and beyond the categories.

---

[38] Williams, *Immoveable Race*, 96–98.

The description of the primary revelation clearly indicates the change in perspective. This revelatory goal for Allogenes' ascetic activity becomes also an image of his own perfection:

> He is a primary revelation and a knowledge of himself who alone understands himself. Since he is not anything of those things which exist, rather he is another more exquisite of those exquisite ones. But like that which he possesses and that which he does not possess, neither does he participate in an aeon, nor does he participate in time, nor does he usually receive anything from another, nor is he diminished, nor does he diminish another, nor is he diminished. For he is a comprehension of himself, as something so unknowable as more exquisite than those who are good in unknowability. (63.14–32)

Defined as one who knows and understands himself, one who is more exquisite than existent beings, beyond aeons and time, beyond being influenced, diminished, or diminishing, the primary revelation is exquisitely self-comprehended and unknowable.

This revelation, moreover, does not emanate, or move, or show relationship with other cosmic and noetic forces, because his primary characteristic is rest:

> He possesses blessedness and perfection and silence—not the blessedness or the perfection with silence, but he is another who exists, one whom it is impossible for another to know him, and he is at rest. < . . . > but they are things which belong to him which are unknowable to them all. For he thus is unknown to all of them in any form. And through all of them, he is within them, not only as the knowledge which is unknown which is what he is. And he is joined by the ignorance that sees him. (63.33–64.14)

Although it is not clear precisely what distinction is being made, the Powers of the Luminaries distinguish those blessed and perfects ones who *are* silent, from those who are *with* silence. This one is totally at rest, and since at rest, he is beyond being known, except in ignorance.

In the final section the Powers of the Luminaries begin to connect again with the revelation from Iouel. For the first time, the Powers of the Luminaries graft Iouel's revelatory material on to their resting god. Iouel's material again revolves about the search:

> Or how is he knowable? Whether there is one who sees him as he exists in every form, or whether there is one that would say about him that he exists as something like knowledge, he sinned against him, he has a judgment, namely that he did not know god. He will not be judged by that one, the one who is not concerned about anything, nor has any desire, but (the judgment is) from himself alone because he did not search for the origin which truly exists. (64.14–30)

The judgment, the risk, is that Allogenes will not search for the original truly existent God, but will be sidetracked into lesser knowledges which are characterized as "impieties." The Powers of the Luminaries seem intent upon claiming a higher revelation than that of Iouel, the discovery of which for Allogenes constitutes a true piety and true knowledge.

The Powers of the Luminaries call those who take the wrong path blind because they do not see the rest which is the highest revelation:

> He became blind apart from the eye of revelation which is at rest, the one that is activated, the one from the triple power of the first thought of the invisible spirit. (64.30-36)

The reference backward to the "triple power" and "the first thought of the invisible spirit" in the context of the resting eye of revelation, subsumes that prior revelation to the Powers of the Luminaries'. The Powers of the Luminaries then present their revelation as superior to Iouel's. The Powers of the Luminaries' revelation is of a god at rest beyond Existence and

> a beauty and a first emanation of stillness and silence and tranquility and unfathomable greatness. When he appeared, he had no need of time, or anything from an aeon, but of himself he is unfathomably unfathomable. He does not activate either himself in order to become still, nor is he an Existence lest he be in want. On the one hand, he is a corporeal being in a place; on the other, he is incorporeal being in a house. He possesses a nonexistent Existence which exists for all of them. . . . (65.17–34)

> Nor does anyone activate him according to the Unity which is at rest. For he is unknowable. For he is a breathless place of boundlessness. As he is boundless and powerless and nonexistent, he was not giving existence, but he bears all these things resting [and] standing out from the one who stands at every time, since an eternal life has appeared, the invisible spirit, and triple power, the one who is in all those who exist. And it surrounds them all being higher than all of them. A shadow [lacuna 15+ lines] which was . . . he was filled by a power and he stood earlier than they, giving power to all of them. (66.20-67.19)

The Powers of the Luminaries' orientation revolves about the ascetical achievement of rest and quietude which mirrors the divine state of noetic beings.

The Powers of the Luminaries' instruction signifies an individual's formation by a group. This community has a unified voice and guides Allogenes from the philosophical formation to ascetical experience. This implies that philosophical formation best emerges from a relationship with a singular guide and ascetical formation best occurs in a community. This community's method of formation is through a developed system of "withdrawal."

Iouel and the Powers of the Luminaries, as guides, have each presented their narratives. Some material has overlapped, but essentially their guidance has moved in different directions. The Powers of the Luminaries develop minor themes from Iouel's teaching, as their major theme. Whereas Iouel taught Allogenes to search and understand, the Powers of the Luminaries led him to interior reflection, withdrawal, stability, rest, and an existence beyond the categories. These two instructional narratives show an interlocking movement forward at a number of different levels: in content from the Triple Power to the Platonic Triad; in method from searching to rest; and in style from understanding and appropriation of material to rest and transcending categories of thought. These narratives, however, are not the final story: Allogenes recreates them in his own account to Messos.

Allogenes' Narrative to Messos

Allogenes' spiritual guidance to Messos is the main narrative of the treatise. Iouel's and the Powers of the Luminaries' narratives have been incorporated into this larger narrative structure so that Allogenes as the narrator of events to Messos may interpret the content and form of information given by them to Allogenes, the character in their narratives. It cannot be presumed that all three narrative sections are relating the same events; rather it seems that the diversity of narrative elements argues for Allogenes' reinterpretion and nuancing of the divine figures' revelations. Allogenes, moreover, sets forth his narrative to Messos whom he wishes both to receive his revelation and to proclaim it to others (68.10-69.19). Allogenes, thus, at once constitutes Messos as spiritual disciple and himself as spiritual guide. This represents the most important shift in the narratives from Iouel and the Powers of the Luminaries to Allogenes. In the former narratives, Allogenes, as the disciple, receives formation by the divine figures. In this last narrative perspective, Allogenes becomes the divine figure and Messos the receiver. Messos, then, has been constituted as a disciple twice: once in his "overhearing" of the narrative from Iouel and the Powers of the Luminaries to his director Allogenes, and once directly from Allogenes' narrative. Messos receives all the prior revelations, but suitably interpreted and digested by his spiritual guide Allogenes.

Allogenes' first narrative speech makes this shift in roles explicit. In responding to Iouel's first, complex revelation, Allogenes directs his response, not to her, but to Messos:

> But when I heard these things, my son Messos, I became afraid and I turned
> toward the multitude . . . think [lacuna 2+ lines] gives power to those who are

able to understand these things through a revelation which is much greater. But I was able, even though a flesh lay upon me. (49.38–50.10)

Allogenes' immediate remark to "my son Messos" places Messos at the fore of the narrative situation. Allogenes explains to Messos his reaction of fear and his desire to avoid the situation of receiving esoteric knowledge, while at the same time claiming for himself a special power of receiving revelation even though he is still "in the flesh."

It is interesting that Allogenes presents his reactions to his own formation. This gives *Allogenes* its unique place in the spiritual literature of the third century. King has observed the surprising cohesiveness of this treatise.[39] She writes that *Allogenes* is not a collection of disparate materials and sources brought together, but a coherent text which follows its own logic which she locates in the content of the revelations. That internal logic, however, relates more to the interpenetrating narrative structures of the treatise, than to the specific content of any one of the narratives. In other words, Allogenes' formation constitutes the logic of the text.

Allogenes also discloses the purpose or aim of his narrative at the very beginning:

I heard these things because of you (ⲚⲦⲞⲞⲔⲔ̄)[40] and because (ⲈⲦⲂⲈ) of the instruction within them. The thought within me distinguished those things which are exalted beyond measure and those which are unknowable. Because of this I am afraid lest my instruction function as something beyond (παρά) what is fitting. (50.10-17)

Although Allogenes questions his instruction, he clearly establishes himself as one capable of making distinctions between the exalted and unknowable for Messos. The teaching environment determines for Allogenes, as it did for Iouel, the content of instruction. Allogenes reduplicates Iouel's method. The *Disc. 8–9*[41] also contained disclaimers about previous educational formation

---

[39] King ("Allogenes," 39–40) identifies the complex style as a result of the esoteric genre of the treatise which attempts to conceal or reveal the Sethian mythology and philosophy. This can only be the case if the interconnecting narratives are ignored. The logic of the work is not in the mythological or philosophical interpretation, as King would have it, but in the subordination of all narratives to what Messos receives. It is, then, not an esoteric text at all, but a text whose intent clearly is to present as much information as possible in as usable a form as possible.

[40] The Coptic ⲦⲰⲠⲈ in its various forms implies a sort of instrumentality, "by the hand of." The preposition ⲚⲦⲚ̄ (ⲚⲦⲞⲞⲦⳢ), according to Lambdin (*Sahidic Coptic*, 289) means "(1) from, from the hand of, from by; (2) with, by, beside; in the hand of; (3) because of, through." Neither the instrumental, nor the locative make sense in this narrative, because the direct address is to Messos, who is not the origin of the revelation. It would seem, then, that the meaning must be "because of you," in a sort of parallelism with the ⲈⲦⲂⲈ phrase which follows.

[41] Each one of the texts, in fact, have a similar disclaimer. In Gregory Thaumaturgos, the edu-

so that Allogenes' disclaimers seem not simply to be a topos, but an attempt to indicate that the new revelation takes precedence over the old.

Allogenes' narrative continues with the affirmation that Iouel has become manifest and teaches him: "And then, she, Iouel, the one to whom all the glories pertain, spoke to me again, my son Messos. She became revealed to me" (50.17–21). Allogenes, the narrator, emphasizes that she "uncovers" or "reveals" herself to him. What might have been esoteric knowledge given to Allogenes, becomes exoteric knowledge for Messos. The revelation is not secondary, but primary in that she manifests herself and speaks directly to him. This immediacy, hidden at the narrative level from Messos's direct apprehension, further underscores Allogenes' prestige as spiritual guide and medium of revelation. Iouel confirms this in her next revelation which presents Allogenes' election and the parallel description of the spiritually formed Aeon of Barbelo.

Allogenes' narrative next describes his divinization. That this divinization precedes all the other events in the narrative is significant.

> My soul became weak. And I fled. I was agitated greatly. And I turned myself toward myself alone. I saw the light which surrounded me and the good which is within me. I became divine. And she, Iouel, the one to whom all the glories pertain, anointed (or: touched) me again. She gave me power. (52.6–15)

The vividness of this description expresses the drama of Allogenes' own spiritual formation. The revelation weakened him, he fled and became agitated. These negative experiences caused him to withdraw within himself in which state he had a vision of the religious environment (the light which surrounded him) in which he found himself and a discovery that he was good. He was divinized, and then Iouel anointed and empowered him.

The narrative sequence implies a causal process: these are not isolated events which happen serially to Allogenes, but a gradual unfolding of Allogenes' spiritual formation. Allogenes' weakness and agitation lead him to a self-discovery in which he becomes divinized. Once he is divinized his spiritual guide anoints and empowers him. It is curious that Allogenes describes his divinization as a prelude to his anointing and empowering, and that Iouel seems to have no part in his divinization. Iouel prepares the environment for Allogenes' agitation and divinization, and then she responds to his own work,

---

cational biographical section clearly sets out a hierarchy of learning and formation which has been superceded by Gregory's teacher. In Porphyry, the chronological development of the treatises are superceded by the noetic organization. There seems to be an important sense of the current revelation and knowledge taking precedence over all others. The disclaimer gives greater authority and weight to the new material.

but she is not the agent of his divinization. After empowering him, Iouel gives the speech on his completed instruction and the revelation of the Triple Power.

Iouel did not indicate to Allogenes that this agitation and withdrawal would lead to his divinization. Rather she told him that his ability to make distinctions (50.29–33) would guide him to salvation (50.33–36). Only later in her characterization of his experience does Iouel refer to his divinization. Here Allogenes begins to set out his own method of guidance for Messos who should understand philosophy as an agitating force leading to the disciple's divinization. Allogenes maintains that only when the disciple has been divinized, the relationship of guide to disciple leads to empowerment and anointing. The difference between Iouel's and Allogenes' subject orientation becomes evident here. Iouel's teaching method, not the philosophical content, plays the major role in triggering Allogenes' responses. Iouel's instruction forces Allogenes into an *experience* within himself, not into an understanding or knowledge.

Iouel then begins to invoke angelic beings. Allogenes understands her invocation as the appearance of a power in stillness and silence:

> And the power appeared by means of a function [or: activity] of being still and silent. She gave voice in this way: 'zza zza zza.' But when she heard this power, and she was filled. . . . (53.32–38)

Allogenes experiences the power conferred upon him by Iouel as stillness and silence. Iouel gives voice to that silence by a sound, which, when she hears the power, becomes for her an invocation of angelic beings. A similar prayer and vocalic language occur in *Disc. 8–9*; here, however, the external force emerges as a series of divine names in direct address.

As in the *Disc. 8–9*, the disciple has a vision following the invocation of the divine figures. Allogenes narrates:

> But I, when I heard these things, I saw the glories of the individual, perfect and all-perfect ones, those who exist together with the all-perfect ones who are before the perfect ones. Again then Iouel, the one to whom all the glories pertain, said to me. . . . (55.11–18)

In the following speech Iouel explains that these glories are chronologically anterior to the Triple Power. That Allogenes simply narrates Iouel's invocation and then states that he had a vision of the glories implies a causal connection between Iouel's invocation and Allogenes' vision. The spiritual guides' invocation is the instrument of the disciples' vision.

Allogenes relates that he had a vision after Iouel's empowerment, anointing, and invocation. This vision occurs, according to the Powers of the

Luminaries' narrative, only after the withdrawal to Existence, and it is not mentioned by Iouel in her description. Allogenes' narrative organizes the events differently, with the first vision related to cultic invocation rather than ascetic withdrawal.

The vision is followed by a revelation. Allogenes prays for a revelation: "And then I prayed that the revelation would happen to me. And then the one to whom all glories pertain, Iouel, said to me . . ." (55.31–34). After this statement that Allogenes prayed, Iouel presents Allogenes with her final revelation in which she describes what his experience of formation will be. And then Allogenes narrates that Iouel departs: "But when she, Iouel, to whom all the glories pertain, said these things, she separated from me; she left me" (57.24–27). Iouel's revelation, her constituting of Allogenes as a subject of formation, and her description of Allogenes' experience have been instrumental in his formation, but not determinative. She does not initiate Allogenes into any sort of mystery: she tells him who he is, what is happening to him, and what will happen to him in his formation.

Everything which has preceded this point in Allogenes' narrative has been preparatory for a revelation for which he now prays. The narrative text's sequence of preparation is this:

1. Allogenes hears a revelation which he desires to teach to Messos, even though that revelation leads him to doubt the validity of his previous teaching.
2. Iouel appeared and spoke to Allogenes again.
3. Iouel's instruction weakens Allogenes, so that he fled and became greatly agitated.
4. His agitation led him inward, and he saw the light surrounding him and came to know his inner goodness.
5. Allogenes becomes divine.
6. Iouel anoints and empowers him, which leads her to invocation.
7. Allogenes has a vision of the glories, the perfect, and the all-perfect ones.
8. Allogenes prays for a revelation.

Iouel's departure as a character from Allogenes' narrative signifies her preparatory status in his formation. She is not mentioned again, although aspects of her revelatory material will emerge in the other formative narrative which Allogenes encounters in the Powers of the Luminaries. Allogenes, then, may be said to supercede Iouel's revelation, because he perdures long after she has departed.

Allogenes ratifies Iouel's description of his experience. His ratification does not imply that Iouel's guidance had no merit, or value, but that it had a limited purview and function, and that it set Allogenes on a continuing progression of spiritual growth:

> But I did not lose my grasp of the words which I heard. I prepared myself in them, and I counselled with myself for a hundred years. But I rejoiced in myself greatly, existing in a great light and a blessed road, because, on the one hand those things which I became worthy to see and again those things which I became worthy to hear, those things which it is fitting for the great powers alone [lacuna 5+ lines] of God. (57.27–58.6)

After Iouel's work, Allogenes takes responsibility for his own formation. He grasps Iouel's words and ruminates on them for a hundred-year period of self-counselling. In this interlude, Allogenes leads a blessed, happy life: he has been made worthy to follow a blessed road, to hear and see revelations. He now lives in the light which he discovered before his divinization. The focus revolves entirely about Allogenes who has, in a sense, constituted himself in this section as a spiritual guide independent of other guides. Related to other previous revelations, Allogenes nonetheless commands his own spiritual formation.

The hundred-year interlude bears no clear meaning. Allogenes does not indicate whether it is to be interpreted literally or metaphorically. It does, however, signify a long period of time during which the divinized Allogenes lives according to his status as a great power, having received auditory and visual instruction, and awaits a subsequent revelation.

At the end of this hundred years, Allogenes narrates the benefits of his labor:

> When the completion of the hundred years came it brought me a blessedness of eternal hope full of goodness. I saw the good, self-generated (Autogenes) god with the savior who is the three-male, perfect child, and the goodness of that one, the first-appearing (Protophanes) Harmedon, the perfect mind and the blessedness of the Hidden one (Kalyptos), together with the first origin of the blessedness, the aeon of Barbelo, full of divinity, and the first origin of the one without origin, the triple powered, invisible spirit, the All which is higher than the perfect. (58.7–26)

Allogenes' interpretation introduces concepts which Iouel had not indicated: he received a blessedness of an eternal and auspicious hope. Allogenes does not indicate that he worked for this hope, but that it came naturally as a result of the hundred-year interlude. By a personal revelation, Allogenes also received a clear understanding of the relationships of the divine figures who had originally been described by Iouel. Iouel's description was muddled and unclear, mixed in with a discussion of the way it was presented to the community and to Allogenes. Allogenes' summary of his vision clearly organizes Iouel's revelation without explaining their relationship to each other: Autogenes and the thrice-male savior god stand together; their goodness appears as Protophanes Harmedon who is the Mind of Kalyptos; the aeon of Barbelo is the divine origin of blessedness; the Triple Powered Invisible Spirit; and the All.

Allogenes then narrates an experience of being taken up to a holy place. Iouel had not indicated this ascent to a holy place for a vision:

> After I had been taken by the eternal light from the garment (ἔνδυμα) which clothed me, and I had been taken up on a holy place (τόπος), that (place) which it is impossible for an image of it to be revealed in the world (κόσμος), then (τότε) through a great blessedness (μακάριος), I saw all those things about which I heard and I praised them all. I stood upon my knowledge (γνῶσις). I turned toward the knowledge (γνῶσις) of the All, the Aeon of Barbelo. (58.26–59.3)

This scene has been conflated with the withdrawal description to produce a celestial journey motif. Allogenes, however, does not give that specific information. He relates that "the eternal light" took him "from the garment which clothed me." Iouel, in her characterization of Allogenes as a disciple, explained that the Father of All clothed Allogenes with a great power so that Allogenes could make distinctions (51.24–33). Allogenes' stripping, then, does not refer to his removal from the flesh, but to his being stripped of the power of distinction in which he was clothed by the Father of All. The great light in which he existed (58.33) for a hundred years stripped him of this power and led him to a holy place. Allogenes describes this place as unimaginable in the world, without specifying what that means. At the holy place, Allogenes sees all that Iouel had told him and he praises it. The praising reverberates with Iouel's invocations.

Allogenes achieves his stability in this experience. "I stood upon my knowledge," and "I turned toward the knowledge of the All, the Aeon of Barbelo." Stability, taking the stand in knowledge, is the goal of the Powers of the Luminaries' instruction, which Allogenes anticipates in his narrative to Messos. This stability inclined toward universal knowledge, concretized in the Aeon of Barbelo, who was central to Iouel's instruction.

This intermediary period, from Iouel's withdrawal through the hundred years, and culminating in the stability achieved in a holy place, seems to describe an experience of negative theology. At first clothed in power to make distinctions, Allogenes is stripped of that power, achieves his own vision and stability, and inclines to his former instruction. Allogenes has experienced Iouel's "ignorant knowledge" (55.19–21) in this.

The narrative sequence of this intermediary period might be delineated in this way:

1. Iouel separates from Allogenes.
2. Allogenes ruminates on her teaching for a hundred years, while existing in a great light on a blessed path.
3. After a hundred years, Allogenes receives a hope and renews his former teaching for himself by a personal revelation.
4. The Light strips him of the power in which he had been clothed to recieve the revelations from Iouel.
5. He is led to a holy place; sees the vision for himself; and praises.
6. He achieves stability.
7. He has a vision of the powers of the Luminaries of the Aeon of Barbelo.

Allogenes reappropriates his former teaching through a process of being stripped away from it, encountering it directly without intermediary, and achieving a stability in that knowledge.

These intermediate experiences lead to the third phase of his formation by the Powers of the Luminaries of the Aeon of Barbelo. These are related to the Aeon of Barbelo whom Iouel characterized as the one who works successively and individually "by a craft, or by a science, or by a special nature . . . to rectify the sins from within nature" (51.21–24, 29–32). The Aeon of Barbelo is a paradigm of a spiritual master, and these powers are the agents, or functions, through which that formation happens:

> And I saw holy powers by means of the illustrators of the male virgin Barbelo; they (the powers of the luminiaries) said to me that I will find the power to test what happens in the world. (59.4–9)

The Powers of the Luminaries will provide Allogenes with the power to discern in the world. Their goal for Allogenes' formation revolves about his ability to live and discern in the world. Their revelation relates to Allogenes' series of withdrawals to Vitality and Existence. Allogenes describes the effect the revelation about withdrawal had upon him:

> These things then I heard them as they were being spoken, namely, these (very) things. A stillness of silence existed within me. I heard the blessedness, that through which I knew myself as myself. (60.12–18)

Allogenes describes a sense of being fully present, hearing the oracle at the very moment that it is being spoken.[42] That immediacy of hearing creates in him a stillness of silence, in which he knows himself fully recollected.

---

[42] Gregory Thaumaturgos describes a similar phenomenon in his oration to Origen. Gregory's teacher also has been transferred to another realm where such revelations are possible. Intertextually, this probably defines a theme related to the Neoplatonic myth of ascent to salvation.

The narrative continues with Allogenes' description of the stages of his withdrawal. The Powers of the Luminaries warned Allogenes about fear and desire regarding the stages of withdrawal, but Allogenes does not mention fear. He describes rather what he saw and experienced at each level. The first withdrawal is to Vitality:

> And I withdrew upward to the Vitality, seeking her. And I entered into it with her. And I stood not firmly, but quietly. And I saw a movement, eternal, noetic, undivided to which all the powers pertain without form, without limiting him in a limitation. (60.19–28)

Allogenes identifies the withdrawal with a search for Vitality into which he enters. Within the Vitality, he was not so much stable as quiet. His vision is of a noetic movement. This movement or activity characterizes Vitality, and within such movement it is not so much stability as quiet which Allogenes achieves.[43]

The second withdrawal is to Existence:

> And when I wished to stand firmly, I withdrew upward to the Existence which I found standing and resting according to an image and a likeness of that which clothes me through a revelation of the undivided one and the one who rests himself. I was filled with a revelation from a primary revelation from the Unknown one. As though I were ignorant of him, I understood him and I received power from within him. (60.28–61.4)

Again, it is affirmed that the movement between stages is a function of desire for stability. It is not automatic. Existence reflects as image and likeness[44] the one who is undivided and resting. In existence, Allogenes is filled with a primary revelation of the Unknown One whom he understood in ignorance and from whom he recieved power.

Allogenes further explains his experience in Existence:

> Since I received an eternal strength, I knew him who exists within me and the triple powered one and the revelation of that which is unreceivable from him.

---

[43] Williams, "Stability as a Soteriological Theme in Gnosticism," in Layton, *Rediscovering Gnosticism*, 2. 821.

[44] The possible reference here to the Genesis creation of Adam in the image and likeness may indicate a Jewish mythology in the background of the Sethian tradition behind *Allogenes*. There is nothing else in the text which mentions so overtly any Jewish origin or concept. Could this One who stands and rests be the creator God of Genesis who rested after the completion of creation? The Platonic Existence, then, would be joined to the Genesis demiurge in an interesting mixing of early and late theologies. For the Jewish origins and themes, see Turner, "Literary History," 56–59; and Stroumsa, *Another Seed*, 17–34.

And by a primary revelation of the first One unknown to all of them, God who is higher than perfect, I saw him and the triple power who exists within them all. I was seeking after the God, the ineffable and unknowable. This is the One who if one should know him at all, one is ignorant of him, the mediator of the Triple Power, the One who dwells in stillness and silence, and is unknowable. (61.4–22)

Allogenes describes his visions at a number of different levels: first there is the One who dwells within him and the Triple Power; then the Unknown One, the God higher than perfect and the Triple Power who exists within everyone, the Mediator of the Triple Power. Their relationships, or identities cannot be certain, but it is clear that they operate in two realms: the inner realm of those who dwell within, or who recieve power, or mediate; and the realm above all existence, the unknown and ineffable Ones. Those who function in the inner realm can exist in the categories of an unknown stillness and silence, all others function beyond categories. Then the Powers of the Luminaries confirm Allogenes in his advancement and they instruct him regarding the negative theology.

There follows a section which is difficult to describe. The characters are not sure. Either it is the Powers of the Luminaries or another character speaking to Allogenes (a "we"), or it is Allogenes speaking to Messos about the limitations of his knowledge. The text is too fragmentary to be fit easily into either the instructive material or into Allogenes' narrative.

Allogenes finally receives instructions from a masculine singular character to write the revelations down:

Write these things which I will tell you and which I will recall to your mind for the sake of those who will be worthy after you. And you will place this book upon a mountain. And you shall adjure the guardian, "Come, Horrible One." (68.16–23)

This masculine singular figure then withdraws from him. It seems most likely, given the interest in the Powers of the Luminaries' narrative, that this figure is the Aeon of Barbelo who emerges from within the final section of the narrative to conclude the instructions. At any rate, then Allogenes narrates to Messos what he experienced. In a sense it constitutes a summary of the entire process:

And after he said these things, he separated from me. But I was filled with joy, and I write this book which was appointed me, My son Messos, so that I might disclose to you those things which were proclaimed in my presence within me. And first I received them in a great silence, and I stood myself. These are those things which were disclosed to me, O my son Messos [lacuna lines 2–13]

Proclaim them, O my son Messos, these five seals of all the books of Allogenes. (68.23–69.19)

The departure of all the other instructors and guides leaves Allogenes as Messos's sole guide. Allogenes, filled with joy, relates to Messos that he wrote the book.

Messos emerges here again, as at the beginning, as a focal point for the instruction. What Allogenes has learned he has given to Messos in the book. The end product of Allogenes' formation is the production of the text which contains the instruction for Messos. Messos's authority as a guide depends upon his possession of the text, not upon his verbal instruction from Allogenes. The authority pointed throughout the treatise to authoritative teaching with verbal and visual revelations, but in the end, the authority rests with the text.

This final sequence of events in Allogenes' description of his formation by the Powers of the Luminaries is as follows:

1. vision of the Powers of the Aeon of Barbelo;
2. the immediate hearing; experience of silence; the sound of the blessedness of self-knowledge;
3. withdrawal to Vitality; quiet among movement;
4. withdrawal to Existence; rest and stillness;
5. primary Revelation with reception of power and ignorant knowing;
6. description of the aspects of the primary revelation: the two realms;
7. instructions regarding the production of the book;
8. the departure of all other instructors;
9. the writing of the book; and
10. Iouel's final instructions.

This final phase of Allogenes' instruction emphasizes the senses, hearing and sight predominate, but rest and stillness also play a role. Allogenes' descriptions indicate that this final stage, as announced in the discernment goal by the Powers of the Luminaries, is oriented toward existence in the cosmos, in the sensible world.

Conclusions

This ascription of authority to the text gives a curious twist to the ending of the narrative. The sensible writing replaces the revelatory speeches of divine or divinized figures, even though the entire treatise has been built upon the transfer of information from Allogenes to Messos. This interest in the sensible world also resonates with the sensible (auditory and visual) dimensions of the final phase of Allogenes' formation and with the sensible descriptions of

Allogenes' experience throughout the text. The narrative structure of the text, with its overlapping of content and its succession of guides prepares the reader, idealized in Messos, for a discerning life in the cosmos. The orientation is not extracosmic, or out-of-body, but embodied sensible living.

There are three phases. Iouel's instruction is the first phase which gives Allogenes all the philosophical information he needs to begin to form himself. Allogenes begins to search following her instruction. In the intermediary phase, Allogenes builds on what he has learned from Iouel and withdraws into himself, for his own spiritual growth and nurture. In the final phase, the Powers ascetically guide Allogenes back into the world having taught him the methods of withdrawal into Life and Existence. Their teaching is a sort of inner withdrawal while living in the world.

The instructors for these three phases also have sign-value. Iouel is a female philosopher and teacher. She is primarily responsible both for the heuristic focus of the treatise and for the intensely concrete philosophy of being. The Powers are a group. They are related to Iouel and her instruction: they are deployed by her and fulfill the beginning of the instruction when Allogenes has developed sufficiently to return to the world. Their relationship, although entirely derivative from hers, continues her program, but with a different and more practical (ascetical) orientation. And then there is Allogenes, Iouel's disciple, self-formed, and capable of discerning life in the world. He transmits to Messos all that he has experienced, digesting and reforming that which he has heard and seen so that the final product is much greater than all the parts. And finally there is Messos. Really he is the reader who is given the opportunity to hear and to see, to understand and to have interpreted for him, to experience, and yet to hold back and not be drawn into the narrative. Outside and yet fully informed, Messos is the real center of the story, the hinge upon which all of the complex series of narratives hang.

This investigation of the underlying narrative structure in *Allogenes* has produced an embarrassment of riches far in excess of this study's capacity to calculate: three guides interacting in their narrative structures to form each other, a cooperative effort which grants access to a significantly wider perspective both for ancient and modern readers; a female guide whose heuristic methods contrast markedly with her male counterparts, but whose divine status evidences both her power and her authority; community guides who provide ascetical formation as a stage in the individuation and corporate development for one of its members; a guided guide whose narrative processed, interpreted, and reformed the benefits of his own formation for his disciple; and finally Messos who receives direct and indirect formation, a text, and a commission to proclaim the formation which he has inherited. It is an embarrassment of riches which in subsequent study as well will become a storehouse of knowledge about third-century spiritual guides.

6

A Concluding Essay

Every treatise surveyed in this study has been oriented in some way to texts: writing texts has been specified as an integral aspect of spiritual formation in three of the four works; the fourth substitutes the interpretation of text for text-production in the formative process. While on the one hand texts have been given primacy, on the other they have also consistently been denigrated as inferior to formative relationship. The texts betray a bias against texts in favor of personal relationship with a spiritual guide. This bias warrants some consideration before proceeding to the more global questions of the cultural systems underlying the descriptions of the spiritual guide's relationship to the disciple.

When Athanasius described Anthony's relations to his spiritual guides, he described only verbal or visual contact between them: Anthony heard the gospel read in the Church, he visited ascetics to observe their way of life, and he imitated their ascetical practice. Likewise Athanasius described others who came to Anthony for spiritual guidance and formation as listeners, observers, and imitators. For Athanasius, the entire process revolved about sight and sound, observation and dialogue.

I. Hadot evidences this same perpective in his conclusion regarding Late Antique spiritual guides. He states that Neoplatonists remained skeptical about the possiblity of the written word acting as guide because the formation occurred through the dialectic, friendship, and intellectual community of the leisured and entitled communities of friendship.[1] Clearly Porphyry's "Life

---

[1] Hadot, "The Spiritual Guide," in A. H. Armstrong, ed., *Classical Mediterranean Spirituality: Egyptian, Greek, Roman* (New York: Crossroad, 1986) 436–39, 448–49.

and Books'' opposes such a view. The bias against textual guidance emerges even more strongly about Christian spiritual formation so that Sr. Donald Corcoran can summarize the early history of spiritual guidance without any reference to reading or textuality.[2]

Both the ancient presentation and the modern conclusions, however, do not describe the texts just surveyed. Although each text, like Athanasius, described a personal dialogical and interactive relationship between guide and disciple, the descriptions were literary creations of significant complexity. The duplicity that initially led into semiotic analysis has also directed attention to the sophisticated literary development of these four texts. The written texts subvert themselves by presenting the immediate, nontextual basis of the relationship as superior to all textual and written spiritual guidance. Even in Gregory Thaumaturgos's speech which describes his teacher in a fine example of a deictic oration, the illusion is created that he is speaking and not writing about his teacher, although it is virtually impossible to decide whether the original genre of the work was written or oral. The other three texts explicitly include the production of text as part of their program of spiritual formation: Porphyry writes to introduce and to authenticate Plotinus's books to their readers; *Allogenes* and *Disc. 8–9* both give direct instructions regarding the production of text as the encapsulating event in their relationships to their guides. The treatises themselves direct attention away from textual to personal guidance while at the same time again directing attention to the production of a text within the text. The treatises create the impression thereby that they are secondary to relationship: the treatises lead Hadot to his conclusion that Neoplatonists were suspicious of textual formation; and Corcoran to her exclusively relational view of guidance.

This is ironic because, at least on the basis of the treatises studied here, third-century spiritual guidance advocated the importance of textual production as the summary of formative relationship, while proposing that texts are only appropriate as a propaedeutic to formation. These treatises literarily create the spiritual guide as characters who disparage literary (textual) formation; the written dynamic of the text creates the illusion of a superior direct relationship between guide and disciple. For Gregory Thaumaturgos, the fiction of a dinner speech creates the illusion of actuality; for Porphyry, the ironic juxtaposition of books and person; for *Disc. 8–9*, dialogue form itself; and for *Allogenes* the person of Messos as recipient. But in all of them, only the text provides the spiritual guidance; the guides themselves remain

---

[2] Sr. Donald Corcoran, ''Spiritual Guidance,'' in Bernard McGinn and John Meyendorff, eds., *Christian Spirituality: Origins to the Twelfth Century* (New York: Crossroad, 1986) 444–52.

fictional creations within the text because these textual guides do not primarily refer to historical people. The sophisticated literary working of the text creates the literary fiction of historicity while in fact fashioning literary characters. Gregory does not describe Origin, the historical person, but a teacher whom he created as a character in a speech. Likewise the Plotinus of Porphyry's "Life and Books" presents only Porphyry's literary and intellectual formulation. And the divine characters, Hermes Trismegistus, Iouel and the Powers of the Luminaries of the Aeon of Barbelo, exist only as the literary creations of the texts, referring not to cosmological systems or to other sets of relationships among divinities, but to literary and textual creations.

This bias against text leads the reader away from the text to reconstruct the presumed reality which it describes. The realities described by the texts, however, result from the texts' own literary artifice (linguistic, metaphoric, referential, generic); these realities are fictive. And the texts create spiritual guides as characters, actors, in a narrative of spiritual formation while claiming for these characters a reality and authority uncircumscribed by artifice or textuality. Although attempting at once to disguise their artifice and to claim a historical referent, these texts actually provide the spiritual formation through reading.

Each text has included magical or mystical languages, oracles, visions, and ecstatic praise as a part of its formation program. The presence of such phenomena may underscore its verisimilitude, but more likely portrays the text itself as transmitting agent of the divine, a phenomenon made explicit in *Disc. 8–9*. The texts function more analogously, then, like a transforming theurgic ritual with the literary spiritual guides as hierophants. Gregory Shaw[3] has argued that an "embodied apotheosis" in later Neoplatonists (Porphyry, Iamblichus, Proclus) achieved through theurgic rituals constituted an "embodied soteriology" in which physical means were employed to divinize and to save people while they were still in the cosmos. This "emphasis on embodied deification and salvation," believed to be consistent with earlier Platonic teaching, evolved from the philosophical position that a soul must both ascend and descend again to be complete. Shaw writes:

> For post-Iamblichian Platonists the salvation and apotheosis of the soul demanded that the soul's *anagoge* arouse a reciprocal descent of demiurgic powers in the theurgies of the embodied soul. After all, in a cosmos that was considered a theophany, and with matter created by god, the body was

---

[3] "Apotheosis in Later Platonism: Salvation as Theurgic Embodiment," in Kent Harold Richards, ed., SBLASP (Atlanta: Scholars Press, 1987) 111–19.

understood to be a divinely created vehicle—however weak—and one perfectly
appropriate for the human soul, the lowest divinity of the Neoplatonic cosmos.[4]

This positive cosmic and theurgic attitude toward embodiment and embodied
activity does not seem to be only a late understanding of Neoplatonists
because the four treatises in this study convey a similar orientation.

None of these treatises had a negative view of embodiment, none
disparaged the physical realm of existence, or condemned the physical aspect
of their own or their disciples' lives. On the contrary, the literary world
created in these treatises specifically promotes the possibility of apotheosis,
divinization, or perfection for their disciples physically. Each one holds out
the promise and presents the method for achieving a higher status of living
while still in the world: Gregory learns from his teacher how to ascend and
return to become a teacher; Porphyry claims that Plotinus may only be
known in the books which he wrote and which bring him forth at any time
that the reader wishes; Hermes initiates a disciple into the mysteries which
the disciple experiences immediately, in his present life; and Iouel gives
revelations to an Allogenes who himself already has a student who will carry
forth the methods of formation. The treatises themselves become the means
for such instruction to happen: not the experience forming the treatise (this is
another illusion created by the text), but the treatise creating a spiritual guide
who through the textual writings effects the divinization or apotheosis within
the reader.[5] The language of the texts forms the experience, not the experience finding expression in the language: the treatises bias the reader against
their own method.

The antitextual bias implicates the methods of formation presented in the
treatises. The underlying systems of meaning which enable communication
represent textual strategies, the skillful use of artistic methods to present (if
not create) a particular understanding of spiritual guidance. The texts strategically create particular guides to promulgate their understanding of formation within specific cultural and religious traditions. The guides and the rela-

---

[4] Ibid., 117.

[5] This recalls Reitzenstein's theory of the "literary mystery" which is described in this way:
"Anyone who published these mysteries as books expected that the reader, if God chose to favor
him would, upon reading them, feel the same effect as Thoth felt upon hearing; the miraculous
power of God's message functions even in the written word: the vision, the experience, occurs.
But he also expected that the unbeliever into whose hand the book might fall would not understand it; indeed, for him it must remain dead, just becasue the vision does not occur" (*Mystery-
Religions*, 62). Reitzenstein posits a primary experience behind the text which enlivens the text;
my position is that the literary creation of the text is itself the experience and the fullest expression. Although some experience may lie behind the text, the text, as a complex literary construction, refers not to the experience, but to itself.

tionships result from the textual strategies, not from a description of historical reality. This will become evident from the exploration of two central textual strategies: the divine status of the guide, and the sexual encoding of the relationship between guide and disciple.

The divine status of the guide does not address questions about the origin of the guide's power or knowledge. The treatises never raise the question regarding the authority which permits the guide to instruct, nor do they betray an interest in developing a divine lineage for knowledge like the Christian apostolic line or the Neoplatonic succession of teachers. Even in Porphyry's "Life and Books" where he relates Plotinus's intellectual lineage he gave it only peripheral importance within his own literary agenda. The divine status of the guide rather addresses the question about the reader's own final formation: the textual strategy regarding divine status models the reader's expectations about the end result of his own formation, not the guide's lineage.

It is likewise in the question of the sexual encoding of the relationship. The sexual metaphors do not address the question about the sexual activity between guide and disciple, but rather characterizes the intensity, the work, the singularity of the inner dynamic of the relationship. Like sexual intercourse, the relationship of guide and disciple becomes an exclusive and pleasurable work. The sexual dimension, as a textual strategy, reveals the interior workings, the dynamic of formation in common, graphic and memorable images. Both of these strategies need closer scrutiny, and in the process the range of significations and underlying cultural systems enabling the description of the guide to disciple will be surveyed.

The treatises ascribe divine status to the guides. Two textual strategies emerge for the acquiring of divine status for the guide. First, as Gregory's teacher and Plotinus, the guides may achieve divine status through their own effort. Their work may revolve either about an ascetic practice of migration (Gregory's teacher and Plotinus's union with the One) or about an esoteric study with a master (Plotinus and others with Ammonius). Second, the guides may be described as divine figures (Iouel and Hermes) who descend from the higher realms of the cosmos to give instruction. These already divine figures develop more intense and immediate relationships with their guides: unlike the intellectually distancing oratorical or biographical genres, both these figures relate intimately to their disciples in dialogue and dialogical narrative. The sexually encoded interaction in *Disc. 8–9* and the closely regulated instruction and formation by Iouel in *Allogenes* undergird the intensity of their relationship.

The guides, moreover, display an advanced level of education. Three of the guides (Gregory's teacher, Plotinus, and Iouel) present philosophical material in the course of their formation programs; one guide (Hermes) presents cosmic revelation, while another develops an ascetical system of negative theology. The specific content of these programs depends upon the cultural and religious environment, but the fact that every guide teaches has been consistent. The guides also consistently function from the higher part of the anthropology, either by virtue of their divine origin (Iouel and the Powers), or because they are noetic (both Hermes and Plotinus) or have received special revelation (Gregory's teacher and Allogenes).

The texts differentiate between these higher guides and other lesser ones. Gregory Thaumaturgos listed his parents, rhetor, and law professor among the lesser group, and his divine *paedagogus* among the superior. Porphyry distinguised between the lesser guidance of scholars and textually based instructors (like Longinus) and the guides who taught by personal relationship (like Ammonius and Plotinus). Porphyry ironically mirrors his own opinion in Longinus's: Porphyry argued, while justifying the production of books, that Plotinus taught by relationship. In *Disc. 8–9*, the guide purposefully replaced all earlier educational formation by the initiation which he supervised. And in *Allogenes*, the character Allogenes claims a superior status to Iouel's and the Powers' formational systems. Moreover, the treatises, in subordinating all of these other systems to the higher guidance of their chief spiritual guide, ascribe an increment of numinosity to the chief guides. Gregory's teacher was a "holy man"; Plotinus operated only from the *nous*; Hermes declared himself "Mind"; and Allogenes presented himself as divine.

Women also displayed advanced educational status. Iouel, both as philosopher and as spiritual guide, and the women in Plotinus's coterie of philosophical associates provide evidence that gender did not prohibit educationally or socially privileged women from becoming spiritual guides.

The strategy of ascribing divine status to the chief spiritual guides, in contrast to all others, models the outcome for the disciple (within the treatise) and the reader (outside the text). The guide's divine status represents that for which the disciple works; it mirrors the disicple's own development; it makes concrete and tangible what the disicple can expect to achieve. Each text portrays the guide divinizing the disciple in its own way, according to the guide's divinity. Among the texts in which the guides progress by their own labor, the disciple receives, by implication, the assurance that, should he ascend in similar fashion, he too will become like the teacher. Gregory Thaumaturgos does not claim his own divinity, but he does claim that his departure from his teacher is like leaving paradise: the completion of his studies in the paradise, as he calls it, implies that he has achieved everything that the teacher has been able to transmit; he has received the benefits of the teacher's ascent. Porphyry already claims that his understanding and structure of Plotinus's mind's work gives order to what is chaotic, structure to what is elusive. By giving voice in their narrations to their guide's lives, they display their superiority and claim a higher position for themselves. This becomes evident in Allogenes who portrays his own divinization independent of Iouel's instruction and yet carefully organizes (and supercedes) the formational model of his predecessors.

In the case of those figures who are already described as divine (Hermes, Iouel, and the Powers), they directly assist their disciples to become divinized. They bring their disciples to the point either of their own divinization, as Allogenes, or through the process of divinization, as in Hermes' son's initiation. In each case, the divine status does not relate primarily to the guide, but to the possibilities envisioned for the reader in the text.

The use of sexual language also represents an important textual strategy. Sexual signs have carried intense and powerful messages from Plato to today because they signifify powerful emotional and psychological responses.[6] The Hermetic literature presented the sexual dynamic of the relationship of guide to disciple in a direct and nuanced manner. Gregory Thaumaturgos dealt with the sexual implications of the teacher-student relationship only indirectly in his connotative systems. And Porphyry introduced the possibility of sexual relations only to dismiss it summarily. Allogenes, the only text with a woman guide, did not mention the sexual dynamic at any level. These texts have presented a fourfold spectrum of sexual encoding: the fully discussed and very important (Hermetism); sexually connotative descriptions and important (Gregory Thaumaturgos); mention and denial of any value or importance (Porphyry); not mentioned and (presumably) not relevant (Allogenes). Only the first (Hermetism) and the last (Sethian Gnosticism) have presented the sexual dynamic unambiguously: the Hermetic literature indicated that the sexual dynamic both defined and explained the relationship; Iouel, the Powers, and Allogenes did not find it to be an important strategy for communication.

Gregory Thaumaturgos and Porphyry invested the sexual dynamic with great power by dealing with the subject less directly. Their innuendo and refusal to discuss the sexuality of formation seems defensive, or, as another strategy, titilating. The indirect signification (by connotation and mention) titilates the readers' interest in and desire for more information with the implication, of course, that there is more to know than is being written about. Their indirect method of discussion produces desire. As a textual strategy, such titilation involves the reader not only in speculating about Gregory' teacher and Plotinus, but also confronts the readers' own sexual expectations,

---

[6] The most influential study of male homosexuality has been John Boswell, *Christianity, Social Tolerance, and Homosexuality: Gay People in Western Europe from the Beginning of the Christian Era to the Fourteenth Century* (Chicago: University of Chicago Press, 1980) 61–166.

thus drawing them to explore the potentiality of their own formation. This textual strategy provides a classic protreptic to formation: it creates the desire and interest in subsequent study. This desire, of course, has been made explicit in the Hermetic *Disc. 8–9* where the initiate's desire both began and sustained him throughout his initiation. What this treatise made explicit, Gregory and Porphyry used indirectly to achieve the same results.

In the Hermetic literature the question revolves about the manner in which sexual intercourse represents visually and intellectually the relationship of guide to initiate. Since the topic is directly discussed, the only question is *how*. In Allogenes, the problem becomes more complex because the absence of sexual encoding of the relationship raises the question *why*. Since every other text explored in some way the sexual dynamic of spiritual formation, why did not *Allogenes*, a text with three spiritual guides? Hermes, as a divine guide, would indicate that the omission was not because the sexual metaphor was inappropriate for a divine figure like himself or Iouel. Nor, as in Porphyry's "Life and Books," does it appear to be morally reprehensible, because Allogenes does not even mention sexuality. Two possible reasons, then, remain: the sexual metaphor when it applies to a female guide would not communicate the same message as with a male guide, whether human or divine. The same underlying systems of meaning would not be activated by the sexual relationship of female guide to male disciple, so it was not used. The second is that Allogenes' formation relies more heavily on individual initiative in the context of community: Allogenes teaches, through his narrative level, the means to self-formation. Messos's formational instruction teaches him, as an individual, both how to relate to philosophical education and communal asceticism, but without in any way attaching such relationships strongly to one individual guide. Iouel and the Powers of the Luminaries provide Allogenes, and thus Messos, with aspects of the formation which Allogenes himself manipulates. This strong sense of individual formation also mitigates against the sexual encoding of the relationship.

This absence for the median texts on the spectrum (Porphyry's and Gregory Thaumaturgos's) implicates their relationship, not in the suggestion of sexual activity, but in the nature of their relationship. Hermes Trismegistus openly states that the reality of the mystery of initiation mirrors the reality of heterosexual intercourse. The strong and dynamic language reveals the inner workings of the relationship. In both Gregory's and Porphyry's text this same intensity is implied, but never directly expressed. For Porphyry's description of Plotinus, a suggestion of the sexual dynamic would direct attention away from the primary orientation, to sell books. Porphyry dismisses sexuality, but in fact, more accurately dismisses the relational aspect of the formation, as he did the social aspect of Plotinus's life as well.

Only the books, not the relationship or potentiality for relationship, embody the reader's relationship with Plotinus.

Gregory's description, however, presents the full relationship of guide to disciple. Again, the sexual dynamic, as an underlying system, suggests the inner workings of the relationship. Gregory describes his conversion to the teacher and through the teacher to philosophy, a conversion which was like a dart of friendship which captured him and like a spark of erotic love being planted in his soul. This intensity, however, signifies even more because the teacher has ascended as a human and descended as a divine figure: the relationship manifests the compelling, transforming, loving relationship of human being to God. Gregory gathers a multitude of available means, every conceivable and appropriate system of signification, to describe the relationship. His purpose, however, was not simply to characterize his own teacher-student relationship, but to draw others into the sort of spiritual formation which his teacher advocated. Gregory's purpose was to create desire, a desire as strong and significant as sexuality itself.

The sexual dynamic, as a textual strategy, does indeed prepare the reader to understand precisely the interior workings of the guide-disciple relationship: its power, attraction, and demand for exclusive attention; its fulfillment, enjoyment, and pleasure; its work, exercise, and ascetic dimension. Hermes Trismegistus rightly identified its iconic value as a strategy of communication.

When third-century writers created their spiritual guides, they searched for the textual and literary means most graphically and immediately to communicate them to their disciples. They created the illusion of immediate and intense relationship by describing the relationship sexually. They prepared their disciples to know the end result of their labor in the description of the divinity of the guide. But most of all they created treatises to be the spiritual guides. Treatises, enshrined as in the Hermetic temple, were the true offspring of formation: those who were formed, who became the religious leaders, were nurtured by the treatises which guided.

If Athanasius were more true to the history of third-century formation presented here, he would have shown Anthony reading a book, or hearing an ascetical treatise being read aloud, or searching for the written wisdom from ascetics or Scripture. Anthony would not only have observed others, but written about his observations as a means of forming other monks. Anthony would not only have conversed, but he would have recorded his conversations for the edification of his fellow monks. What Anthony did not do, however, Athanasius did for him: he created a text to be a spiritual guide.